Understanding the Risk Society

Understanding the Risk Society

Crime, Security and Justice

Gabe Mythen

First published 2014 by
PALGRAVE MACMILLAN

Palgrave Macmillan in the UK is an imprint of Macmillan Publishers Limited, registered in England, company number 785998, of Houndmills, Basingstoke, Hampshire RG21 6XS.

Palgrave Macmillan in the US is a division of St Martin's Press LLC, 175 Fifth Avenue, New York, NY 10010.

Palgrave Macmillan is the global academic imprint of the above companies and has companies and representatives throughout the world.

Palgrave® and Macmillan® are registered trademarks in the United States, the United Kingdom, Europe and other countries.

ISBN 978–0–230–55531–0 hardback
ISBN 978–0–230–55532–7 paperback

This book is printed on paper suitable for recycling and made from fully managed and sustained forest sources. Logging, pulping and manufacturing processes are expected to conform to the environmental regulations of the country of origin.

A catalogue record for this book is available from the British Library.

A catalog record for this book is available from the Library of Congress.

Printed in China

For Vix and for Harry.
I know. I don't need to talk to you about risk.

Contents

Figures

Acknowledgements

I am grateful to a number of people who have helped and supported me from the inception of this book to its completion. Emily Salz offered firm direction and enabled me to find a clear focus for an initial sketchy set of ideas. Anna-Marie Reeve worked tirelessly in encouraging me and gently pointed out the woods when I was busy staring at the trees. Nicola Cattini at Palgrave Macmillan provided sound editorial advice in the final stages of the project.

In my undergraduate days, I was fortunate enough to have been taught by several inspirational academics who sparked my interest in social theory and arrested what should have been a less taxing journey into employment at the local sports centre. Con Lodziak, John Tomlinson and Steve Taylor are primarily to be thanked – or indeed to be blamed – for this. Over the last ten years, I have benefitted immensely from working with Sandra Walklate to whom I owe a debt of gratitude. As this is not a joint production, the rougher edges – usually knocked off with tact and precision – unfortunately remain. I am also privileged to have been mentored by Ulrich Beck whose ideas continue to captivate and enthuse me.

The University of Liverpool has provided a fertile ground for research, and the collegiate atmosphere has been uplifting during a choppy period in the sector. Listening to the ideas of academics in the Department of Sociology, Social Policy and Criminology has both challenged and sharpened up my thinking. I would particularly like to acknowledge the positive effect on my thoughts of folk in the *Publics and Practices* reading group: Peter Campbell, Lynn Hancock, Ciara Kierans, Michael Mair, Susan Pickard and Dave Whyte. There are several cohorts of long-suffering SOCI 320 students out there whose patience I have stretched while sounding out some of the ideas in this book. Apologies, one and all.

Working with colleagues on a range of research projects has helped me loosen the risk blinkers. In this regard, Hazel Kemshall, Fatima Khan, Ross McGarry and Liz Peatfield have educated me in new ways of seeing the world. I have been lucky enough to both encounter and engage with the work of a number of scholars working in and around risk. To this end, thanks are due to Louise Amoore, Alison Anderson, Claudia Aradau, Evelyne Balliergeau, Didier Bigo, Patrick Brown, David Denney, Rob Flynn, Frank Furedi, Jonathon Gabe, Joanna Gilmore, Ana-Marta Gonzalez, Steve Hall, Dirk Helbing, Imran Irwan, Mike Levi, Willem de Lint, Lasse Lindekilde, Deborah Lupton, Stephen Lyng, Peter Mascini, Derek McGhee, Karenza Moore, Pat O'Malley, Kenneth Pettersen, Scott Poynting, Francesco Ragazzi, Sara Salman, Basia Spalek, Christine Schwobel, Peter Taylor Gooby, Joost van Loon, Ole Waever, Lucia Zedner and Jens Zinn.

I am very grateful for the enduring support and motivation provided by the following colleagues turned friends and friends turned colleagues: Mark Banks, Adam Burgess, Luke Goode, Paul Jones, Richard Ronald, Nicole Vitellone, Teela Sanders and Iain Wilkinson. A final mention for ex-tennis coach (turned fear of crime guru), Murray Lee. Although I remain indebted for the advice on my backhand technique, I would point out that my unbeaten record remains intact over three continents. That would have been four had he not 'forgotten' his racket in Argentina. Thanks all the same mate.

Introduction

What better way to start a book on risk than by contemplating the ultimate threat: the extinction of human life on the planet. Notwithstanding the 'end is nigh' prophecies of placard-carrying prophets of doom, concerns about the perilous condition of the world have been readily expressed in recent years by politicians, religious leaders, scientists, academics and social commentators, from the seemingly ceaseless problems of drought, malnutrition and disease in the Horn of Africa to the endemic economic crisis in Southern Europe and the complex and violent conflicts raging between government, militia and citizens in countries across the Middle East. All of these examples suggest that we are living in troubled times. Such a view would certainly be shared by the members of the *Bulletin of Atomic Scientists*, which includes 18 Nobel Laureates. The Board of Directors make annual assessments of the state of human security with reference to a Doomsday Clock. Designed to reflect the extent to which the human race has become vulnerable to catastrophic threats, the hands of the clock are altered in accordance with fluctuating world affairs. If we do reach a point at which the clock chimes midnight, human life will become extinct. Since its inception in 1947, the clock has been altered on 18 occasions, an average of once every three and a half years. In the last decade, the Board have seen fit to tinker with the clock face with greater frequency than in previous eras. The minutes currently left before midnight strikes are few. With the Cold War coming to an end, the dismantling of the Berlin Wall and the Velvet Revolution which followed in former Eastern bloc countries, by 1991 the hands of the clock were a comforting 17 minutes away from midnight. After the 2001 terrorist attacks in America, the time had been pushed on to seven minutes to midnight. A decade later, in January 2012 the clock was advanced further still to five minutes before 12. This is the closest to midnight the clock has ever been and serves to reflect the grave anxieties of the Board about the future of the planet. The forwarding of the hands of the clock was made with reference to the proliferation of countries seeking to develop nuclear weapons, unprecedented climate changes and the threat of global terrorism:

> The challenges to rid the world of nuclear weapons, harness nuclear power and meet the nearly inexorable climate disruptions from global warming are complex and interconnected. In the face of such complex problems, it is difficult to see where the capacity lies to address these challenges. The political processes in place seem wholly inadequate to meet the challenges to human existence that we confront.
>
> (*Bulletin of the Atomic Scientists*, 2012)

Taking a glance at the turmoil that exists in many regions of the globe, it is tempting to concur that we are indeed teetering on the brink. As the summation of the Board infers, human interventions do not appear to be reducing major societal risks. It is clear that the misguided military interventions in Iraq and Afghanistan have spectacularly failed to ease ethnic and tribal tensions, and violent struggles have surfaced in several countries in the Middle East, including Egypt, Yemen, Libya and Syria. While it would be easy to point to the historical omnipresence of political, economic and social instability and to dismiss the Board as little more than fretting do-gooders, the coupling together of contemporary global conflicts with upcoming environmental and energy challenges brings into view the prospect of an unsettling future. Environmental campaigners, citizen's groups and critical politicians have forewarned about the brewing of a 'perfect storm' in which combustible elements combine to bring about harm on a hitherto unseen scale. The UK's former Chief Scientific advisor John Beddington has posited that such a storm – in which the sum becomes much greater than the parts which constitute it – is likely to erupt within the next two decades (BBC News Online, 2010). In his view, as the world's population continues to grow at a rapid rate, scarcity of food, water and energy will intensify. As food prices escalate, a greater number of people will become malnourished and migrants will flee en masse from the worst-affected regions, causing subsequent overpopulation and resource shortages in host countries. What makes the situation more troubling is the escalating nature of the problem, with the component processes catalysing one another. The deployment of intensive agricultural methods, for example, uses up large amounts of water and energy, while climate change not only deteriorates the environment but also affects the food chain. Beddington estimates that by 2030 the world's population will have risen from six billion to eight billion, ramping up demand for food and energy by 50 per cent and water by 30 per cent. According to the charity Oxfam (2011), unless dramatic changes are introduced in environmental management, food production and energy consumption, our actions up to this point will simply be exacerbating rather than alleviating the problem.

Insofar as the bigger global picture is disconcerting, it is not just the future of the planet that Western citizens have to worry about. Risk has become an omnipresent feature of contemporary life that surfaces in a range of domains, including personal relationships, work, housing and health. Given the depressed nature of global markets, it is the ramifications of the financial crisis that are uppermost in many people's minds and lowermost in their pockets. As well as impacting on individuals, the financial meltdown has produced shockwaves that have rocked private companies, public service providers and the State (see Davies, 2010; Lanchester, 2010). Far from being a random news item that flitters across consciousness, the economic crisis is having profound effects on employment, welfare provision, pensions and healthcare. In their best-selling book *The Body Economic*, Stuckler and Basu (2013) use a range of quantitative indices to demonstrate the harm that the financial crisis has wreaked in Europe and North America. They argue that over 10,000 additional suicides and around a million extra cases of depression have been recorded across the two continents since the inception of austerity programmes. In the United Kingdom, the market triumphalism that characterized New Labour's term in office has long since receded and been supplanted by a period of cost-cutting and biting austerity measures. The Conservative–Liberal coalition's attempts to reduce a gaping budget deficit have involved cuts to frontline services, rises in public taxes and exhortations to community and voluntary agencies to become partners in the delivery of health, welfare and penal provision (see Mythen et al., 2012).

Set against such a canvas, it is unsurprising that there has been a spike in interest in risk over the last two decades within the mass media, politics and culture more broadly. The spectre of risk lingers over a veritable mélange of social ills, including the problems of knife-crime, predatory paedophiles and teenage drug consumption. In addition to episodic moral panics about such threats, critical incidents such as 9/11, the Banda Aceh tsunami, the earthquakes in Kashmir and the terrorist attacks in Norway have served to embolden the global significance of risk. Nonetheless, aside from the human devastation caused by such incidents – and going against the grain of common sense wisdom about the precariousness and dangerousness of life in the twenty-first century – if we follow stock material indicators of health and longevity, such as life expectancy, disease rates and levels of infant mortality rates, contemporary Western cultures appear to be relatively safe and secure places to live (see Taylor-Gooby and Zinn, 2006: 272; Wilkinson, 2009: 1). In this regard, there is more than a grain of truth in Furedi's (2007b: 2) assertion that modern anxieties about risk are not connected to probabilities of harm. As Bauman (2006: 101) notes, the contemporary Western world is something of a paradoxical habitat: remarkable in terms of wealth production and technological sophistication, but populated by people that are disturbed by feelings of insecurity, disquietude and helplessness. As Wilkinson (2009: 1) observes, well over one in ten people in the United Kingdom are living with neurotic disorders, while it is estimated that one in four people will suffer mental illness at some point in their lives (Singleton et al., 2001). In a fast-paced and demanding world, statistics on the prevalence of depression among young people are disquieting. A recent large-scale study of 16–25 year olds in the United Kingdom found that one in five had suffered from bouts of depression, with one in three having contemplated suicide (Mindfull, 2013). A studious gaze at the ostensibly comfortable curves of capitalism reveals that many are sliding along without brakes, with the worst affected considering whether or not to fling themselves off the ride. For Bauman it is not so much risk which engenders anxiety, as the rapid pace of flux, the constant disembedding of social relations and the disruption of cultural bonds that characterize contemporary life. As he puts it: 'the only permanence in society is change, and uncertainty is the only certainty' (Bauman, 2012: 26). In Bauman's estimation, the winners in society – those who are well resourced and nimble – profit from the routine undulations of 'liquid modernity', while the losers are left floundering. Amidst the maelstrom of modernity, Bauman sees the individual's capacity to live with uncertainty and to manage the multiple risks that spring up as the key to surviving and thriving in the modern world. Developed in parallel with Bauman's 'liquid modernity', Ulrich Beck's proposition that we live in a 'risk society' has been the subject of heated academic debate (see Beck, 1992; 2009; Mythen, 2008; Strydom, 2002). While Bauman distinguishes between the winners and losers of the ruptures and transitions that course through society, Beck speaks more of a generalized society of dangers. In the risk society, all individuals and classes are imperilled by the systemic production of manufactured uncertainties.

From this opening discussion, we can observe that not only are the boundaries between risk and uncertainty blurred, we need to recognize from the outset that when we talk about 'risk', the past, present and future often merge together, such that it becomes difficult to separate out the hypothetical from the probable and/or the actual. Of course, while the meta-narratives of Beck and Bauman provide useful anchors for discussion, there is some worth in distinguishing between risk as a concept that is debated in the social sciences, risk as a problem which is managed by social institutions and risk as it is experienced by individuals in the course of everyday life (see Arnoldi, 2009). While there are multiple joins and overlaps, those 'risks' that become institutional and/or individual priorities outwith the academy are not necessarily those that are the most thoroughly researched within universities. Asking searching questions about what constitutes a risk, for whom and under what conditions, brings to the fore some of the contradictions, dilemmas and disputes that we will be grappling with. Given the increasing significance of local/global interplays for the future safety and security of the planet, it would seem to be a prescient moment to be writing a book about risk. As the potential scope of the subject matter is vast and academic debates are voluminous, this contribution will seek to specifically examine both the presence and the role of risk in the spheres of crime, security and justice. Not only are these spheres interconnected, but they have high social significance. Taken in the broadest sense, crime, security and (in)justice tangibly effect and materially shape the lives of citizens within and outside Western Capitalist countries. It is worth briefly separating out each of these entities to render this observation concrete and to underscore their import.

The problem of crime is omnipresent in society and is one of the most talked about issues in Western cultures. The frequency, causes and effects of crime have been endlessly debated in the media, among academic experts and by members of the public. Crime control has become a ubiquitous subject of debate in the public sphere and a crucial element of political manifestos, with major parties attempting to out-muscle each other on how 'tough' they can be in punishing law breakers. Since their public dissemination in the early 1980s, national crime statistics have become a source of wonder and consternation, with the accompanying debate about 'fear of crime' rather unhelpfully encouraging pole clustering. At one end of the pole, the debate has involved an over-dramatization of fearfulness and anxiety among the public which is then mobilized as a rationale for the government to 'do something about the crime problem', invariably via the introduction of stricter forms of regulation and more punitive deterrents. At the opposite end of the spectrum, rational risk sceptics have highlighted the gap between public anxiety about crime and the actual probability of becoming a victim. Such discussions in the broadsheet newspapers have invariably involved comment about the lamentable 'irrationality' of the public in making judgements about crime rates and a fair deal of chastisement of low brow tabloid media for amplifying the crime problem. As we shall see in Chapter 4, both of these frequently heard refrains take a dim view of people's ability to make informed choices based on previous life experiences, knowledge of the locale in which they live and tacit judgements about personal security. Further, they assume the existence of an unfeasibly homogeneous citizenry prone to the ideological whims of the media, rather than a diverse set of publics making sense of crime in different ways. Whatever the shortcomings, interest in crime proliferates way beyond discussions about crime rates or the current agendas of political parties. Within popular culture, the range of media products focussed on violent crime have expanded almost to saturation point, from prime-time television dramas to computer games and popular music. Advances in technology and new forms of social media have also increased the range of channels for dialogue to take place about crime, with Internet pressure groups forming to adopt particular stances on both generic and specific aspects of crime and punishment. The competing positions of groups supporting and opposing the prosecution of Amanda Knox for the murder of the British student Meredith Kercher in Perugia stand as a case in point. Of course, this is not to comment on the informational quality nor the depth of engagement facilitated by exchange of information and views about risks on social media sites such as Facebook or Twitter. As Bauman (2011: 27) counsels, new media technologies certainly assist in speeding up communication, but 'profound ideas needing contemplation and reflection' may not be best suited to such platforms. The cementation of crime as a popular interest in the cultural domain is suggestive of a public fascination with the topic (see Mooney et al., 2004). Yet the examples cited above reflect a relatively narrow account of crime and one that is fixed on eye-catching offences such as rape, murder and sexual assault. This rather partial view is not unique to popular cultural products and reflects dominant trends in politics and academia. Sailing against this prevailing wind, I would encourage a broadening out of the concept of crime. As Hillyard (2009) points out, crimes routinely dealt with by the criminal justice system are but the tip of the iceberg in comparison with other forms of harm perpetuated outside its jurisdiction. Following the zemiological tradition, an expanded definition of 'crime' would include acts of violence routinely perpetrated by nation states represented by police, military and security personnel, by employers causing injury and death to employees by flouting health and safety legislation, by corrupt marketeers and bed-feathering bankers who encouraged rash investment and lending policies while the global economy overheated and by polluting companies in the pursuit of profit over public good (see Almond, 2013; Benson and Simpson, 2009; Christie, 2004; Coleman et al., 2009).

The concept of security has visible overlaps with crime. In certain circumstances, in seeking security we may be trying to avoid becoming a victim of crime. Much of our security-seeking behaviour is geared into the quest for a safe life, untroubled by external forces, violence or unwarranted intrusion. The range of measures that we take to try to reduce our risks of becoming a victim of crime are sizeable, from installing security lighting and burglar alarms in the home to carrying personal alarms and avoiding what we perceive to be 'no-go' areas after dark. Of course, at the same time as we search for the available means and resources for managing our own security, the State is charged with governing the security of the nation. Yet the governance of nations has changed markedly in the last three decades and the idea that the State has sovereign responsibility for the safety of citizens has receded (Shearing and Wood, 2007). In a globalized world, national security management is an increasingly diffuse process which involves a range of international alliances as well as mixed public and privately funded partnerships designed to protect communities, groups and individuals (see Zedner, 2009: 2). Besides its association with crime, security also has more deep-rooted ontological connotations. Whether we feel secure is not only contingent on our ability to avoid victimization. It depends upon many more things than whether we, the agencies of the State or private enterprises can create conditions of safety. We must remember that security is also about how happy we are in ourselves, how safe and clean our environment is and how free we are to express what we think and feel, politically, socially and culturally.

And so too is justice. When we speak about 'justice', we often use the term allegorically to find a way in to broach a cognate collection of social goals such as parity and equality. At its heart, justice is about moral fairness, which is determined by adherence to a set of equitable principles or rules. While this definition is somewhat expansive, we can also locate a more restricted version of 'justice' as it is understood and applied within the confines of the criminal justice system. In this restricted version, criminal justice structures are designed to operate by regulating behaviour and ensuring that the ordered environment in which justice can survive and thrive is maintained. Moving outwards from legal definitions, justice is not solely about the rights of the accused to get a fair trial or to receive reasonable treatment in custody. It is also about meeting the needs of those that are routinely victimized. Justice is thus fundamentally about the maintenance of morality, about creating conditions of fairness as well as punishing and rehabilitating those deemed to have transgressed. This produces disputes and controversies, around who is classified as a perpetrator, who is deemed to be a victim and which people or groups are able to evade the principles of justice. Here, the maintenance of justice depends upon punishing individuals for actions which breach shared rules enshrined in law. For the condition of justice to exist, there have to be limits to freedom. In liberal democracies, justice is meaningful only insofar as those that flout it can be rendered accountable. Thus, seeking and securing justice depends crucially upon the actions, policies and interventions of a range of agencies. Without a sense of justice, the foundations of society are thrown into turbulence. As the political scientist John Rawls (1999: 3) puts it: 'justice is the first virtue of social institutions'. Nevertheless, justice is an adaptable rather than an absolute virtue. For some social groups justice maybe taken for granted, for others it has to be fought for (see Hudson, 2006; Mythen, 2012b). As with crime and security, justice comes in many forms and each is associated with different principles, be they retributive, restorative or redistributive. If we can commit to a more expansive definition of *social* rather than *criminal* justice, we are able to shine a light on a broader range of ills, suffering and harms. Justice then becomes not only about whether the sentences dished out to violent offenders match the severity of the crime but also about the responsibility of Western nation states to effectively deal with the issue of climate change or to address the dire plight of those suffering from malnutrition in the developing world.

Despite our somewhat peremptory introduction, the discussion above indicates just how interconnected issues of crime, security and justice actually are. In order to talk about meeting the goal of justice, one first has to decide which processes and practices may be harmful or detrimental to whose security, under what circumstances and to what end. These are not likely to be easy or tidy judgements. There are, as always, different views, competing values and alternate perspectives at stake. If we consider, for instance, the aftermath of the 7/7 bombings in the United Kingdom, the contested nature of justice becomes palpable, as does the range of stakeholders involved in its determination. In this instance, the possibility of directly pursuing criminal proceedings against the perpetrators was not an option, as each had extinguished their own life in the attack. Thus, the question of how the families of victims and the surviving wounded would be able to 'get' justice became more complex. In the light of such complexity, media attention fixed most fully on concrete issues such as the effectiveness of intelligence and surveillance by the security services, the efficacy of the emergency response to the incident and the robustness of counter-terrorism legislation. Among the families of those that perished in the attack and the survivors of the incident, divergent perspectives emerged about what might be done to prevent similar attacks occurring in the future. Some called for much stricter counter-terrorism regulation and police surveillance. Others, such as the author and academic John Tulloch (2006), rallied against knee-jerk legislation and counselled instead for wider and deeper understanding of the grievances felt by young Muslims in Britain. Tellingly, so far as the political harnessing of risk is concerned, the day after 7/7, the UK Government announced a detailed 12-point counter-terrorism plan which included proposals for detention without charge for terrorist suspects to be extended to 90 days, the setting of higher thresholds for British citizenship and new powers to close down mosques on security grounds (see Prince, 2010). Putting aside accusations of political opportunism, in this and in other cases, history has shown that acting with alacrity to somehow supply 'justice' using magic legal bullets after the trauma of a malevolent incident are prone to failure. As far as attaining the conditions in which a broader social justice may thrive is concerned, there is little unanimity of approach and there are certainly no quick fixes or simple solutions. Social justice is less an end point that one is likely to arrive at through punishment and more a manner of travelling in which people's needs and rights are valued and the responsibilities and obligations of institutions and private companies upheld. The composition of justice – who administers it and who receives it, why and under what conditions – remains a matter of discord and struggle.

From this introductory discussion, we can begin to discern how and why issues surrounding crime, security and justice not only intertwine but also are at the forefront of public concerns, political dialogue and media debates. In connecting crime, security and justice to and through risk, I am striving in this book to achieve three broad objectives. First, I want to illumine some of the central social and political problems and issues that constitute the patina of the age, drawing on a range of illustrative vignettes. Second, I intend to offer some critical insights into the contemporary dynamic between social structure and human agency and, in so doing, draw attention to the symbiotic relationship between institutional formations and everyday lived experiences. Third, I wish to embark on a thorough conceptual exploration of risk. A good chunk of this journey will involve detailing and scrutinizing the competing theoretical perspectives on risk that have emerged in the social sciences in the last three decades. This third objective, although important, will be connected to rather than detached from the first and second. Throughout the book I will be keen to engage theory with practice, illuminating particular incidents and events by applying elements of risk theory. The casing risk sections that appear in Chapters 3–6 of the book are intended to provide food for thought and to illustrate the ways in which theoretical tools can be used to make sense of social happenings. Although the torchlight may be directed towards specific risk incidents, these case studies also tell us much about what is going on in the shadows. To this end, I hope to demonstrate how power networks shape the ways in which risk impacts *on* people and, conversely, how risk is impacted *by* people.

Heeding the shot across the boughs issued by Bourdieu and Wacquant (1992: 233), I hope to avoid being sucked into 'the vacuous discourse of grand theorizing'. Nor do I intend to develop an acute case of 'riskitis', a condition in which the sufferer subjects the full gamut of societal processes and practices to scrutiny using the solitary lens of risk. These concerns indicate my desire to offer a truly critical appraisal of the uses and abuses of risk, both in academia and in wider society. I am motivated to consider both what risk reveals and what it may conceal. I will thus consider the ways in which theories of risk can provide us with apertures through which we can view the social world, while remaining mindful that, if misused, risk can act as a blackout blind that unhelpfully obscures issues that may be taking place behind the screen. To this end, we will consider the drawbacks to the 'turn to risk' and some of the negative effects of viewing lived experience and social transitions through the confined lens of risk. Responding to this task requires much more than outlining and mulling over competing theories of risk. To become overly ensconced in theory is to reside comfortably but neglectfully in the sanctuary of the abstract, tucked away from the tiring, dirty world of data-gathering and distanced from the ongoing turmoil and troubles of individuals living 'out there'. Thus, the latter part of this journey will bring me back to the start, to question whether scholars of risk are able and willing and capable of developing robust tools of analysis that can grapple with the ills that blight contemporary society.

So, to the specific sections of the book. In the opening chapter, I lay the contextual ground by considering definitions of and meanings attributed to risk, both synchronically and diachronically. Before delineating the key theoretical perspectives, it is first necessary to catalogue the various properties of risk and to contemplate the processes underpinning its ascendance. Here the primary features of risk are considered alongside the inflection towards it as a mechanism for understanding social behaviour. I wish to offer an account of the rising popularity of risk as a sociocultural referent, documenting the events and decisions that have incrementally led to risk becoming a common – if heterogeneously interpreted – language and discourse. As well as cogitating on the rise of risk as a social descriptor, I will also delineate the contours of the academic 'turn to risk', outlining the reasons why risk has become such a recognizable and well-worn currency. This context-setting exercise paves the way for an explication of the foundational theories of risk that have been developed within the social sciences in Chapter 2. As we shall see, within the broad theoretical church of risk, there are multi-faith congregations. Insofar as theoreticians have collectively sought to inquire into the social effects of risk, different congregations have been underpinned by distinct beliefs, values, objectives and methodological approaches. At this juncture, I map out the central tenets and the contributions made by particular risk perspectives. Given the extensive range of work on risk, this is by necessity something of a selective exercise. I have pragmatically chosen to cover what I see as the main theoretical currents in detail, rather than attempting to provide potted summaries of each and every perspective. I am inclined to think that a slight reduction in breadth is a reasonable sacrifice to make to achieve analytical depth. The perspectives that are accorded priority – namely the risk society, governmentality, anthropological and culture of fear perspectives – act as portable anchors.

Having set the context in which the turn to risk has occurred and unpacked foundational social science theories of risk in the opening chapters, in Chapter 3 I begin to excavate the long-standing association between crime and risk. Central here is the emergence and consolidation of risk in the assessment, management and regulation of crime. Focussing on crime prevention and policing, I wish to elucidate the axial role of risk in criminal justice and the wider governance of security. These issues strand over into the next chapter where the representation and changing nature of criminal victimization takes centre stage. Returning to debates around public anxieties, the functions of the media as a conveyor of notions of victimhood are highlighted and I also draw out some of the limitations of mainstream criminological research into 'fear of crime'. While the themes of crime and justice are foregrounded in Chapters 3 and 4, they are superseded in Chapter 5 by that of security. Here questions about the construction and maintenance of national and international security are paramount. The magnitude and geographical range of the 'terrorist risk', dominant ideologies and discourses about the threat posed by 'new terrorist' groups and the effectiveness and legitimacy of established modes of combating terrorism are all topics considered here. I will argue that the discursive construction of the present threat as unique and catastrophic has ideationally underpinned a sweeping material phase of State securitization. This process of securitization has had dramatic consequences for those affected by military incursions and deleteriously impacted on minority groups unjustly targeted by blanket forms of surveillance, regulation and scrutiny (see Abbas, 2011; McGhee, 2010: 59). In Chapter 6 we move into the broader terrain of environmental risk, examining the ecological damage caused by anthropogenic activities and the consequent effects of environmental despoliation on the planet. Focussing on the production, distribution and regulation of environmental risks, it is my intention here to concentrate on the systemic generation of harms and the inability of capitalist institutions to halt – less still reverse – global warming. Having considered the nodal points at which risk, crime, security and justice intersect, in Chapter 7 the limits to risk as an analytical tool are addressed. Having dwelt on the capacity of risk perspectives to open up understandings of the social, in the last chapter I want to ask how well equipped current theories of risk are to wrestle with current and impeding trans-territorial problems. This involves broaching the difficult question of what it is that goes missing if risk is prioritized as a prism through which the world is viewed.

In any enterprise of this scale, it is important to declare up front one's allegiances and sympathies. In truth, I write this book as something of a risk agnostic. Having been captivated – but not completely persuaded – by the risk society thesis in my early days as an undergraduate student, I went on as a young scholar to critically assess Beck's work and to engage in broader debates about the theoretical utility of risk. Following on from this, my appetite for exploring the dynamics of risk led me to empirical examination of the subject in contexts around crime, security, employment and the environment. In the course of this journey – a period during which risk has moved from the margins towards the centre of academic dialogue – my sympathies and proclivities have ineluctably shifted. It is fair to say that my initial optimism about the capacity of risk to explain aspects of the social world has been balanced out over the years by a more sceptical approach marked by concern about the liberal application of risk as an explainer for all manner of dilemmas. The stellar rise of risk – both as a cultural category and as an area of academic concern – hastens the need for a sober examination of what exactly it is that framing social issues in terms of risk reveals. Rather than advocating risk scholarship in a partisan manner, this book is instead an attempt to capture the reasons why it has become such a popular and well-worn concept. In so doing, I wish to both outline and interrogate the burgeoning theoretical and empirical literature in which risk is expounded as a social referent. In seeking to develop a frank account, I want to travel beyond risk and to consider its relationship to rather less fashionable – but nonetheless vital – concepts such as power, inequality, coercion and harm. One of the age-old tasks for the social scientist has been to examine the nature of the dynamic between structure and agency (see Wright Mills, 1959). One way of broaching this issue is to explore the connections between individual behaviours and decision making around risk and the macro social processes that are institutionalized in wider political, economic and security policies. It is essential that social scientists within the academy are involved in such discussions in order to grapple with and elucidate some of the problems facing the world, such as the uneven distribution of environmental risk, the unfolding economic and energy crises and the upsurge in religious and political violence. In accounting for the rapid historical ascendancy of risk, this book represents not so much an attempt to reject, tether or tame risk, but rather a way of establishing a clearer sense of its diverse contents, fields of application and limitations. In advance of this, it is first necessary to take a step back from the present day and to track the birth and evolution of 'risk' in Western culture.

CHAPTER 1

The Turn to Risk

Defining risk

Although the different theoretical perspectives that we will encounter in Chapter 2 may have distinct trajectories, their proponents are agreed on one thing: that risk has become an increasingly important social phenomenon. A range of writers have sought to account for the ways in which risk has become a quotidian feature of everyday life, as people seek to protect and insulate themselves against the many uncertainties and anxieties that arise in the modern world (see Bauman, 2007; Beck, 2009; Tulloch and Lupton, 2003). Yet in historical terms, couching social problems and understanding cultural experiences in terms of 'risk' must be seen as something of a modern fetish (see Giddens, 1999b). In this chapter I will offer an account of the underlying factors involved in the 'turn to risk' in popular culture, academia and governance. This account will involve the excavation of what are rather tangled etymological roots, a considera-tion of contemporary meanings of risk and some mapping of the assorted properties of risk. Providing a context for the foundational theories of risk that will be elaborated in Chapter 2, I wish to first venture towards the conceptual by discerning discrete aspects of the 'turn to risk' in the social sciences. Prior to this, it is worth mulling over the various historical meanings of risk in order to distinguish how contemporary definitions have been arrived at and which dimensions have become accentuated or attenuated over time. Such contemplation may yield some vital clues not only about the ancestry of risk but also about its future uses and applications. As we shall see, accounts of the emergence of risk as a concept and a technology of regulation are marked by ambiguity and dispute.

Before we consider some of the impacts of risk-based governance in specific domains such as crime, national security and the environment, it is important to reflect on the origins of risk. Linguistically speaking, 'risk' is a relatively novel phenomenon, which has seeped into European language over the last four centuries. It is widely believed that the English word 'risk' finds its roots in the Latin *risco*, which is a derivative of the verb *riscare*, meaning to run into danger (see Giddens, 1999b; Lupton, 1999a: 5). As the meaning between the two languages is coterminous, it is thus probable that Italian language is the most likely parent of the English word 'risk'. However, there is no con-sensus about the origins of the word. Some etymologists, for instance, believe that risk derives from the Greek word *rhiza*, meaning cliff face. Such interpretations cast risk as a term that was initially used to describe the practice of sailing dangerously close to rocks (see Ayto, 1990: 446). In this reading of history, risk originated as a naviga-tional device used by sailors entering uncharted waters. Interestingly, those that perceive risk to derive from the Latin *risco* also note its use to describe hazardous cliffs or reefs possessing the capacity to puncture sailing vessels (see Arnoldi, 2009: 25; Ewald, 1991).

Regardless of the precise lineage, it is probable that risk can be traced back to the development of principles of maritime insurance. Archival evidence suggests that risk was commonly used by insurers to express the balance between acquisitive opportunities and potential dangers for explorers taking to the sea in search of foreign lands (see Giddens, 1999a; Wilkinson, 2001: 91). Indeed, the prosperity of the insurance industry today remains dependent on the gamble that a comparatively small number of risks will actually materialize as harms. By offering their services to consumers, insurance companies are certainly taking a risk, albeit one where they are able to stack the odds in their favour. In setting premiums insurers are banking on the probability that the adverse effects that they have sold insurance for will not transpire and that their customers will not make a significant number of simultaneous claims (see Lombardi, 2004: 362). While maritime attributions of risk were focussed on space and place, later definitions focussed on temporality. As Giddens (1999b: 3) points out: 'the idea of risk is bound up with the aspiration to control and particularly with the idea of controlling the future'. In addition to the management of upcoming processes and events, this derivational genealogy introduces something of a neutral hermeneutic slant, in that it lends itself to an appreciation of the possibility of gains as well as losses. What is noticeable in contemporary times is that the positive dimensions of risk appear to have been all but subsumed by negative overtones of threat and harm. The *Oxford English Dictionary* (2011), for instance, defines risk as:

(1)   A situation involving exposure to danger;
(2)   The possibility that something unpleasant will happen;
(3)   A person or thing regarded as a threat or likely source of danger.

Across these definitions the accent is slanted towards threat, whether it be related to incidents, events, people or objects. While it is difficult to settle on a multipurpose definition of risk, if we take a broad overview of the contemporary properties associated with it, we might want to settle on five elements that tend to be – in varying degrees – present in situations where the word 'risk' is used. First, as the dictionary entry suggests, risk refers to situations of *danger* that may result in harm to individuals, people, institutions and/or the environment. Alongside danger, risky situations are also characterized by *uncertainty*. As Giddens (1998: 27) notes, if outcomes are certain, events cannot be strictly classified using the register of risk. Risk can only be meaningfully mobilized to describe a process, activity or event that contains some degree of indeterminacy and unfinishedness: 'the essence of risk is not that it is happening, but that it might be happening' (Adam et al., 2000: 2). Risk emerges in cases where outcomes are yet to be defined and thus necessarily involves engaging with the discomforting territory of the unknown. Third, as risk directs us to impending outcomes, it is intrinsically linked to *futurity*. Risks are incidents and/or consequences that may – or may not – transpire over time (see Bernstein, 1998: 1; Lupton, 1999a: 74). Thus, when experts assess risk, they are seeking to forecast future outcomes based on available data about past occurrences. In this regard, institutional forms of risk management can be understood as attempts to predict upcoming dangers in order to prepare for negative eventualities (Sparks, 2001: 160). Fourth, given their association with uncertainty and futurity, risks are attached to *probability*. The history of risk is very much bound to the development of mathematics and, in particular, the evolution of probability theory (see Lombardi, 2004: 362). Probability calculations produced by risk assessments seek to provide numerical estimates through which harm can be gauged. As Ewald (1991: 207) reasons, established institutional methods of risk assessment are indicative of a desire to mathematize the future. As risks are identified, a panoply of tools can be used by experts to try and calibrate and assess the extent of threat, which areas and groups might be affected, how and under what conditions. It is through judgements about probability that relative categories of safety and vulnerability are established. The mathematical birth of probability can be traced back to the seventeenth century and the work of the French mathematician and philosopher Blaise Pascal. Pascal was born in Clermont-Ferrand, France, in 1623 and demonstrated an early gift for mathematics and science. When he turned 13, his father introduced him to a Parisian discussion group called the *Académie Mersenne*. It is here where Pascal made acquaintance with both the philosopher René Descartes and an outstanding mathematician called Pierre de Fermet. Pascal's debates with de Fermet were to lead to the perfecting of a computational method, the seeds of which had previously been sown by pioneering mathematicians, including Zhu Shijie and Gerolamo Cardano (see Mlodinow, 2009: 72). Through his sustained correspondence with Pierre de Fermat, Pascal is attributed as having founded probability theory through the development of the arithmetical triangle.

The outcomes of Pascal and de Fermat's early experiments with calculation form the basis for contemporary probability models in Western society. In essence, probability theory makes it possible to estimate the chances of an outcome occurring in the future (Arnoldi, 2009: 21). Pascal's advance was to pioneer a method of systematizing what previously appeared to be random sequences of events (see Mlodinow, 2009: 68). Although consideration of probabilities may be a routine venture in today's world, Pascal's exposition of probability theory is a critical moment which has informed the deployment of risk as a method of measurement and categorization from the Enlightenment period through to the present. Thus, the rising significance of probability can be traced from early experiments in mathematics, through maritime insurance and on into the modern world where an 'avalanche of numbers' are used to quantify all manner of processes, situations and concerns (Hacking, 1990: 27). As Beck (1995: 7) reasons, in the course of capitalist industrialization a concatenation of processes encouraged the formation of a specific 'calculus of risk', involving methods of risk assessment being allied to the principles of probability. Despite pre-dating the Enlightenment, probability remains a critical factor in institutional decision making, economic investment and scientific, technological and medical development. Ewald (1991: 202) shines a light on the way in which the application of probability principles enables the calibration of hazards:

> When put in the context of a population, the accident which is taken on its own to be random and unavoidable, can (given a little prudence) be treated as predictable and calculable. One can predict that during the next year there will be a certain number of accidents, the only unknown being who will have an accident, who will draw one of existence's unlucky numbers.

Although probability assessments can generate information that can be used to improve the management of risks, when and where harms might occur remains a matter of conjecture. We should remember too that predicting risk is not an art that is exclusively practised by institutions. Potentially threatening situations invoke horizon scanning and probability estimates on behalf of individuals as well as institutions (see Sunstein, 2005). Flanking the properties of harm, uncertainty, futurity and probability, we can also identify a fifth element: *opportunity*. As we shall see, although opportunity was central to the origins of risk, this element has become somewhat muted. Notwithstanding the current accent placed on the negative aspects of risk, we need to recognize that situations of risk often involve the promise of opportunity, acquisition or gain. Indeed, some historians maintain that the derivation of risk stems from the Arabic word *risq*, meaning to acquire good fortune or wealth (see Wilkinson, 2009: 17). Although the idea of *taking* a risk in order to accrue financial benefit, achieve ontological satisfaction or simply experience sensory pleasure has been afforded scant attention in the social science literature, risk still connotes activities which involve the possibility of gain as well as loss. Nowhere is this more evident than in the economic functions that form the bedrock of global capitalism, such as banking, mortgage loans, stock market investments, private insurance and pension schemes. Risk is at the very heart of such activities and courses through the routine decisions of brokers, market makers, actuaries and financiers. Indeed, some thinkers, such as Anthony Elliott (2009), postulate that risk can be viewed as *the* central driver of the global economy. Both the negative and the positive facets of risk can emerge simultaneously, but produce disparate effects. As we know from the aftermath of the financial meltdown, profits and bonuses gained from the risk-taking activities of some may have negative knock-on consequences for others (see Rebonato, 2007: 11). Attempts to reduce the considerable fiscal deficit in the United Kingdom that resulted from the over-borrowing of the State and reckless mortgage lending in the private sector have produced tangible harms in the public sector in terms of unemployment and pension cuts for those seemingly uninvolved in the initial generation of the crisis. Far from being absolute, definitions and attributions of risk are contingent and labile. Different stakeholders with competing interests and goals may choose to talk up or redact particular elements of risk in line with priorities and objectives:

> Knowledge of risk may now be used on one side to highlight 'chance' and 'opportunity' and on the other to accentuate 'uncertainty' and 'danger'; where 'taking risks' in the spirit of enterprise tends to embrace its positive meaning, those that identify themselves as standing 'at risk' seek to draw attention to the potential for the future to visit us with danger.

(Wilkinson, 2009: 22)

As Wilkinson's observation infers, the five elements of risk outlined above are far from distinct. By way of example, a fusion of the properties of risk can be located in the emergence of global financial crisis. Although the causes of the current economic malaise are contestable, it is evident that standard probability models were overlooked by profiteers seeking to fill their boots through speculation and irresponsible lending, leading to huge economic losses, endemic uncertainty about the future and a gamut of harms to individuals, ranging from higher unemployment in the West as a consequence of debt reduction and cost cutting, to escalating problems of hunger in developing countries due to the upsurge in the cost of basic foodstuffs, such as wheat, rice and sugar. Clearly, different circumstances bring variant blends of elements, interchange between particular components occurs and groups and individuals may choose to highlight or downplay particular properties in line with overarching worldviews, personal expedience or instrumental motivations (see O'Malley, 2010: 15; Szmukler, 2003; Walklate and Mythen, 2010).

Inflecting towards risk

Over the last two decades the idea of risk has had a marked impact in the social sciences as well as at the level of popular culture, politics and policy making. Prior to the 1980s, risk was a relatively marginal subject in the social sciences, being commonly considered as a phenomenon both determined and utilized by those working in science, technology, engineering and medicine. The relative disinterest in risk in the social sciences can in part be attributed to historical values, institutional proclivities and professional preferences. By and large, risk has traditionally been associated with geo-physical rather than social processes and conceived by scientific experts to pertain to the objective, technical measurement of harms (see Adams, 1995). However, a number of focal incidents in the early 1980s brought to the fore important questions about the institutional management of risk and raised public sensitivities about environmental issues. Accordingly, currents of research in the social sciences became trained on these and other incidents and prominent thinkers such as Ulrich Beck and Anthony Giddens popularized new theoretical frameworks which mobilized risk as an axial principle. By the turn of the twenty-first century, risk had become established as an accepted unit of analysis within the social sciences (see Adam et al., 2000; Beck et al., 1994; Lupton, 1999b). In the first decade of the new millennium, the stock of risk has continued to rise. Indeed, one might argue that global processes and happenings have led to the academic and political significance of risk resounding at a higher pitch than at any other point in human history.

Much has been made of the cultural ubiquity of risk within contemporary society and the ways in which risk pervades the lived experience of citizens in Western cultures. Within the literature, it has been noted that risk filters through a range of cultural practices and social engagements, including work, relationships, food consumption, leisure activities, finance, personal security and health (see Beck, 1992; Caplan, 2000; Culpitt, 1999; Denney, 2005; Mythen, 2005a). The surge of academic interest in risk has led to the concept becoming a key term of reference for debate in the social sciences. Mirroring what became known as 'the cultural turn' in the 1980s (see Hall, 1980), it is plausible to talk about a 'risk turn' within the social sciences in the last two decades (see Mythen, 2008). Before we examine the academic currents that have characterized this turn, it is first necessary to collect up the underlying factors that have fuelled the turn to risk. Which underlying social and political processes have been instrumental in this rotation?

Insofar as seeking safety and security are innate aspects of human life, over the last three decades the language of risk has proliferated in the media, politics and within everyday discourse (see Boyne, 2003; Mythen and Walklate, 2006a; Taylor-Gooby and Zinn, 2006). While developments in biology, medicine and science have enabled us to identify a number of risks that would have remained unknown in the past, as Beck (1992; 1995; 2009) is at pains to stress, capitalist globalization has simultaneously produced a series of potentially dangerous technologies, such as nuclear power and genetic cloning. It is incontestable that the process of globalization facilitates the rapid movement of people, information, products and services. Yet speed can be seen as a burden as well as a blessing, aiding the pace by which risks travel across continents (see Tomlinson, 2007). The risks generated by globalization are highly portable and challenge the regulatory mechanisms historically developed within the sovereign boundaries of nation states. Citizens in the West may well have become accustomed to living with risk in its various guises, but it is important to recognize that the modern turn to risk in the social sciences is novel. Prior to the 1980s, risk was customarily seen as a technical term associated with 'hard science' modes of calibration and assessment. While engineers, physicists, medics, meteorologists and economists have historically deployed risk as a mode of measuring objective hazards, social science engagement with risk is relatively new. Given a predominant focus on the cultural and the subjective, social science approaches to risk have come to serve as a corrective to the dominant objectivist risk framework established in the natural sciences. In the 1980s iconic incidents such as the Chernobyl reactor explosion, the Union Carbide disaster and the BSE crisis came to symbolize the crystallization of public scepticism about scientific truth claims and public distrust in expert institutions. The high profile of these catastrophes in the media – allied to wider technological developments which aided the circulation of information about social hazards – was instrumental in raising public awareness about environmental and technological harms and putting risk firmly on the political agenda. Undoubtedly, the ubiquity of the traditional mass media, coupled to growing personal use of newer technologies such as the internet and mobile phones has played a part in raising public consciousness around risks in society (Anderson, 2009). Television and news media in particular seem to be magnetized to situations involving human catastrophe and scientific uncertainty, with extensive coverage being assured in cases where the experts disagree on the nature, causes or the extent of threat. Examples include the H1N1 flu epidemic, the safety of the MMR vaccine and the furore over emissions of radiation from mobile phone masts. Further, the fluidity of video and image transfer that mobile phones and the internet facilitate has enabled instantaneous sharing of communication about risks, hazards and accidents (Mythen, 2010). Risks now 'go viral' not only in an epidemiological, but also a technological manner.

In many respects, the heightened public awareness of risk observed in the Western world can be seen as something of a double-edged sword. Along the inside surface of the blade, the relatively free and uninterrupted flow of information in the public sphere heightens individual sensitivity to threats. A comparatively advanced state of risk consciousness potentially enables citizens to weigh up harms and to develop appropriate avoidance strategies. But on the outer edge, the very increase in risk awareness may encourage the modern individual to perpetually ruminate on low probability risks that are unlikely to materialize. In modern times, all manner of activities that may in previous generations have been conducted unthinkingly have become subject to risk assessments and probability calculations. Buying food at the supermarket, taking one's child to the swimming baths and choosing a holiday destination have all become practices that are fraught with lurking dangers and require hazard evaluation. As we shall see, thinkers like Furedi (2007a) and Isin (2004) would interpret such mundane modes of risk management as indicative of a noxious climate of social anxiety in which issues of personal security have come to colonize everyday life and personal autonomy is curtailed. For others, such as Beck (1999; 2009) and Bauman (2002; 2005) the age of risk is more ambivalent, opening up the capacity for personal mobility and the prospect of progressive political change. While I will grapple with these competing perspectives shortly, what it is incontrovertible is that risk has become a hallmark of the contemporary age, whether it manifests itself in the world financial meltdown, concern about exhaustion of energy supplies or large-scale violent conflicts. Just casting an eye over a morning newspaper is enough to raise sensitivities to a surfeit of threats that could easily send the most rational of people scrambling back under the duvet covers. Marmalade dropping headlines about the pensions 'time-bomb' and violent crime nestle up against warnings about terrorist sleeper cells primed to attack. Risk, it seems, is everywhere that we turn. Under such conditions, it is expectable that various assertions and claims will be made about the role of risk in the modern world. While Ulrich Beck has popularized the idea that we live in a risk society, others, such as Furedi (2002; 2007a) subscribe to the view that powerful stakeholders and social institutions have strategically cultivated a culture of fear. Although the comprehensiveness of such perspectives are up-for-grabs, various opinion polls support the view that Western citizens are both increasingly sensitized to risk and relatively anxious about contemporary problems and issues (see Eurostat, 2010; Gallup, 2005; Worcester, 2001). Nevertheless, despite the commonly held view that levels of personal anxiety have increased, we need to be careful that we do not confuse cultural and political representations of risk and assumptions about people's 'fearfulness' with the diffuse reality of individual and collective perceptions and worldviews. Although the data about mental health problems presented earlier indicates that a considerable number of people in the West are living with conditions of depression and anxiety, beneath the bald statistics such psycho-social problems are multi-factorial in nature and certainly cannot be read off as evidence of 'public fears about risk'. Although representations of a fraught and febrile world offered by scientists, politicians and the media might encourage us to see the world as a dystopic habitat, it is sagacious to retain a grasp of the relatively secure conditions in which we exist and to be appreciative of the traumas and suffering experienced in previous epochs. How we presently view society, the way in which we classify threats and how we treat other people – in this context those that are either vulnerable to harm or likely to produce it – are socially contingent and contextually rooted. The issue of risk – and our obsession with its identification and management – has come to the fore as a result of the coalescence of a range of factors including the dynamism of globalization, techno-scientific developments, mass institutionalization and increasingly rapid social change. With this in mind, it does not take a learned scholar to appreciate that risk is a filter through which Western cultures observe, organize and regulate people, products, places and events. A steady advance in the language of risk in media, politics, social policy, academia, culture and society is apparent not only in anecdotal terms but also at an empirical level. Over a decade ago, Lupton (1999a: 10) used media databases to search for references to the term 'risk' in the main headline and text of Australian daily newspapers between 1992 and 1997. During this five-year period alone references to risk had doubled. Furedi (2002: xii) conducted a similar exercise in the United Kingdom, tracking use of the term 'at risk' across UK daily newspapers between 1994 and 2000, finding that the term appeared nine times more frequently in 2000 than in 1994. For social constructionists such as Lupton and

Furedi this kind of exercise raises the critical question as to whether the dangers faced by Western society are actually escalating or whether such figures are reflective of a more risk sensitive and risk aware culture, both mirrored in and refracted by media products.

While it has become almost second nature for social scientists to tut disapprovingly at 'the media' for sensationalizing and amplifying social risks, we also need to be cognizant of the role played by the academy in the proliferation of risk discourse. Academics are as much a source of risk amplification as politicians, media professionals, scientists or cultural commentators. Academics conduct funded projects with public and private agencies, share their findings about risk with the public and other stakeholder groups and corporate communications professionals within our Universities promote our research to media outlets and potential investors. Simply typing the word 'risk' into an electronic academic search engine such as *Google Scholar* yields well over three million hits. This suggests that academics in the natural and the social sciences have played an important role not only in communicating about risk but also in cultivating the language of risk. In the social sciences risk has become something of a lingua franca, facilitating inter-disciplinary debate betwixt scholars in sociology, social policy, international relations, geography, politics, criminology and cultural studies (see Mythen and Walklate, 2006a; Taylor-Gooby and Zinn, 2006). It should also be pointed out that much of this interchange has taken place within and between what are classified as affluent advanced nations. Looking at the 'global' prevalence of risk using *Google Trends* might well confirm the importance of risk in terms of the number of searches conducted by internet users, but if one tabs down to the regional interest section to track the geography of these searches, the patchiness of the map is striking. Internet searches in countries such as the United States, Canada, the United Kingdom and Australia abundantly feature risk and this tells us something important about exactly where and why the language of risk has gained a foothold.

Despite the propagation of an abundance of work oriented towards or around risk, the glut of literature paradoxically provides a clue as to its 'risk'. In an academic world in which risk has been used to explain everything, then somehow it runs the risk of explaining nothing. As I will go on to argue, in some cases, overuse of risk in academia and its misapplication in the media and politics has obscured rather than elucidated social problems. In short, in a world where all things are risky, it is easy to lose sight of gradations of harm. Due to its tendency to flatten out social hierarchies, thinking in terms of risk may mask rather than reveal core questions, such as which threats are the most pressing, who is the most vulnerable and which efforts need to be made to reduce exposure. As such, there remains a need to get a critical fix on exactly which social phenomena risk is and isn't capable of explaining and to be bold enough to challenge instances where risk is mobilized to obfuscate or put to work as a foil for politically convenient actions. While it is used in common parlance to signal the unwelcome spectre of harm, it needs to be recognized that, when technically applied, risk also acts as an instrument for observing and surveying populations. Further, it is the utilization of risk as a technology for understanding and planning for potential adversities that generates tiers of social regulation (see Ewald, 1991; O'Malley, 2010). As the apparatus developed in science, technology and medicine allow us to detect a greater range of threats, so too do social institutions become duty bound to manage such dangers. As such, risk (re)produces and sustains itself. It perpetuates productive macro forms of structural regulation and micro forms of self-management. Despite acquiring a historically unprecedented array of knowledge about threats to the individual, society and the environment, endeavours to predict and reduce risk are not always successful. What we choose to do at an individual level to limit our risk may sometimes result in exposing ourselves to higher rather than lower probabilities of harm. To cite one striking example, following on from the September 2001 terrorist attacks, in the months of October, November and December air travel in the United States fell by 20, 17 and 12 per cent respectively. In these three months, 353 more people died in road traffic accidents compared with the preceding year, a rise of almost 10 per cent (Begley, 2004). The inference here – which cannot, of course, be causally determined – is that as more people decided not to fly and traffic increased on the motorways so too did the number of fatalities. As this unfortunate statistic reveals, we cannot design risk out, despite individual and institutional efforts to do so. Our attempts to protect ourselves from one risk may inadvertently render us vulnerable to another.

There is, nevertheless, some justification for the rise of risk as a lens through which social problems and social issues are viewed. If we concur that risk is about possible exposure to harm, it is clear that many macro level processes and micro level interactions and decisions are saturated by risk (see Fischhoff and Kadvany, 2011: 4; Mythen, 2004). As Beck (2009) maintains, making meaningful interventions in the cycle of environmental destruction or attempting to jump-start the ailing economy requires grappling with risk at the level of strategies and policies. Yet as we shall discuss in Chapter 6, such 'global' risks are at once local, being affected by our everyday decisions and behaviour, from consuming environmentally friendly products and recycling waste, to retaining economic commitments in working pensions and trust funds. Thus, risks exist both for – and in the interface between – the individual and the society. As a result of this, we are all both bearers and subjects of risk, whether we like it or not. We should also keep at the forefront of our minds that risk is a plastic concept that generates multiple meanings. In differing circumstances, it can be a catch-cry, a warning, an appeal, a tool for blame, an enticement, a technology of regulation or a scare tactic. In political dialogue risk is frequently set against its antonym, safety. In exhorting us to help in limiting social bads – obesity, cancer, terrorism, identity theft, burglary – politicians simultaneously promote notions of a good life of safety and security. Such contrasting and pliable meanings reveal both the beauty and the beast of risk. It may allow freedom of representation and application, but so too can it lead to definitional confusion and conflicting interpretations. The very liquescence of risk enables its appropriation as a tool of persuasion that can aid and abet those using it for Machiavellian purposes.

Risk has historically been approached in the academic literature as a form of calculation through which harm could be identified. This is unsurprising given that the language of risk had generally been fashioned by the natural rather than the social sciences. Until recently risk had largely been treated in an objective and probabilistic fashion, as a mode of quantifying, communicating and mitigated against threats. Once such risks were identified through assessment – be they environmental, biological or crimogenic – regulations and procedures could be reinforced and enhanced to improve safety. Or so the story goes. As we shall see, in the last three decades various contributions from within the social sciences have sought to critique the narrowness of scientific-objectivist accounts of risk and to draw attention to the subjective and social dimensions of risk. The formative contributions to debates about risk within the social sciences were initially relatively diffuse and scattered across the disciplines of psychology (Slovic, 1987), geography (Adams, 1995) and anthropology (Douglas and Wildavsky, 1982). In the early 1990s, the uptake of risk in sociology moved on apace, largely due to the contributions of heavyweight thinkers such as Beck and Giddens. Arguing in similar grooves, these authors sought to throw light on the social salience of risk and championed risk as a theoretical prism through which macro social shifts could be viewed. Since the publication of Beck's *Risk Society: Towards a New Modernity* (1992), interest in risk has grown steadily. Alongside the band of sociologists inspired by Beck's landmark text, followers of Mary Douglas's work in anthropology and a collection of political and criminological scholars deploying Michel Foucault's work have contributed to elaborate and extensive debates about risk. Today, understanding the evolution, construction, assessment and regulation of risks is a central preoccupation in the social sciences. Reflecting the rise of interest in risk in the media and politics, a voluminous bank of literature has developed and a range of major empirical projects funded by international bodies have sought to investigate the production, assessment and management of risk. As a result of the marked upsurge in interest in risk across the social science disciplines, a great deal has now been written about the ubiquity of risk and the ways in which various threats and dangers impact upon and shape the lived experiences of individuals in Western cultures (see Arnoldi, 2009; Beck, 1992; Gardner, 2009; Lupton, 1999b). Where just two decades ago risk was considered something of a novel subject of focus for social thinkers, it has now become firmly embedded in the mainstream of theoretical advancement and empirical enquiry. A range of journals specifically tailored to the subject have become popular, including *Risk Analysis, the Journal of Risk Research, Risk Decision and Policy* and *Health, Risk and Society*. Furthermore, a host of international centres that promote risk research have developed such as the *Centre for Analysis of Risk and Regulation* in England, the *Harvard Center for Risk Analysis* in the United States, and the *Risk and Crisis Research Centre* in Sweden.

Approaching risk: Paradigms, branches and perspectives

In order to firmly set the foundations, it is worth categorizing macro and micro approaches towards risk and also distinguishing between different strands of theoretical development. In pursuit of clarity, I wish to draw conceptual distinctions between three elements that can help us both define and differentiate between approaches to risk: paradigms, branches and perspectives. As each of these elements is equally important in informing the positions adopted on risk, I refer to these them collectively as the *hermeneutic triumvirate of risk*. When talking about *paradigms*, I am referring to underlying epistemologies and ways of seeing the world. Beneath the paradigm, perceptible *branches* of risk research have evolved. These branches indicate the particular focus of inquiry and the methodological approach adopted. Emanating from different branches of risk research, a range of theoretical *perspectives* have taken shape in the social sciences. It is important to see these three elements of the hermeneutic triumvirate of risk

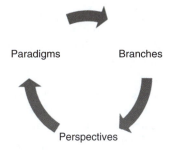

Figure 1.1 Hermeneutic triumvirate of risk

as connected and mutually conditioning. Paradigmatic approaches inform and influence branches of risk research and these branches have in turn fostered the development of specific theoretical perspectives (Figure 1.1).

Let us begin then with the paradigm. I am using the term 'paradigm' in this context to refer to the core set of values and attitudes which shape worldviews on risk. While paradigms are not absolute – in the sense that the complete works of writers and researchers cannot be neatly located within them – we can identify two paradigmatic poles as instrumental in informing branches of risk research and filtering through to discrete perspectives: realism and constructionism. The paradigms of realism and constructionism essentially exist at two ends of a spectrum and inform distinct ideas, notions and values about risk (see Hacking, 1990; Lupton, 1999a). While the natural sciences, medicine and economics have been central in the development of realist approaches to risk, a constructionist tradition has largely taken shape in the social sciences. The realist paradigm that has developed since the Enlightenment period arguably remains more institutionally embedded than constructionism (see Jackson and Rees, 2007). Realists believe that risks are 'real' and measurable phenomena which exist in the natural and social world. For realists, the key task is thus to reveal particular dangers in society and to develop scientific and technical knowledge about these dangers. The positivist philosophy underlying realism is underpinned by distinguishing between cognitive perceptions of risk and the materiality of threats in the real world. For realists, the task is to quantify risks and to track and trace causality. Once risks have been calibrated and probability estimates have been made, it is the duty of experts to disseminate information to the general public to enhance safety and security. Thus, realist approaches have tended to be predominantly quantitative and favoured activities such as identification through tools of assessment, the creation of statistical formula to estimate threat and the implementation of harm reduction strategies. Out of the realist tradition a series of technologies of risk have been used to test susceptibility, reliability and resilience in science, medicine, environmental health and the economy. A range of statistical and technical methods have been developed to anticipate the probability of discrete harms materializing in the future, ranging from adverse weather conditions to terrorist attacks (see Amoore, 2011; Loader and Sparks, 2002). In the course of the twentieth century processes and practices of risk assessment which were previously employed in high risk areas, such as the nuclear, chemical and airline industries have become more common in other spheres. In the contemporary world, a plethora of sectors of social life have to be risk assessed and safety principles agreed to reduce the possibility of harm occurring. Risk assessment procedures are now a routine part of occupational life in many sectors including health, education, policing, immigration, welfare, food production and sport. The creep of risk has been quite pronounced and its tentacles extend into what might previously have seemed unlikely places. Within Universities, for example, Heads of Department are now obliged to compile formal risk registers through which potential threats are identified, undergraduate students are directed to perform risk assessments before undertaking research dissertations involving 'human subjects' and academics are required to risk assess their working environment, computing facilities and electronic security practices.

In contrast to the realist goal of rendering threats to human safety visible, the overriding focus in the social sciences – arguably with the exception of psychology – has been on the social and subjective side of risk. In the constructionist way of thinking, risk is a broad and complex concept that is not reducible to objective assessment or probability estimates. Lending more freely from the principles of social constructionism, branches of risk theory have sought to investigate the ways and means by which risks are culturally constructed, communicated, comprehended and regulated. This work has involved a variety of foci but is collectively propelled by the quest to understand the role that institutions, policies and social processes play in shaping what people think and do about risk. We can see from this division that the natural sciences have primarily approached risk as an extant tangible entity, whereas the social sciences have generally been more concerned to tease out the ways and means by which risks are produced, labelled, represented and managed. Paired down to archetypes, the realist approach leads technical experts to report 'objective' facts about risk, while the constructionist perspective examines the role of social structures in influencing 'subjective' knowledge about risk. Social constructionists do not set out to uncover the reality of risk but rather to understand the social interactions and processes through which risks are brought to public attention (see Le Coze, 2005). As tensions between the public and experts over failures in institutional risk communication and risk management suggest, at the extreme ends the realist and constructionist paradigms make incompatible bedfellows. The gap between experts and the lay public in interests and priorities around risk has traditionally been mirrored by conflict between scientists schooled in realist methods of risk assessment and social scientists seeking to find out how risks are made to mean by individuals and social groups (see Wales and Mythen, 2002; Wynne, 2002). Szmukler (2003) defines the process of evaluating risk as containing two components: numbers and values. The latter, which refers to the estimation of adverse events occurring has been the dominant preoccupation within the realist tradition, whereas the latter which relates more to perceptions of risk and the values attached to them have preoccupied social constructionists. Insofar as the realist tradition has historically been dominant in the natural sciences, within the social sciences two branches of inquiry inspired by both constructionism and realism have become popular. In constructing a typology of risk research we can refer to these branches as those of *risk analysis* and *risk theory* (Figure 1.2). Risk analysis has largely been developed within psychology and has produced a prolific range of academic outputs. In contrast to risk theory, risk analysis has been strongly influenced by technical/calculative approaches and is underpinned by the assumption that risks can be accurately measured by scientists, medics and climatologists. As such, the prime focus

Paradigm	Realism	Constructionism
Branch	Risk analysis	Risk theory
Perspectives	Psychometric approach Heuristics and biases Mental modelling	Risk society thesis Anthropological approach Governmentality Culture of fear

Figure 1.2 Typology of risk research

of risk analysis as it has evolved in psychology has been to assess how people cognize, mentally organize, rank and respond to specific risks. Proponents of risk analysis are essentially seeking to evaluate various facets of risk perception and patterns of information processing in order to determine which components of risk people find frightening and how accurate their perceptions of risk are. Within the risk analysis tradition we can identify three intersecting perspectives: the psychometric approach, heuristics and biases and mental modelling. In the most popular and well developed form of risk analysis known as the psychometric approach, researchers have built up knowledge about the 'social' dimensions of risk including how people rank harms and how people respond to expert information about risk. Academics deploying psychometric methods have sought to measure people's tolerance to a range of risks and their attitudes towards different types of risk. Key work in the psychometric field conducted by the Oregon School led by Paul Slovic (1987; 2000) indicates that estimates of harm given by lay people often do not match the likelihood of a particular risk occurring. These psychometric studies show that people tend to over-estimate the incidence of 'low probability, high consequence risks' such as nuclear accidents and terrorist attacks and underestimate the harms caused by high probability and high frequency risks such smoking and alcohol consumption (see Wilkinson, 2009: 39). Through an ample bank of empirical studies, Slovic and his colleagues have found that the acceptability or otherwise of a risk for the individual is contingent on several factors which relate to the perceived nature of the threat. For instance, in circumstances in which a discernible benefit may be gained and the risk is seen to be voluntarily taken by the individual, tolerance of harm is relatively high. Conversely, in circumstances in which a risk is seen to be imposed on the individual without consent tolerance is much lower. Similarly, in situations in which the effects of risks are largely unknown and/or poorly understood by science people will tend to be risk averse rather than accepting of danger. Risks of great magnitude such as terrorist attacks or nuclear accidents have been found to evoke feelings of dread and to be highly unacceptable to many people. In the psychometric approach, the way in which individuals rank risks in terms of their severity has been cross tabulated with estimations of frequency, that is how likely an event is to transpire or how often it materializes over time. Notably, the frequency of risks associated with categories of dread and the unknown are overestimated by individuals and tolerance of them is low.

In a similar vein, work into the cognitive shortcuts that people use in making judgements about risks and the preferences they exhibit in estimating harm has been conducted. In what is known as heuristics and biases research a confluence of factors have been found to influence judgements about risk. Embedded social practices such as relating risks to personal experience or estimating threat according to whether people in proximity have been affected by a particular threat. While these heuristics are in some senses inevitable and useful, they can also lead to certain biases emerging which can lead to inaccurate judgements being made. Work in the area of heuristics and biases draws attention to two common errors that people make when they make judgements about risk: availability bias and optimistic bias. Optimistic bias describes the tendency for individuals to have an unrealistically sanguine view of their health in the future. Empirical studies which have reported the existence of optimistic bias reason that people wish to psychologically insulate themselves from the negative effects of dealing with potential upcoming adversities and expect that threats will affect others rather than themselves (see Taylor and Gollwitzer, 1995; Weinstein, 1980; Weinstein and Klein, 1996). Optimistic bias frequently occurs when people are asked to consider risks which affect their own health and safety, including harmful effects of smoking, drinking and drug consumption, crime victimization and mental illness (see Joffe, 1999: 56). Alongside optimistic bias, a famous study by Amos Tversky and Daniel Kahneman (1974) found that people use a number of cognitive codas in evaluating information about risk. The work of Kahneman and Tversky has been instrumental in uncovering the shortcuts that people take in addressing social problems and issues and the ways in which cognitive preferences affect decision making. Mlodinow (2009: 28) alludes to a common question used in tests for availability bias: 'Which is greater: the number of six letter English words having "*n*" as their fifth letter or the number of six letter English words ending in *ing*?' Empirical studies show that the majority of people choose the latter rather than the former. The explanation connects to the relative availability of the two options. Because we frequently come across and use 'ing' words they are more retrievable in memory. Of course, the correct answer is the former – i.e. those words that have '*n*' as their fifth letter – as this group of words includes all of the six letter words ending in 'ing'. The shortcuts that people use in decision making are alluded to as *heuristics* and the errors that people frequently make in assessing risk were attributed to *biases*. In relation to risk perception, the availability heuristic accounts for the way in which recent exposure to a risk – either personally, among family or friends or through media consumption – can sensitize people to a particular threat and cause them to over-or underestimate harm (see Lombardi, 2004: 367). Rather than making judgements based on objective indicators, people instead tend to use the information which is available and proximate to them. Of course, this availability bias can generate errors which span either way, from the 'Crimewatch effect' whereby we may become anxious about our personal safety immediately after watching television programmes featuring violence, to reasoning that alcohol cannot be that bad for you because an elderly relative of yours has lived a long and fulsome life, despite having imbibed several pints of Stout a day.

Alongside research into heuristics and biases and the psychometric approach, a third cognate area of risk analysis has sought to investigate people's mental landscapes of risk and risk incidents. Primarily developed in the area of risk communication, the mental models methodology seeks to establish differences between the beliefs and cognitive maps constructed around particular risks by different stakeholder groups (see Fischhoff and Kadvany, 2011: 107). The primary objective of this research has been to shed light on the mental representations of risk that underlie perceptions of risk and shape decisions about preferences and tolerances (see Flynn et al., 1993; Morgan et al., 1992). Aspects of mental modelling have been used to advance knowledge about human decision making, while other studies have sought to rectify gaps between stakeholders by determining tools to aid better communication and more effective decision making (see Atman et al., 1994; Bostrom et al., 1992).

In many respects, the findings from the mental models methodology, heuristics and biases research and the psychometric approach align (see Kahneman et al., 1982). Considered collectively, they show that individuals generally overestimate the probability of certain risks occurring and underestimate those that are actually likely to affect them. Given the emphasis on cognition, perception and communication, one might be tempted to think that forms of risk analysis such as heuristics and biases and the psychometric approach have been primarily informed by the constructionist paradigm. Although there are residues of constructionism in evidence, I would argue that those involved in risk analysis have been more strongly influenced by the realist paradigm. Such an influence is evidenced by the pre-setting of calculable risks to be considered in experiments, the assumption that physical hazards can be ranked according to magnitude, the separations drawn between expert and lay actors, the proclivity towards hypothesis-based research and the favouring of quantitative methods and statistical modes of analysis. Importantly, despite seeking to access certain 'social' dimensions of risk, the epistemological assumption underpinning risk analysis is that harms can be accurately quantified by experts in order to compare them with public estimates of danger, media communications of threat and responses of stakeholders. The overarching problem with risk analysis undertaken in this *oeuvre* is that it is overly focussed on defining the public by lack in terms of perception, interpretation and communication of risk. Consequently, policy initiatives stemming from the findings of risk analysis have focussed on designing educative programmes to 'correct' errors in judgement and to align public perceptions with the 'real' probabilities of harm as defined by experts. Unfortunately, all of this glosses over several important caveats that destabilize the assumption of scientific expertise and lay lack. In the first instance, certain risks may be scientifically unquantifiable. Second, scientific estimations of risk are fallible, as a range of historical incidents from Windscale to the Fukushima nuclear disaster indicate. Third, scientific experts often disagree about the extent, nature and possible consequences of risk. Fourth, the expertise of lay people and their capacity to make reasonable judgements regarding risk is underplayed. It needs to be remembered that in some instances members of the lay public end up producing accurate estimates of harm, while scientists make inaccurate predictions (see Wynne, 1992; 2002). Arguably, the risk analysis tradition has over-emphasized the differences between lay people and experts and under-emphasized the similarities. It must be remembered that scientists are themselves members of the public with their own worldviews and values. Simply donning a lab jacket does not lead to the exorcism of cultural values, political beliefs or personal assumptions. Despite striving for objectivity and attempting to embed it via professional methods, scientists cannot insulate themselves against exhibiting biases.

Thus, despite its moniker, we should not presume that risk analysis is distinctly analytical, nor indeed critical, so far as examining the perception, communication and production of risk is concerned. Indeed, a strong methodological focus on individual cognition within the risk analysis tradition has often led to an inadequate appreciation of both group dynamics and social context (see Joffe, 1999: 71). Particular studies in the risk analysis tradition have been criticized for being experiment centric and gathering data under unrealistic laboratory conditions. At worst, studies have been reliant on unrepresentative samples – most notably a ready pool of American college students – and have paid little attention to the everyday contexts in which people encounter and negotiate risk. Nevertheless, the branch of risk analysis has been influential in informing government policy and is supported by a raft of journals devoted to disseminating its findings. Critics of risk analysis such as Wilkinson (2001; 2009) have argued that the bulk of work in risk analysis remains detached from the experiences, needs and problems of the large majority of the World's population. While studies investigating public perceptions of low probability threats such as food contamination and chemical leaks are routinely published in risk-oriented journals, dire global problems of malnutrition, poverty and disease seem to lie outside the ambit of interest. Perhaps partly as a consequence of their rolling temporalities, such harms have received a distinct lack of attention in the branches of both risk analysis and risk theory.

The realist inflection within the risk analysis branch of research can be contrasted with the predominantly constructionist inspired branch of risk theory. Arguably, it is the different sets of assumptions, beliefs and worldviews with which researchers approach their academic activities which helps us account for the parallel development of the two branches. The distinct paradigmatic accents have led to risk analysis and risk theory following largely separate and autonomous trajectories. Those involved in the development of risk theory have taken little heed of the findings of those working in the predominantly empirical field of risk analysis. In contrast to the experiment-focussed empirical bent of risk analysis, developments within risk theory have offered competing conceptual narratives of the place of risk in contemporary society. Informed by the constructionist paradigm, work along the branch of risk theory has led to the emergence of various perspectives including the risk society thesis, governmentality, the anthropological approach and the culture of fear thesis. While risk analysis has undoubtedly had a greater impact in psychology, risk theory has been most fully developed in sociology, cultural studies, politics and criminology. Of course, the typology of risk research I have sketched out here is intended to provide a broad brush picture of developments in the social sciences. As such, it cannot reflect the complexity or the diversity of the full gamut of approaches and does not capture anomalous examples. For instance, some work by those situated in the risk analysis tradition has sought to test the applicability of theories of risk (see Dake, 1991; Marris et al., 1998). Similarly, as perspectives within risk analysis have different paradigmatic inflections, theories of risk such as the risk society perspective are informed by both constructionist and realist paradigms (see Lupton, 1999a; Mythen, 2004). In line with their respective impact in these disciplines, in the remainder of the book I wish to unpack and scrutinize theories of risk and to consider their applicability and resonances in the contemporary world. This chapter began by grappling with the slippery issue of risk definition. Casting back to the etymology of risk and reflecting on the various narratives surrounding its evolution, it becomes apparent that definitions of risk are mutable and culturally relative. This is a caveat for us to bear in mind through the course of the book.

2 Theorizing Risk

Introduction

Having contemplated the linguistic origins of risk, the drivers of the recent turn to risk and the contribution made by scholars of risk analysis, it is now time to focus more methodically on the foundational perspectives which constitute risk theory. In Chapter 1 both the underlying processes involved in the popularization of risk and the constituent properties of risk were discussed. In mapping out the hermeneutic triumvirate that informs and defines risk research in the social sciences, we have deliberated on the paradigmatic assumptions that inform the study of risk, accounted for the different branches of risk research that exist and identified the major theories that have gained credence in the social sciences. Insofar as the approaches developed within the predominantly realist branch of risk analysis have been relayed, it is now necessary to elaborate the perspectives that have emerged out of the constructionist tradition of risk theory. My aim in this chapter then is to provide extended outlines of key perspectives, noting their origins, chief proponents, architectural features and analytical scope. Rather than making a hurried conceptual deposit, I will, in upcoming chapters, be putting each theory to work through specific cases of application which demonstrate how specific situations, processes and incidents might be viewed through the lenses of different perspectives. Instead of attempting to cover the gamut of risk and risk-related theories, I wish instead to centre on those which I consider to be the most impactful and those that have been most frequently utilized and debated in the social sciences, before subjecting them in later chapters to more rigorous conceptual interrogation. In adopting a selective approach to the literature, I provide a summary of four key perspectives that have sought to understand the consequences of risk for human experience and the institutional uses of risk – namely the risk society, governmentality, anthropological and culture of fear perspectives. Although some commentators have flagged the relevance of risk to other theoretical perspectives – for example, systems theory and actor network theory (see Arnoldi, 2009: 61; Boyne, 2003: 69) – the perspectives on risk I concentrate on here have undoubtedly been the most impactful in sociology, cultural studies, social policy, politics and criminology. Focussing on a limited number of perspectives will enable us to assemble a broad theoretical base from which to systematically broach issues around crime, security and justice. In considering the development and application of theory, it is important to avoid risk centrism. As we shall see, although a red thread of risk runs through the spine of risk society and anthropological theories, academics advancing the governmentality thesis and the culture of fear approach set out to define a more diffuse set of conditions that describe processes of social ordering and cultural control rather than being tethered to the concept of risk per se. Thus, we should note from the outset that both the emphasis and the accent on risk varies considerably within and across social science perspectives.

The risk society perspective

Insofar as the risk society thesis has been cultivated and promoted by a range of thinkers, including Anthony Giddens (1998; 1999b), Beck et al. (2000) and Piet Strydom (2002), the German sociologist Ulrich Beck is undoubtedly its progenitor and standard bearer. More than any other text on or about risk, Beck's *Risk Society* (1992) generated a spike of interest in risk and served to popularize the subject in sociological circles (see Mythen and Walklate, 2006a; Taylor-Gooby and Zinn, 2006). Since its ascendance in the 1990s, the risk society thesis has been applied across a range of social science disciplines to enhance understanding of a range of activities and processes including fear of crime (Hollway and Jefferson, 1997), global futures trading (Boden, 2000) environmental disaster management (Bennett, 2012), home ownership (Ford et al., 2001) and the regulation of terrorism (Mythen and Walklate, 2006b).

Over the last two decades, Beck (1992; 1995; 2000; 2009) has continued to write about the production, effects and regulation of risk, while also devoting attention to associated projects on individualization, globalization and cosmopolitanism. Heralded as one of the most important sociological thinkers of the age, Beck has now relinquished his role as Director of the *Institute for the Study of Reflexive Modernization*, but remains an Emeritus Professor at the University of Munich. He has also retained visiting roles at the London School of Economics and Harvard University. Beck has been widely feted as a social science luminary and a public intellectual who has made important contributions to politics, media debates and the formation of public policy (see Boyne, 2003; Ekberg, 2007; Elliott, 2002). Beck previously acted as an informal advisor to German Chancellor Gerhard Schröder, was a member of the Future Commission for Saxony and Bavaria and has written numerous thought pieces in newspapers in Germany and the United Kingdom, including *The Guardian*, the *Frankfurter Allgemeine Zeitung* and the *Süddeutsche Zeitung*. An extraordinarily prolific academic, he has amassed an August body of work, having published over 20 books. He is also something of a polymath, writing on a range of subjects, including the flexibilization of work, intimate relationships and transformations in religious belief. Despite such diffuse interests, it is Beck's work on risk which has made the most substantial impact within the social sciences (see Elliott, 2009; Mythen, 2007b). First published in Germany in 1986, under the title *Risikogesellscaft: auf dem weg in eine andere moderne*, Beck's magnum opus documents the deleterious side effects of technological and economic development and the incapacity of social institutions to regulate volatile threats. The meta-theoretical style of the risk society thesis follows a Germanic sociological tradition established by Marx and Weber and consolidated by Adorno and Habermas (see Lash and Wynne, 1992: 2). Inspired by the blossoming of the environmental movement in Germany, *Risk Society* (1992) tapped into a growing mood of public concern in Germany in the 1980s about the reluctance within science, business and politics to provide adequate safeguards against disasters and to address cumulative environmental problems (see Wilkinson, 2011). It also struck a chord in other parts of

Europe where a number of high-profile incidents and accidents had heightened public sensitivity to the harmful effects of nuclear and chemical technology on the environment (see Allan et al., 2000; Boyne, 2003: 17; Wynne, 2002: 459). Against the backdrop of challenges to the competence of expert systems in the media and growing public distrust in social institutions, it is, in retrospect, easy to see just how and why the risk society perspective became modish in the late twentieth century. Beck's thesis acted as a popular lexicon that enabled academics to develop *au courant* conceptual tools to engage with the threats and anxieties which characterize the modern age. Furthermore, in the twenty-first century the term 'risk society' has transcended academic boundaries and become a moniker that is used by journalists, politicians and policy makers. Despite the undoubted purchase of the risk society thesis, as we shall see, various blind spots and limits to its exploratory reach have been identified. Before we examine these, let us first sketch out the central principles of the risk society thesis. What exactly does it mean to say that we live in a 'risk society'?

In a nutshell, Beck and his followers argue that Western cultures have experienced a seismic shift from a first modernity or 'industrial society' into a second modernity, or 'risk society'. The hazards that characterize the first modernity are relatively predictable, localized and controllable. Operating hand in glove with Beck, Giddens reasons that such dangers are treated as unfortunate accidents whose consequences can be relatively comfortably predicted and managed: 'external risk can be fairly well calculated – one can draw up actuarial tables and decide on that basis how to insure people. Sickness, disablement, unemployment were treated by the welfare state as accidents of fate, against which insurance should be collectively provided' (Giddens, 1999a: 4). By contrast, the larger scale 'mega-hazards' of the risk society are global and escape established institutional practices of threat assessment, insurance and regulation.

The original articulation of the risk society thesis sought to draw attention to the diffusion and the transformative capacity of two interlinked macro-social processes. Firstly, Beck argued that the unrelenting churn of capitalist development was leading to the reproduction of unmanageable 'side-effects' that threatened the future stability of the social system, such as global warming, chemical contamination and the leaking of nuclear waste. The generation of such manufactured risks – which occur through scientific development, intensive production of goods and mass consumption – effectively renders the second modernity 'a problem for itself' (Beck, 1997: 5). Secondly, Beck was concerned to raise awareness of the social consequences of a sweeping process of individualization which was leading to an increased accent on personal choice, decision and self-reflexivity on the one hand and introspection and reformation within social institutions on the other. These two processes of risk production and individualization are cast as dynamic and symbiotic, with each acting as a catalyst for the other. For example, recognizing the role of human activity in the production of air pollution fuels a net rise in public awareness of environmental risks and this in turn generates greater personal reflection regarding production of goods, individual consumption preferences, modes of travel and chosen leisure activities. As manufactured risks defy institutional forms of social, legal and political regulation, the burden of risk migrates from the systems world into the sphere of individual decision making (Beck, 2000: 53). Although the two processes are conceptually fused together, academic take up of the individualization strand has been more pronounced in Germany, while in most other European and

North American countries it is the risk strand of the thesis that has attracted most attention. Beck avers that radical transformations in the nature of risk are representative of a fundamental shift in the nature of politics and in patterns of social distribution. For him, the sporadic macro production of manufactured risks as a side effect of techno-scientific and economic development has generated deleterious consequences across a range of domains including health, the environment, security and politics. Meanwhile, the embedding of an everyday culture of risk management has placed recursive demands upon the self, forcing individuals to reflexively order their lives as planning projects to be designed and articulated.

Beck's claims regarding the transference from previous historical eras into the risk society is predicated on an analytical separation between 'risks' and 'natural hazards'. In previous epochs, 'natural hazards' – such as earthquakes, famine and floods – adversely affected human existence. By contrast, in contemporary Western cultures, the catastrophic force of natural hazards has largely been reduced by proactive human interventions in terms of regulation and management. Yet the advancement of science and technology and unfettered mass production for profit has inadvertently created a batch of 'manufactured risks', such as global warming and nuclear accidents. While human exposure to danger is by no means a novel phenomenon, Beck wishes to differentiate between the effects and consequences of the two forms of danger. The natural hazards of previous epochs are localized, amenable to regulation and attributable to either gods, demons or the destructive force of nature (Beck, 1995). In contrast, risks are anthropogenic, incalculable and unconstrained by temporal and spatial boundaries. Anthony Giddens (1999b: 3) offers an analogous vista:

> Life in the Middle Ages was hazardous; but there was no notion of risk and there doesn't seem in fact to be a common notion of risk in any traditional culture. The reason for this is that dangers are experienced as given. Either they come from God, or they come simply from a world which one takes for granted.

Notwithstanding the questionable temporal lines established in the risk society narrative, Beck argues that it is the very volatility of manufactured risks which undermines the authority of social institutions in the second modernity. The generation of 'boomerang effects', whereby affluent risk generating countries become exposed to adverse side-effects of risks of their own creation, makes real the possibility that techno-scientific and economic development will irreparably damage the lived environment and bring about the destruction of the planet. Although Beck is influenced by certain realist assumptions about the nature and magnitude of environmental threats, his argument also seeks to explicate the ways in which risks are socially constructed through 'relations of definition' (Beck, 1992: 227; 1995: 116). In contrast to the centrality of the 'relations of production' in Marxist theory, the term 'relations of definition' is used to describe the critical role played by institutions which set rules and regulations and create knowledge about risk, including scientific and technological bodies, national governments, the legal system and the mass media. Allied to responsibilities for defining threats, these institutions are also involved in risk assessment and management. For example, policy makers, the State, scientific experts and legislators are all involved in calibrating risk, setting levels of risk acceptability and determining compensation packages in cases of harm. Although the historical angles of the argument are somewhat underdeveloped, Beck believes that in the late nineteenth and early twentieth century calculative insurance systems evolved to assess the probability of accidents and to determine liability for compensation payments. By the middle of the twentieth century, legal systems were firmly involved in risk regulation and the welfare state functioned as a social support mechanism to insure against illness and harm. In this period, the rules and regulations embedded within the relations of definition were designed to deal with tangible and identifiable risks, such that the public could be protected, guilty parties punished and compensation packages awarded to victims. Thus, in the first modernity, the general public lobbied the various institutions that comprise the relations of definition to press for the fair distribution of social 'goods', such as employment, income, health care and housing. Conversely, in the risk society, individuals and political parties are not exorcised by the pursuit of goods but are instead bound up with trying to avoid unmanageable social 'bads'. Beck posits that in modern society, the legitimacy of the calculus of risk has been undermined by transformations in the nature of risk. What is more, this sea change in social logic is indicative of an ontological as well as a political transformation:

> The dream of class society is that everyone wants and ought to have a share of the pie. The utopia of the risk society is that everyone should be spared from poisoning ... the driving force in the class society can be summarized in the phrase 'I am hungry!' The driving force in the risk society can be summarized in the phrase 'I am afraid!'.
>
> (Beck, 1992: 49)

This fundamental shift is suggestive of a wider point about the democratization of social distribution under the logic of risk. While the defining logic of the class society is hierarchical – some win and some lose – the logic of the risk society is horizontal. Ultimately, everyone loses. What Beck (2009) determines as the foremost threats in contemporary society – financial meltdown, ecological crises and global terror networks – have the capacity to damage rich and poor alike.

In offering a critical commentary of Beck's contribution, I have suggested that the risk society thesis is founded on three pillars (see Mythen, 2004: 17). First, the argument rests on the assumption that the geographical scope of manufactured risks is comparatively greater in contemporary society than in preceding times. In stark contrast to the temporally compact hazards common in pre-industrial cultures, dangers in the risk society cannot be time or place limited. Second, manufactured risks are of unprecedentedly high consequence, possessing greater potential for causing widespread human harm. Not only do manufactured risks span the globe, they also generate catastrophic effects. In the risk society, the intensification of techno-scientific development accelerates rather than reduces the production of harm: 'the risks of terrorism exponentially multiply with technological advancement. With the technologies of the future – genetic engineering, nanotechnology and robotics, we are opening a new Pandora's box' (Beck, 2002: 9). Third, the catastrophic force of 'worst imaginable accidents' (WIAs) shatters existing principles and practices of social insurance, leaving a regulatory power vacuum.

Beck's style of communication is at once politically uncompromising and socially provocative. He is not motivated by empirical precision, nor is he concerned with the minutiae of formal methods of calculating, assessing and regulating risk. Instead he wishes to issue a warning about the impending environmental and social catastrophe that will eventuate unless current modes of production, consumption and regulation are reconfigured (see Wilkinson, 2011). Although Beck is motivated to illuminate the endemic self-generated problems of capitalism, he is relatively sanguine about the future, plotting a number of possible ways out of the present crisis. For him, the changing nature of risk has the capacity to reproduce positive subterranean social shifts and modifications in cultural practices that can serve as a stimulus for political change. In essence, the scale and extent of manufactured threats force citizens to consider risk in political terms. Given that public concerns cannot be satisfactorily expressed through the traditional routes of the formal political system, the diffusion of risk undermines traditional power bases, making society susceptible to social upheaval and political restructuring. Through self-co-ordination and direct action citizens are able to debate and contest vital issues affecting the economy, welfare, health and the environment. In this way, the adverse global effects of capitalist expansion, economic globalization and unchecked technological development make real the need for political change and encourage the construction of fledging political constellations (Abbinnett, 2000: 115; Beck and Willms, 2004: 195). As we shall discuss in Chapter 6, through direct actions – including protest marches, blockades, petitions and consumer boycotts – individual citizens have the capacity to collectively associate in order to challenge national policies and engage with wider international issues around social justice and economic exclusion. There are no shortage of examples that serve as sources of hope for Beck's subpolitical revolution, ranging from the global Occupy movement to the Arab Spring. Nevertheless, both the theoretical validity and the empirical case for the risk society thesis have been subjects of much discussion in the social sciences. A number of theorists have advocated the politically progressive dimensions of the risk society thesis (Bronner, 1995; Strydom, 2002), while others have developed trenchant critiques of the risk society thesis (see Atkinson, 2007; McMylor, 2006). In response, Beck (2007; 2009) has both countered specific criticisms and sought to modernize particular aspects of his theory.

The epistemological standpoint assumed by Beck is quite complex and placing it squarely within a particular paradigm would not do justice to the complexities of the argument. Indeed, the extent to which the risk society thesis is primarily informed by realism and constructionism has spawned a debate in itself. Depending on the evidence marshalled, the case can be argued either way. For what it is worth, I have maintained that although Beck draws from each paradigm the thrust of Beck's thesis is aligned with the constructionist tradition (Mythen, 2004: 98). Although there are traces of realism in the way in which Beck casts environmental risks as imminent threats and the way that he attributes extreme physical dangerousness to genetic cloning and nuclear power, he is predominantly motivated by recounting institutional deficiencies in the communication and regulation of risk. This means that at the heart of his project is the social as well as the material construction of hazards and the policies and practices put in place to manage risk. Exhibiting a characteristic distaste for orthodoxy, Beck (2009: 89) has refused to subscribe to either paradigm and voiced his unwillingness to fall in line with 'simple oppositions'. For him, aligning with paradigms is a archaic practice that hinders free expression, reflexivity and sociological development. In forwarding what Lupton (1999a: 33) describes as 'weak constructionism' and Beck (2009: 88) refers to as 'constructivist realism', the author subscribes to a blended approach to risk which draws across the traditions. Although the controversy surrounding the epistemological foundations of the risk society thesis will doubtless continue, it is clear that Beck sees risk as a master key through which the most pressing social problems of the age can be unlocked. In shaping his thesis Beck is motivated to pass comment on the inadequacies of social theory and the inability of traditional sociological categories and concepts to grasp the problems facing the modern world. Launching a critique on the sociological canon, Beck claims that the discipline has served to perpetuate 'zombie categories' that remain alive in social science textbooks, but are peripheral to the major problems that people face in their lives as well as the ways in which the majority articulate their social experiences. For him, the prioritization of analytical modes of class or gender analysis within social science is a questionable endeavour in a world in which such forms of stratification have receded as markers of identity. Instead, Beck urges that we recognize that the world has changed dramatically as a consequence of the production of potentially catastrophic manufactured risks and advocates that citizens politically mobilize from the bottom up to challenge an unresponsive and outmoded system of formal party politics. Nevertheless, as we shall see, the attempt in the risk society thesis to capture not only major societal transformations but also large tracts of human experience via a grand narrative means that all manner of processes, issues and incidents – from intimate relationships to the war in Iraq – are branded with the stamp of risk. While the conceptual elasticity of risk enhances its capacity to be stretched across different contexts and practices, there is a degree of shoe-horning in Beck's attempts to encourage us see the world through risk. This raises a set of wider concerns that I will turn to later regarding the problems and issues that arise when academics, politicians and policy makers use risk as a central category through which to organize and categorize micro level lived experience and macro social transformations. At a time in which the framing of social issues in terms of risk in affluent Western nations has become customary, we need to remember that different types and degrees of risk manifest themselves in different contexts. Here, simple and stark figures – such as the bleak reminder that almost half of the world's population are surviving on less than $2 a day (Elliot, 2009: 257) while 1000 million people are malnourished (Oxfam, 2011: 31) – transport us soberly back from the plain of risk theory to the stark material realities of poverty and deprivation that scar the everyday lives of many.

The governmentality perspective

Where the risk society thesis is unquestionably the brain-child of Ulrich Beck, the governmentality perspective is rooted in the diffuse writings of the French social theorist Michel Foucault (1978; 1980; 1991b). In contrast to risk society scholars, Foucault and his followers have been less interested in the detrimental environmental impacts of risk and more concerned to document the ways in which discourses of risk are constructed, normalized and reproduced through everyday social practices. Hence, Foucauldian thinkers have attempted to unspool the ways in which the State and State institutions have mobilized risk as a mode of governance to order, categorize and control populations. In concert with the trajectory followed by Mary Douglas, Foucault's work spans a latitude of subject areas, including sexuality, imprisonment, ageing and mental illness.

Since his death in 1984, strands of Foucault's work have been conceptually developed within the governmentality tradition by academics interested in a range of social problems, including ill-health, criminality and obesity (see Dean, 1999b; Lee, 2007; O'Malley, 2010). As Wilkinson (2009: 52) observes, what coalesces these disparate interventions is a concern to connect risk to politics and, moreover, the exercise of power.

During his life, Foucault combined periods of travelling in Europe and North America with employment at a number of Universities (see Miller, 1993). It was as Chair of the History of Thought at the College de France in Paris – and through the much heralded public lectures that he gave during this time – that Foucault became acclaimed. A much vaunted and highly controversial academic, Foucault involved himself as an activist in political campaigns concerning the abolition of prisons, homosexual rights and human rights abuses. The shadow cast by Foucault's work remains large today and his ideas have been influential in a number of disciplines. In comparison with alternate perspectives on risk, the governmentality approach is represented by a relatively disparate group of scholars working *inter alia* in the fields of political studies, sociology, criminology, geography, education, history and international relations. It is important to note that although risk is an important ingredient within Foucault's writing, he was not motivated to study risk as a standalone concept. Rather, his central preoccupation was the relationship between knowledge and power as expressed through the idea of governmentality. Governmentality thinkers endorse and champion Foucault's 'genealogical' method, in which the sources and origins of institutional and individual practices are subjected to scrutiny. In contrast to Beck, Foucault was deeply absorbed in historical detail and his work represents an attempt to describe the establishment of order over time through prevailing social discourses and forms of institutional control. The historical analysis which is privileged by genealogists seeks to reveal fluctuations in knowledge, discourses and power over time and space in order to develop an archive of forms of governance and their impacts on citizens. Given the emphasis on historical change and a dependence on archival methods of analysis, the genealogical approach can be located firmly within the constructionist tradition. Although based on archival research, Foucault perceived the genealogical method to be much more than a descriptive form of data gathering and documentation. Rather, genealogy represents an attempt to historically ground the relationship between structure and agency. By developing a genealogical method Foucault (1993: 202) aspired to understand 'the constitution of the subject across history which has led us up to the modern concept of the self'. Moulded in Foucault's image, the genealogical tradition involves critical examination of language and discourse and the interrogation of conditions in which historical practices and functions arise (see Rose, 1984; 1996; 2000). As such, the genealogical approach is intended to 'cultivate the details and accidents that accompany every beginning' (Foucault, 1984: 80). For Foucault, a long historical view and an ability to think beyond contemporary trends was a necessary pre-requisite for understanding contemporary societies: 'the genealogist needs history to dispel the chimeras of the origin' (ibid). Geared towards analysis rather than description, the governmentality perspective involves analyzing the underlying basis of regimes of power that have prevailed in different epochs. Foucault specifically developed the notion of governmentality in his later work to scrutinize shifts in the nature of government that began to arise in the eighteenth century in Western Europe and took shape thereafter. Prior to the Enlightenment period, monarchs and feudal lords held sway and power was exerted either through a mixture of force and divine claims to sovereignty. The processes of the Great Transformation – most notably capitalism, industrialization and urbanization – acted as a stimulus for reconfigured modes of government. In order to deal with the complexity of new formations and to maintain control over populations experiencing social change, more elaborate modes of governance were required. Crucially, Foucault's notion of the 'history of ideas' assumes that there can be no knowledge without power. Similarly, without the exercise of power knowledge cannot exist:

> Knowledge linked to power, not only assumes the authority of 'the truth' but has the power to make itself true. All knowledge, once applied in the real world, has effects, and in that sense at least, 'becomes true'. Knowledge, once used to regulate the conduct of others, entails constraint, regulation and the disciplining of prac-tice ... there is no power relation without the correlative constitution of a field of knowledge, nor any knowledge that does not presuppose and constitute at the same time, power relations.

> (Foucault, 1977: 27)

In a much celebrated sequence of essays published shortly before his death, Foucault built on his previous work to refine the idea of governmentality, or, as he described it: 'the conduct of conduct' (1982: 221). In these essays, Foucault's attention is drawn not only to the role of Government in promoting social control but also the broader web of institutions involved in social regulation. Drawing on particular case studies of the education system, hospitals and prisons, in his later work Foucault described the seg-mentation of life into discrete institutional fields, bound by forms of governance, such as the family, work and welfare (Foucault, 1991a: 96). Using these institutions as filters, the neo-liberal State is depicted as securing the compliance of populations through a combi-nation of embedding disciplinary discourses and customs and enforcing statistical forms of categorization (see May and Powell, 2007). In comparison with preceding eras, the operation of power in contemporary society is perceived to be diffuse not direct, rooted in dominant discourses and achieved through the active consent of citizens rather than the direct application of force (see Dean, 1999a: 19). In capturing this motion from direct physical control to more oblique forms of control, Foucault alludes to the development of a 'science of the State', which involves an assemblage of surveillant practices through which institutions seek to observe and monitor citizens. Within Foucault's 'science of the State', risk is operationalized as a technique of social ordering through which people are surveyed and classified. In the famous 1975–76 public lecture series, Foucault drew attention to the strategies used by the State in the eighteenth and nineteenth centuries to organize processes of disease and mortality, highlighting the role of mathematics in pro-ducing risk statistics that serve to distinguish social groups and concretize ideas about (ab)normality (see Cooper, 2008: 7).

Following the genealogical method, governmentality scholars have analysed the ways in which risk calculations are used to assess, measure and order populations (see Lupton, 1999a: 87; Rose, 2000). Neo-Foucauldians such as Ewald (2002) for instance, have followed up this work by looking at the use of actuarial strategies that incorpo-rate risk as an ideational measure. Integral to the ordering of society through risk is the abstract and stretchy notion of discourse. Although discourse is usually linked to language in common parlance, a broader definition of the concept has been developed by governmentality thinkers. In Foucauldian dialect discourse refers to language, ideas and practices that act as channels for the representation of knowledge. Dominant institutions disseminate discourses that lead to the formation of discrete forms of knowledge that define what is knowable and thinkable about a particular subject, event or issue. Through the operation of discourses, particular forms of knowledge gain credence while others are excluded. The governmentality perspective assumes that expert institutions strategically deploy discourses not only as a means of neutrally channelling information about social harms to the public, but also to reinforce dominant values that lessen potential opposition to the status quo. In effect, discourses discipline and restrict human agency by generating 'truths' about society which then become interiorized by individuals (Foucault, 1978; 1980). In contradistinction to the operation of ideology in classical Marxism, discourses are practically as well as ideationally embedded. The interiorization of discourse through social practices functions through adherence to dominant social norms that enable people to function and make sense of the world. Thus power relations in contemporary society are reproduced not by diktat but through the reproduction of discourses by which people bring themselves to order (Allen, 2004: 39).

In *Discipline and Punish* (1979) Foucault focussed on the birth and evolution of prisons, drawing analogies between the operation of the prison as an institution and forms of regulation and monitoring in other institutional settings. Here he provocatively poses the question: 'Is it surprising that prisons resemble factories, schools, barracks, hospitals, which all resemble prisons?' (Foucault, 1979: 228) Inspired by his contribution, modern Foucauldian theorists have studied the relationship between institutional power and the implementation of rationalities, techniques and practices of risk. The management of populations through actuarial risk-based techniques is seen by Foucauldians as a fundamental mechanism through which power operates. Forms of risk analysis and prevalent discourses devised within and promoted by expert systems – for instance in economics, the natural sciences, medicine and psychology – inform discursive formations of risk that shape public perceptions of dangerousness. In opposition to the realist paradigm, risk is not so much a touchable material entity and more a mode of calculative rationality or 'moral technology' (see Castel, 1991; Dean, 1999a; O'Malley, 2006). Neo-Foucauldians argue that through the course of socialization individuals are surrounded by discourses of risk which are embedded in social practices. Children are taught from an early age to be cautious of strangers, sex education programmes warn teenagers about the risks of 'promiscuous' behaviour and in the workplace we are encouraged to adhere to multiple edicts around our health and safety – including frequent missives from human resources professionals that we ought to be keeping our bodies fit and healthy for work. The idea of governmentality then lays bare the will of neo-liberal States to govern risks to the population through various modes of incitement and provocation (Denney, 2005: 35). Through the implementation of forms of threat assessment and management – from crime and policing to obesity and sexual health – risk discourses and rationalities provide a tangible way of organizing people, places, history and the future (Ewald, 1991: 207).

In comparison with other theoretical approaches, adherents of the governmentality perspective have been especially keen to bring to the fore the political quality of risk. Following the line of governmentality thinkers, expert institutions are able to utilize and control discourses of risk to channel information, reinforce dominant norms and stifle political opposition. In Foucault's conception of perfect governance, the ultimate aim of power is to successfully but subtly direct the conduct of others (see Dupont and Pearce, 2001; Wales and Mythen, 2002). Power is exercised by a multiplicity of governing bodies, practices, techniques and rationalities and this in turn influences the range of (im)possibilities for individuals by shaping their fields of action (see Dean, 1999a: 133; Owen, 1995: 500). Foucauldians believe that contemporary neo-liberal institutions strive to activate and responsibilize individuals by making them answerable for the management of risks and uncertainties. What Foucault (1982: 10) described as 'self-subjectification' describes the institutional incitement to individuals to regulate and control their own identities, bodies and actions. He is thus motivated to trace 'techniques that permit individuals to affect, by their own means, a certain number of operations on their own bodies, their own souls, their own selves, modify themselves, and attain a certain state of perfection, happiness, purity, supernatural power' (Foucault, 1978: 74). Such a rendition of power suggests that it is 'productive' in the sense that it generates particular actions and effects. Neo-Foucauldians such as Culpitt (1999), Rose (1996) and Garland (2001) have collectively charted the rising prevalence of the language of risk and its broader usage as way of individualizing social problems and responsibilizing citizens. Rose (1996) avers that the modern tendency to categorize social problems through the lens of risk is indicative of a broader transition of responsibility from the State to the individual in areas of welfare, security, economic management and family life. In this way prevalent cultural discourses both lock into and strengthen the power of dominant groups. Not only do institutional discourses of risk make individuals responsible for their own safety management, they also encourage the attribution of blame by attaching risk to marginalized groups. For instance, in recent history in the United Kingdom, political and media discourses have identified asylum-seekers, single parents and Black and Asian youths as dangerous groups that not only threaten social order but also place a burden on the resources of the State (see Mythen, 2012a; Saeed, 2007).

In summary, the governmentality perspective suggests that discourses condition human behaviour by generating 'truths' about society that are 'interiorized' by individuals (Foucault, 1978; 1980). The interiorization of discourse enables people to make sense of the world and invites them to assume 'subject positions' (Mackey, 1999: 127). In effect, in contrast to pre-industrial epochs, power relations are reproduced not by force, but by discourses that facilitate patterns of self-regulation and conformity. Disciplinary power produces what Foucault (1977: 136–137) calls the 'docility of utility' through which bodies are 'subjected, used, transformed and improved'. Expert discourses of risk, thus provide the boundaries of (in)appropriate action, while the State performs governance by deploying technologies of risk management to regulate social practices and dissipate opposition to the political status quo.

The culture of fear perspective

In as much as Foucauldian theory represents an attempt to historicize the relationship between knowledge and power, the culture of fear perspective seeks to define the prevailing mood of the present age. Despite these disparate trajectories, as we shall see, there are commonalities between followers of Foucault and proponents of the culture of fear thesis, devised by Frank Furedi (2002; 2005a; 2007a; 2007b). Furedi is currently Emeritus Professor of Sociology at the University of Kent and has written extensively about the evolution and consolidation of a fearful, precaution-oriented culture. Like Beck, he is very much a public intellectual, frequently appearing on radio and television and regularly contributing to online political debates. Furedi draws upon key examples – including crime, child abuse and terrorism – to argue that Western citizens are living in a decidedly anxious and risk-averse era in which public fears run out of kilter with the magnitude of harm. Furedi maintains that the language of risk has become culturally ubiquitous, with the omnipresent reinforcement of a range of security threats being symptomatic of a tendency to focus on the negative aspects of everyday life. As such, he asserts that contemporary Western societies are increasingly affected by a 'culture of fear' which is actively promoted by State institutions and those working within media and security industries. In describing the defining features of the current epoch, Furedi (2002: 5) emphasizes the ways in which risk has become an embedded feature of contemporary life. The culture of fear thesis has been taken up by a number of scholars and cultural commentators and applied to a range of threats, including gang violence in schools, drink-spiking and terrorism (see Burgess et al., 2009; Curtis, 2004, Thompkins, 2000). For Furedi, the cultural ubiquity of risk and the tendency to categorize a range of experiences and events according to dangerousness, has resulted in everyday life becoming prone to examination through the lens of safety and security:

> Being at risk has become a permanent condition that exists separately from any particular problem. Risks hover over human beings. They seem to have an independent existence. That is why we can talk in such sweeping terms about the risk of being in school or at work or at home. By turning risk into an autonomous, omnipresent force in this way, we transform every human experience into a safety situation.
>
> (2002: 5)

While Beck sees the mass media as having a potentially positive role in 'socially exploding' hazards in the public sphere (see Cottle, 1998), Furedi takes the contrary view, believing that an obsession with risk in the mass media is socially disabling. As we are alerted to the existence of an array of potential harms – from flesh eating viruses to collision course asteroids from outer space – proponents of the culture of fear perspective argue that a rational and relative view of how safe we actually are slides out of view (see Altheide, 2002; Burgess, 2008). Furedi has it that our obsession with risk serves to shroud the fact that contemporary Western societies are comparatively safe and healthy places to inhabit. If we cast back to the dictionary definitions of risk discussed earlier, it would seem that positive conceptions of risk-taking as a route towards progress – for instance in medicine, technology or the economy – have receded, as the negative facets have come to prominence. Furedi reasons that our collective inability to appreciate the positive features of risk has led to the balance between constructive advances and negative consequences becoming skewed. The media's emphasis on high consequence, low probability harms encourages individuals to monitor their own risks through perpetual assessment of personal safety, health and fitness, hygiene, obesity and diet. It is here that the crossover with the governmentality approach is observable, with both perspectives tracking the ways in which risk management has migrated from the collective umbrella of the State to the life-world of the individual. Yet while Foucauldians such as Garland (1997) draw attention to a process of responsibilization through which independent risk management is undertaken, for culture of fear theorists the net result is the formation of a 'neurotic citizen' who is introspective, untrusting and fearful (see Isin, 2004; Walklate and Mythen, 2010). Our reliance on fear as a lens of categorizing and reflecting on human experience ultimately obscures the fact that – following indicators of life expectancy, health and mortality rates – contemporary Western societies remain relatively safe and secure places to live. Furthermore, Furedi points out that the micro level focus on managing dangers to the self diverts attention away from important unresolved global problems such as poverty, malnutrition and disease. Applying his thesis to the threat of terrorism, Furedi (2005a) contends that what we ought to concern ourselves with is not so much the harm caused by specific attacks but more the way in which the media constructs danger and the ways in which political and military responses to terrorism serve to escalate not reduce levels of violence. According to Furedi (2007b), the sensationalist adjectives which are mobilized to define terrorist attacks – among them 'unimaginable', 'incomprehensible' and 'catastrophic' – discourage engagement with the root causes of political violence. Furedi is troubled by the problem of sensationalism and the way in which media outlets have become inured to endlessly trawling for information about potential disasters and calamities. For him, the presentation of disturbing and dystopic visions of the future serves to blur the line between reality and fiction and promotes unnecessary anxiety among members of the public. In Furedi's opinion, constant consciousness raising around future threats has resulted in fear becoming 'a means through which people respond to and make sense of the world' (Furedi, 2007b: 7). Refusing to be drawn on what Beck sees as the real and catastrophic threat of environmental risks, Furedi sees risk and fear as socially constructed phenomena harnessed and manipulated by politicians, the mass media and securocrats. Furedi (2007a) chastises what he calls 'professional panic-mongers' and 'fear entrepreneurs' for their irresponsible pronouncements and policies that seek to manufacture and trade on alarm rather than allay public fears. It is, in Furedi's opinion, in the interests of such actors to create fear in order that 'safe' solutions can be advocated and sold. A fearful population is one that is malleable, susceptible and one that may be willing to invest in an expansive array of health, safety and security products. Thus, according to the culture of fear perspective, the production of fear is multivalent, operating at different levels of cognition, emotion and experience. In this regard, fear can be understood to be as much of a way of interpreting lived experience than a response to actual harms: 'many of us seem to make sense of our experiences through the narrative of fear. Fear is not simply associated with high-profile catastrophic threats such as terrorist attacks, global warming, AIDS or a potential flu pandemic . . . there are also the quiet fears of everyday life' (Furedi, 2007b: 1). Sharing common ground with governmentality thinkers, Furedi insists that risks are not simply material entities waiting to be uncovered. While institutions are able to draw on risk assessment strategies to calibrate potential harms, such strategies are themselves culturally contingent products of social values and choices:

> The impact of fear is determined by the situation people find themselves in, but it is also, to some extent, the product of social construction. Fear is determined by

the self, and the interaction of the self with others; but it is also shaped by a cultural script that instructs people on how to respond to threats to their security.

(Furedi, 2007b: 5)

As such statements suggest, the culture of fear perspective is avowedly constructionist in nature. Whereas Beck is determined to alert us to the consequences of manufactured risks, Furedi's focus is trained not so much on the risks themselves nor their material effects, but more on the social processes by which objects, people, practices and places acquire riskiness. Moreover, Furedi is seeking to capture and interrogate the processes by which incident specific anxieties fuel a generalized culture of fear:

> It is not hope but fear that excites and shapes the cultural imagination of the early 21st century. Indeed, fear is fast becoming a caricature of itself. It is no longer simply an emotion or a response to the perception of threat. It has become a cultural idiom through which we signal a sense of growing unease about our place in the world.

(Furedi, 2009: 1)

The anthropological perspective

The fourth perspective on risk for us to consider is the anthropological approach that is, somewhat confusingly, also referred to in the academic literature as the 'cultural-symbolic' and the 'sociocultural' approach. Emanating from the work of Dame Mary Douglas (1985; 1992), the anthropological perspective seeks to analyse the social functions of risk within culture. Deceased in 2007, Mary Douglas was one of the most highly regarded British social anthropologists of her generation (see Fardon, 2007). The seeds of the anthropological perspective can be found in the book *Purity and Danger* (1966) and are developed by Douglas and Aaron Wildavsky in *Risk and Blame* (1982). Set against the distinctly macro theoretical contributions of Beck and Foucault, Douglas's perspective was shaped by a pioneering anthropological study of the Lele people of the Kasai in the 1950s. Based on fieldwork observations, Douglas's cross-cultural approach seeks to explain how and why discrete activities and events are attributed dangerousness within different cultures and how risk functions as a means of establishing social cohesion. In the anthropological perspective, nothing is a risk in and of itself. Rather, what we understand as risk and conceive to be risky is shaped by political, economic, historical and social forces. Thus, the extent to which incidents, peoples or processes are deemed to be risky is culturally contingent and indexed to social structure: 'the selection of dangers and the choice of social organization run hand in hand' (Douglas and Wildavsky, 1982: 186). Objects, things and processes are therefore not risky in and of themselves, they acquire dangerousness through social processes of attribution.

According to Douglas (1992: 58), before one begins to consider the materiality of risk, it is first necessary to acknowledge that when individuals encounter dangers they do so with a pre-existent set of cultural beliefs and assumptions. It is at this juncture that overlaps between the anthropological, culture of fear and governmentality perspectives become visible, with Douglas reasoning that understandings of risk are culturally constructed entities that cannot be properly made sense of outside of particular frameworks of shared knowledge. Douglas' approach differs however, in that it is based on the structuralist principle that all cultures possess elemental forms and fixed classificatory systems through which social meanings are generated. Theoretically inspired by the functionalist tradition and drawing on ethnographic observations, Douglas explains how symbolic boundaries between good and bad are established and sustained. According to her, all cultures draw distinctions between purity on the one hand and danger on the other. These binary distinctions between purity and threat are upheld through social structures, traditions and commonly shared narratives. Aspects of culture which are deemed to be pure are celebrated whereas those that connote danger are feared. Douglas observes that different cultures uphold different boundaries between what is deemed to be risky and safe through maintaining traditions, sharing myths and implementing sanctions. At the same time, distinctions are drawn between self and other, where otherness is ascribed to individuals and groups deemed to be outside the accepted dominant culture: 'people select their awareness of certain dangers to conform with a specific way of life' (Douglas and Wildavsky, 1982: 9).

According to Douglas, risk and blame are inseparable concepts. As and when risks eventuate, they become attached to specific social sources and in-groups and out-groups emerge. Those who speak for the victims denounce the actions of those responsible for introducing harm into the community. In this way, dangerous 'others' are identified, blame is attributed and the collective solidarity of the in-group is reinforced. Douglas (1985: 52) reasons that indigenous cultures routinely use feared 'others' as repositories for blame for a range of social ills. In this way, the presence of the 'other' operates both as a safety valve for expressing anxieties and a means of (re)establishing order:

> The ideal order of society is guarded by dangers which threaten transgressors. These danger-beliefs are as much threats which one man (sic) uses to coerce another as dangers which he himself fears to incur through his own lapses of righteousness. They are a strong language of mutual exhortations ... thus we find that certain moral values are upheld and certain social rules defined by beliefs in dangerous contagion.
>
> (Douglas, 1966: 3)

In emphasizing the dynamic relationship between risk and blame, Douglas is seeking to explain why both individuals and cultures are afraid of different risks. According to her, different societies generate different sets of 'cultural biases'. Drawing on the classical sociological work of Emile Durkheim, Douglas posits that cultural biases can be indexed to two socio-structural axes, those of grid and group. Grid describes the extent to which a person's choice is determined by their social position. Group connotes the amount of cohesion that exists within society as a collective body. Cultures characterized by high group have strong internal cohesion and those with low group typically exhibit greater individuality and looser collective bonds. Following the functionalist proclivity for categorization and grouping, Douglas avers that individuals can be associated with one of four cultural types that are shaped by patterns of solidarity and social cohesion (see Manzi and Jacobs, 2008). Each of these cultural types share a characteristic set of worldviews about the lived environment. In accordance with their position at different locations along the grid/group axes, different types of cultural bias and thus different visas of risk are expressed by individuals. Writing with Aaron Wildavsky, Douglas (1982) proposes four ideal types: individualist, egalitarian, hierarchist and fatalist. Individualists have low group and grid and see risk as a potentially positive force that requires individual rather than institutional management. Individualists thus tend to have liberal outlooks on life and see the positive side of risk as a route to enterprise and progress. Egalitarians have high grid and low group, meaning that they identify with the collective and tend to attribute blame for risk to outsiders. As such, egalitarians seek equality in social relations and support social redistribution. Hierarchists have high grid and high group, and also conform to the rules of the collective even if this requires political conflict. However, hierarchists are more conservative than egalitarians and trust organizations to manage risk. Finally, fatalists have low group and high grid, making them prone to feeling a lack of control over their lives and to attribute outcomes to fate rather than human will. Fatalists do not possess strong political worldviews and their attitude towards harmful events is one of helplessness rather than resistance (Figure 2.1).

While risk theories have, in general, had limited impact within the branch of risk analysis, Douglas' typology has found favour with some academics in this tradition and her work has been well used as a tool for exploring divergent understandings of risk according to social solidarity, political worldviews and cultural values. Although the grid/group framework may seem overly prescriptive, it is important to stress that the anthropological perspective does not seek to impose value judgements about which cultural biases are the most rational or socially desirable. Rather, Douglas was primarily interested in questions of structure and her followers have sought to account for divergent risk perceptions between and within cultures while simultaneously upholding the general function of risk and blame as forms of social regulation and cultural bonding. Although certain cultures may express a degree of unanimity, it is possible for ideal types to coexist in the same locale and for individuals to flit between cultural biases according to context. For Douglas, when conceptualizing people's perceptions of risk we should not be making judgements about whether they amount to reasoned vistas of harm at one end or hysterical responses at the other. Rather, risk attitudes and values are seen as expressions of broader worldviews and reflections of degrees of trust in risk communicators

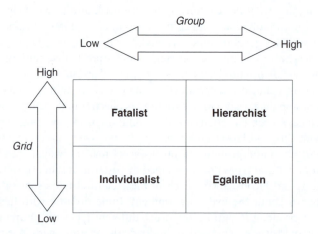

Figure 2.1 Grid and group

and regulators. In Douglas's view public disquiet about risk serves as a reasonable and rational form of displacement activity for wider social concerns. She believes that expressions of risk anxiety – such as those around the demise of the natural environment – act as a valve and serve to strengthen social cohesion, reinforcing what Durkheim (1984) called the 'collective conscience'. Although Douglas is clearly influenced by structural-functionalism, her work on risk falls squarely within the social constructionist tradition and promotes a culturally relativist position which is diametrically opposed to realism. While Douglas (1992) dismissed criticisms that her work was so relativist as too render risks little more than symbolic fictions, her emphasis on cultural diversity alerts us to the different signs, objects and communities which risks are attached to. Firmly rejecting the neutrality claims of the realist tradition, Douglas was dismissive of natural science attempts to objectively calibrate risk. In summary, her academic project urges us to question the rationality underpinning the contemporary trend of risk assessment, suggesting instead that practices such as hazard management and pollution control are simply modern forms of superstition (Douglas, 1985: 34). The ingrained fixation in the West with establishing risk probabilities has, in her opinion, led to a lack of attention being paid to the subjective and culturally situated ways in which people make sense of risk in their lives and the role of risk in the development of moral codes and social bonds. Cast in this light, the turn to risk distinguished earlier may itself be interpreted by proponents of the anthropological perspective as a latent attempt to set out the boundaries of transgression, regulate individuals and achieve social order.

Competing perspectives on risk: Commonalities and contrasts

We will be seeking to extend our appreciation and deepen our grasp of the four theories of risk outlined above in forthcoming chapters by applying each approach to specific examples. Nevertheless, it may be useful here to offer some initial reflections in order to draw out contrasts and comparisons between the perspectives. Before we do that, let us first position each of the theories in relation to the paradigms of realism and constructionism (Figure 2.2).

If we begin by thinking in terms of the top level of the paradigm, it is clear that the governmentality approach is heavily constructionist in nature. This inflection manifests itself in multiple ways, from tracking the role of institutional discourses to examining

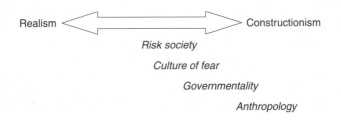

Figure 2.2 Positioning risk perspectives

variant modes of social regulation over time. For followers of Foucault, it is not so much the risk itself which is critical, but who or what risk gets attached to (see Dean, 1999a). The anthropological approach is similarly disinclined to delve into the gritty realities of harm and is more moved to explore the effects of risk at the level of social categorization and ordering. Clustering to the constructionist pole, the anthropology perspective seeks to demonstrate the functions and functionality of risk within culture as a boundary setter and a mechanism for channelling inclusion and exclusion. The culture of fear perspective can also be located within the constructionist paradigm, but arguably unintentional strains of realism are also present. In positing that a culture of fear incites us to needlessly worry about high consequence but low probability risks, an implicit assessment is being made about how 'risky' particular threats actually are. Although weighted towards constructionism, aspects of Beck's risk society thesis are informed by realism. Curiously, in comparing Furedi with Beck, the realist shadows which shade into the work of both thinkers result in them drawing quite contrary conclusions. While Furedi points up the paradox of a comparatively safe society that has become unreasonably risk averse, Beck's sees the world as riven with hazards that endanger the future of the planet and must be tackled urgently to prevent catastrophe. Despite sharing constructionist influences and prioritizing the relationship between risk and culture, the path followed by Douglas and Furedi diverges markedly. For Douglas, risk has a positive function at the level of social solidarity, while for Furedi a preoccupation with risk erodes sociality and undercuts human resilience. Through Douglas's studies we can get a handle on the historical and cultural functions of risk and danger. Whereas the risk society perspective suggests that late modernity throws up a concatenation of highly unique manufactured risks, Douglas's work indicates that concerns about risk constitute a modern form of taboo about danger. As we shall see, this reproduces significant fault lines between the two theories, both in relation to the novelty of risk and its wider social and cultural functions. Douglas has been criticized for her conservatism and a tendency to be too relativistic about risks in order to slot them into an orderly grid (see Arnoldi, 2009: 46). In this sense, disregarding contentions over their dangerousness, those that are labelled as risky, unclean and/or abject are being subjected to norms generated through classificatory systems which are themselves embedded within social structure. Douglas is more inclined to focus on the ways in which extant community forms, cultural rituals and forms of categorization influence constructions and perceptions of risk. She believes that cultures characterized by low social solidarity are more likely to dwell on the emergence of risks and hazards. In such environments, expressions of anxiety around impending disasters can serve as a tool for integration, as individuals collectivize around the shared goals of security seeking and warding off threats. In Beck's work we find little space for competing worldviews about risk and the accent instead falls on the universality of risk. While Beck urges intervention to tackle 'global mega-hazards', Douglas is reticent about the dangerousness of the risks that contemporary Western nations face, viewing risk management as a response to tensions in social structure and cultural (dis)organization. For her, there are parallels to be drawn between the worries and fears of contemporary and preceding epochs. In Douglas' view, in seeking to establish blame, secularized societies have unwittingly replaced the language of sin with that of risk. As Wilkinson (2009: 49) explains:

The concept of risk is the modern device for calling those who have 'sinned against' us to repent for their wrongdoing so as to bring justice and restore order to the world. The main difference is that where the language of sin appeals to the authority of priests and divine law, the language of risk appeals to the authority of science and the prophetic powers of modern rationality.

As well as apparent differences, notable similarities exist between the competing perspectives. Both proponents of the anthropological and governmentality perspectives emphasize the historical contingency of risk as a social category, albeit by virtue of contrasting routes and methods. Douglas, for example, draws upon ethnographic fieldwork to construct a structuralist view of the relationship between sociocultural organization and risk. In contrast, Foucauldian scholars following the genealogical method have deployed archival analysis to show how 'technologies of risk' illuminate the political aspirations of regimes of power. Similarly, there are joins in the risk society and governmentality theses with regards to the ways in which responsibility for risk becomes transferred from the institutional structures to individual agents. While risk society thinkers index the process of 'risk-shift' to individualization, Foucauldians focus upon the responsibilization of citizens in areas of risk management such as health, crime and welfare (see Dean, 1999b; Garland, 1997; 2001). Instead of being regimented and cajoled by direct force, individuals are effectively encouraged to self-police by regulating their bodies, health and lifestyles and by being vigilant about personal security. Such risk-based techniques and modes of governance seek to incentivize the individual and are more thickly veiled than power expressed through direct force (see Dupont and Pearce, 2001: 125). The regulatory uses of risk are also present in the culture of fear perspective, although here the economic goals of the media and security industries are twinned with the moral imperatives of government and State aspirations of social control. Further, while Foucauldians are interested in how discourses of risk may responsibilize citizens to guard their own safety, Furedi (2007: 9) goes on to draw out an instrumental shifting of blame that accompanies this process: 'politicians and officials take the view that if they warn us to be afraid about some impending catastrophe they will protect themselves from the accusation of irresponsibility'. As with their angles of entry on risk, the accent on individualization also varies between competing perspectives. Wilkinson (2009: 56) is instructive on this point:

> While within the bounds of cultural theory and accounts of world risk society, people are understood to become increasingly pre-occupied with risk as part of a response to social pressures towards individualization, according to theorists of governmentality we should rather understand the language of risk as an integral part of this process. It is not so much that individualization gives rise to risk consciousness, but rather that conceptualizing the social world in terms of risk promotes an individualizing world view.

Notwithstanding these differences, the question of relative impact is difficult to judge and claims in this regard are always wont to be conceived as pregnant with interests. Without being drawn into a scholarly beauty contest, the risk society perspective has perhaps proven to be the most impactful theory of risk in the social sciences over the last two decades. Yet the culture of fear approach has gained greater credence among cultural commentators and media producers, specifically with regard to the State's attempts to harness public fears about terrorism (see Curtis, 2004; Oborne, 2006). Of the four perspectives, the anthropological approach has had the largest impact outside academia at the level of policy making and implementation in risk sensitive industries. Douglas's 'grid-group' structure has been developed as an heuristic device in risk analysis and practically deployed to educate policy makers about the needs of stakeholder groups and to improve the quality of risk communications from 'experts' to the public. Finally, the governmentality perspective has arguably attracted the greatest number of academic followers and been deployed across the largest span of academic disciplines.

Conclusion

Having engaged with the concept of risk and documented the turn to risk within the social sciences, it is vital that our grasp of the theoretical issues is not allowed to tail off into the fog. The value of theory lies in its ability to allow us to elucidate key social problems, processes and issues. In this spirit, I hold that we need to judge the worth of theories of risk in line with their capacity to shed light on the dynamics, processes and interactions that characterize and shape the modern world. To this end, we should remain heedful that risk is but one – albeit presently popular – way of framing social problems. I will, in upcoming chapters, be encouraging reflection on the possibilities of theories of risk, but also counselling as to their limits. So far as theoretical preferences are concerned, I would counsel against partisanship. Thinking about risk and choosing one's favoured approach are not processes that take place without bias. Our political leanings, cultural predilections, life narratives and worldviews inevitably nudge us towards some perspectives and away from others. As Flusty (2000: 150) correctly points out: 'how you see determines what you look for, which in turn vectors what you get'. With this proviso in mind, we must appreciate that theoretical perspectives on risk cannot deliver a precisely pixelated image of reality. They are instead created to help us build up a sense of the relationship between micro level interactions and macro level societal processes. It is perhaps sagacious then to assume an open but critical position which allows one to consider the apertures provided by each perspective in relation to given situations, dynamics and processes. To be clear, such an open, critical position is neither a neutral nor, necessarily, an accepting position. It is a position in which merits and disadvantages are considered in an even handed way, according to the subject, process or object under study. In my view, there is more to be gained in grasping the complexities and dynamics of modern society by drawing across competing perspectives on risk rather than religiously subscribing to one and casting the rest asunder. Thus, throughout the book I will be revisiting risk theories to probe their potentialities and also draw out their shortcomings in illuminating aspects of the social world. To do this, it is necessary to engage with both the micro and the macro. First, we need to drill down to the micro level to put theory to work in interpreting incidents, happenings and processes. In so doing, it is also important to step back from the language of risk and to think hard about how we as academics construct and use risk. Being alert at the outset of the political allegiances of authors and their epistemological standpoints allows us to be more critical in our evaluations and more reflexive about how we approach and use perspectives on risk.

In this chapter I have presented capsule accounts of the four perspectives that have been commonly deployed in the social sciences: the risk society, governmentality, culture of fear and anthropological approaches. In order to avoid theoretical pond-skating, in subsequent chapters we will cast a more rigorous eye over these perspectives, applying them to cases and subjecting them to theoretical scrutiny, in accordance with their coherence and comprehensiveness. By building up a macro account of the general applicability and value of particular perspectives we are in a better position to make informed decisions about their relative value and their impact on both the social sciences and wider society. A further note of caution should be sounded about the ways in which we social scientists tend to categorize and box up the world into tidy bite sized chunks. While the historical narrative outlined above puts the realist and social constructionist paradigms in opposition, it needs to be recognized that there is arguably greater mixity than ever before in the way in which risk is conceived both in the natural sciences, the social sciences and society more generally. Perhaps some of the key incidents and controversies of the late twentieth century – among them Chernobyl, Bhopal, Brent Spa and the BSE crisis – have thrust out steep learning curves for scientific experts in that the inherent messiness of risk and the impossibility of establishing certainty has became readily apparent. In the aftermath of questionable institutional actions – in terms of the identification, communication and management of risk – policy makers, government, private companies and scientists have had to take heed of and attend to what is somewhat condescendingly referred to as the 'social' side of risk. As such, the poles of realism and constructionism are less easily identified and less rigidly methodologically applied than in the second half of the twentieth century. Many scientists and politicians now have an appreciation of risk as being about potential harm, while also being aware of the ways in which individuals, cultures and institutions construct and classify events, objects and people. Similarly, social science approaches to risk have evolved from early work in risk analysis which sought to enhance understanding about the technical management of risk through drafting disaster models, to exploring the drivers of risk perception and examining the cultural context in which risks are made to mean. Yet we need to recognize that theories of risk exist along a continuum and do not coherently express nor reflect a singular unified paradigm. Insofar as it is quite reasonable to consider paradigmatic influences it may ultimately be unhelpful to give blanket labels of 'realist' and 'social constructionist' to specific theories of risk. Such categorization is not reflective of the diversity that pulses through perspectives on risk or the range of applications in the field. As always, the brook is much muddier than the text book writer searching for clear water would have us believe. As such, we need to talk about paradigmatic accents, rather than to classify perspectives in absolutes. Beck's realist insistence that we urgently deal with catastrophic harms can be contrasted with his equally impassioned social constructionist passages on the role of the media, scientists and government in the 'staging of risk realities' (2009: 10). Similarly, while most would hold that Furedi's emphasis on the cultural reproduction of fear parks him firmly in the social constructionist camp, his very dismissal of a multitude of threats acts as a kind of contorted realism in which rather than objectively existing, the risks we worry about emphatically don't. In this apparent morass of ambiguity, getting a fair and honest sense of one's epistemological and political standpoint and how this bears on what sense we make of risk is vital. While institutions and social actors have gradually adopted more reflexive attitudes towards risk, it is important that scholars and students of risk do not fall into the trap of imagining themselves and their academic judgements to be somehow surgically extracted from the influences and forces that condition everyday experience.

3 Crime, Risk and Governance

Introduction

In order to provide some solid moorings for our exploration of risk we have considered the presence of risk in contemporary society and differentiated between different epistemologies that inform approaches towards risk. Drawing on a cascade model, I have distinguished between paradigms, branches and perspectives. In the chapters which follow I will build on this platform to assess some of the possibilities of and the limits to theoretical perspectives on risk. Now that the conceptual scaffold has been erected, we will be moving on to apply theory to practice in specific 'casing risk' sections. Before we turn to focus on issues of crime and governance, it is worth pausing for a moment and mapping out the terrain of the remaining chapters. It is my major intention to draw attention to the salience of risk in contemporary debates about crime and security and also to examine the role of risk in shaping policies and practices in the arenas of policing, counter-terrorism, criminal justice and environmental management. In the following chapters, I will be considering the influence of the idea of risk on the political construction and regulation of crime and criminality. As we shall see, in these areas risk functions at a variety of levels and is connected to a panoply of processes including community safety, victimization, punishment, sentencing, crime reduction, the formation of law, policing, surveillance and political strategy making.

In addition to gaining an insight into the impacts of risk on security discourses and practices, we will also be utilizing our four key perspectives to open up avenues of debate and disputation. Given the potential scale of these tasks, it is necessary to pare the analysis down and to focus on those areas which are focal to the principal objectives of the book. To this end, in Chapters 3 and 4 the relationship between risk, criminality and victimization will be our central concern. Situated within this relationship, issues around regulation, policing and control serve as touchstones for discussion. To be clear, the approach towards 'crime' pursued will be broad and include consideration of acts of criminality, the experience of victimization and the workings of the justice system. We will also be considering the factors and motivations that may drive individuals to transgress formal legal rules. Drawing on both classic and contemporary research into criminal risk-taking I wish to stress that the meaning of crime – like the meaning of risk – is culturally specific and historically contingent. In Chapter 4 we will excavate the complex relationship between risk, fear and victimization. Noting changes in attitudes towards both victims and offenders, in this chapter we inspect people's anxieties about crime and the role of the media in exacerbating 'fear of crime'. Following such a line of inquiry, I will go on to interrogate the fear of crime literature and to suggest how and why current perspectives might be broadened out to situate the subject in the context of a range of everyday concerns, rather than arbitrarily isolating 'fear of crime' as an object of analysis and using this as a mandate for correcting 'irrational fears' about crime risks via slicker government communication strategies or public education programmes. The role of the media in the representation and communication of risk will be a central subject of discussion in Chapter 4 and we shall draw on the classic moral panic model delineated by Cohen (1972) to demonstrate the historical tendency within the mass media to sensationalize violent crime. The media is also a significant point of analysis in Chapter 5, alongside other key institutions involved in the social construction of the terrorist threat. In focussing on the ways in which the terrorist risk is perceived and presented in the media, we will be asking whether the political and media attention directed towards terrorist attacks is commensurate with the frequency and magnitude of the risk. I will be focussing primarily in Chapter 5 on issues around the political construction and institutional regulation of risk. Here the post 9/11 social and political context will be unpacked, alongside a critical interrogation of the assumptions surrounding the threat of 'new terrorism'. In the latter part of this chapter, we will move on to consider the efficacy of the introduction of an unprecedented range of counter-terrorism measures in the first decade of the century. We will also be evaluating the effects of particular counter-terrorism measures on the human rights and civil liberties of Muslim Minority communities. In Chapter 6, matters of risk perception and representation remain critical as we ask who is responsible for the production of environmental risks and whether established forms of risk management are proving effective in preventing harm. These discussions will move us towards a sharper awareness of the miscellaneous uses and abuses of risk that will be the principal topic in Chapter 7. Although primarily issue led, the forays in these chapters are also designed to develop and interrogate the theoretical perspectives previously expounded.

And so to the current chapter. In order to examine the ways in which risk is used as a means of quantifying, surveying, managing and reducing crime, I wish to begin by charting the distinct uses of risk in policing and crime control policies, outlining deployments of risk in crime prediction, prevention and harm minimization. Casting back to the governmentality perspective, we consider David Garland's (2001) pioneering work on the formation of a 'culture of control' in Western neo-liberal countries, initiated by Capitalist States seeking to adopt punitive approaches to crime regulation. The Foucauldian perspective is again brought to bear in the case section where Ericson and Haggerty's analysis of the changing nature of policing acts as an example of the deployment of risk as a facet of crime control and its broader mobilization as a tool of social regulation. This discussion indicates that although risk may be a neutral technology, the way in which it is constructed and the uses to which it is put involve establishing moral stances and making political decisions. As we shall see, not only is the culture of control manifest in modern forms of governance, policing and the administration of criminal justice system, it is also sanctioned by the mainstream mass media and approved by sections of the public that endorse punitive and pre-emptive modes of crime regulation. The issue of pre-emptive intervention is one to which we will return to in Chapter 5 in the context of counter-terrorism legislation, but for now we should perhaps log the increasing institutional popularity of preventative modes of managing crime, ranging from early interventions with 'problem children' to attempts to identify signs of 'radicalization' among teenagers (see Hebenton and Thomas, 1996; Mythen and

Walklate, 2010). While much of this suggests a rather top down view of the institutional management of risk, in the latter part of the chapter, I want to highlight the pioneering contribution to the sociology of risk made by the Chicago School and also to address more contemporary developments within cultural criminology which draw attention to the connection between personal motivations, risk and social structures.

So far as both crime policy and prevailing currents of mainstream criminology are concerned, risk has conventionally been approached as a technical entity used to predict and assess crime (see Kemshall, 2003; O'Malley, 2006). There are perhaps good reasons for such an actuarial accent when one considers that probabilistic models and large empirical studies have enabled criminologists to quantify various problems and issues associated with criminal behaviour, patterns of victimization and perceptions of crime (see Loader and Sparks, 2002: 93). Risk has become increasingly central to the ways in which crime, policing and punishment are organized and performed in the modern age. Although risk has long featured as a tool for estimating and measuring criminal behaviour, in the early part of the twenty-first century it has become a critical component of policy and practice for actors and agencies involved in the regulation of crime and the treatment of offenders. Risk has, for example, become an embedded element of software packages which seek to forecast criminality, an analytical device employed in the generation of crime statistics, a driver of strategies of crime prevention and a political justification for the implementation of new law and order measures. In response to the growing presence of risk in the sphere of crime control, in the last two decades sociologists and criminologists have advocated and critiqued theoretical perspectives on risk, with the theories advanced by Foucault, Beck and Furedi appearing as pivot points for debate.

One of the problems that arises when one seeks to address the relationship between crime and risk is the diffuse definitions, understandings and applications that exist among individuals and networks involved in the assessment, prevention and management of crime. As both Walklate (1997) and Zedner (2009) have observed, the term 'risk' has been used with gay abandon in academic and policy literature. Partly as a consequence of contrasting contexts and the pursuit of disparate goals, there remains a lack of agreement within the social sciences about what risk actually means, and, indeed, the value of risk as a facet of regulatory policies (see Ericson, 2007; Mythen, 2008; O'Malley, 2009). It is thus important to be cognizant of definitional disparities and inconsistencies in how risk is defined and operationalized between and within government, the media, academia, the security industries and crime control agencies. Unravelling the kinks and knots in this institutional vortex is a task that is beyond the ambit of this chapter. Nevertheless, I do intend to construct something of a road map detailing the avenues through which risk has travelled in its deployment as a tool for crime prediction, a driver of prevention strategies and a technology of harm minimization. Having considered the impacts of these largely 'objective' technical applications of risk, I wish to engage with some of the common explanations for the 'subjective' risk-taking activities of perpetrators of crime. This shift in accent from social structure to human agency will form something of a bridge to a more detailed appraisal of the issue of risk perception in Chapter 4, where we will consider changing attitudes towards victimization and examine the literature on public fears about crime. Throughout this journey I will continue to encourage an inquisitive and critical approach towards the employment of risk, both as an academic concept and as a shaper of crime prevention and criminal justice policy. Before we delve into contemporary applications of risk, it is first necessary to get a sense of the historical uses of risk in the prediction of crime and the regulation of criminality.

Calibrating and mobilizing risk: Crime prevention and harm minimization

The star of risk has undoubtedly risen over the last three decades among criminal justice practitioners and government policy makers. Today risk is a central feature of crime management and at the heart of criminal justice policy, stretching from modes of surveying ex-offenders to reducing the incidence of crime through urban design. While it is evident that risk has increasingly featured in debates about crime prevention and management in the last 30 years, we should be wary of overplaying the novelty of the association between risk and crime control. Risk is an established mode of quantifying crime and actuarial methods of estimating offending behaviour have a long history, with predictive risk scales first being devised almost a century ago. As O'Malley (2006) observes, Ernest Burgess, one of the founder members of the Chicago School of urban sociology, was instrumental in the development and deployment of actuarial tables which were utilized in the State of Illinois to inform parole decisions (see Burgess, 1928; 1936). Despite their longevity, we can identify the consolidation of an institutional trend towards using technologies of risk in the United States, the United Kingdom and Australia in the early 1980s. There are numerous indicators of the shift towards actuarial crime management over penal sanctions at this time, including the Floud Report (1981) in Britain, which was succeeded by the Greenwood Report (1982) in the United States. As O'Malley (2006) points out, these two documents advocated a sharper focus on risk within the criminal justice system and signalled something of a transformation in the ways and means by which crime was to be managed in future years. In the United Kingdom, the Floud Report – compiled by Floud and Young (1981) on behalf of a Working Party of the Howard League for Penal Reform – raised serious doubts about the effectiveness of penal sanctions in crime reduction and criminal deterrence, advancing the roll out of 'protective sentencing'. As we shall see in Chapter 4, these two reports signalled something of a shift in terms of the salience of the (potential) victim in decision making around imprisonment. Furthermore, the punitive trajectories of these reports demonstrate that both calls for preventative sentencing and a desire to pre-emptively detain the risky are far from modern proclivities. Echoing Flood's recommendations, the Greenwood Report – written by Peter Greenwood and Alan Abrahamse (1982) and commissioned by the US Justice Department – put forward the view that risk assessment measures supported by statistical analysis should be promoted in the quest to identify those most likely to re-offend. Conceived as something of an emergent science, predictive risk scales were promoted as a means of determining which criminals were deserving of lengthy sentences in order to promote the dual social good of deterring future law breaking and protecting the public. Based on a survey of over 2000 prison inmates in three US States, Greenwood and Abrahamse (1982) forwarded the use of predictive scales for identifying high-rate offenders and devised a system of 'selective incapacitation' to limit the risk of future offending. Slightly ahead of this in the United Kingdom, the Floud report recommended a parallel scheme of protective sentencing on the basis that the protection of the public should override the rights of the offender:

> The Crown Court should be empowered, for the protection of others against grave harm by an offender, to sentence him (sic) to imprisonment for a specified period greater than that which would ordinarily be specified, but proportional to the gravity of the anticipated harm and the courts estimate of the duration of the risk.
>
> (Floud and Young, 1981: 155)

Floud and Young (1981: 10) posit that it is entirely rational and reasonable to factor in judgements about future criminal behaviour into decisions about custodial sentences. In order to prevent criminals from causing harm they argued that, much as past intentions are used as a way of determining punishment, future motives should be used to inform sentencing decisions. Notwithstanding the dubious logic on which these assertions are founded, what is interesting to note is that the current debate within society about dangerousness and the appropriate means of managing risky offenders thus has a long historical lineage (see Bottoms and Brownsword, 1982). What is at stake here is essentially a moral decision about which risks are the most acceptable to take and whose rights and security should be prioritized: those of the general public or those of the offender. Although these two reports are undoubtedly important moments in the rise of risk in criminal justice policy and crime control strategy they are certainly not the first applications of risk-based techniques. Adopting a genealogical approach, O'Malley (2008) deftly tracks the history of risk as a technology of crime regulation, pointing out that the contemporary preference for risk governance has deeper roots than are widely acknowledged. Nevertheless, we can certainly chart an acceleration in the use of risk-based modes of regulation in the West in the late 1980s into the 1990s.

The rising use of risk in decision making in sentencing and crime prevention was famously captured by Feeley and Simon (1992; 1994), in their identification of a 'new penology'. The 'new penology' is an attempt to theorize the motion away from the penal modernist emphasis on correctional interventions against offenders towards 'actuarial justice' through which risk probabilities are assessed across populations. The new penology thesis hails the ushering in of novel discourses and techniques of crime regulation. In particular, the language of crime control shifts from a moral tone to one that is actuarial in nature. Such actuarial language invokes techniques of probability, calculation and calibration which ostensibly imbue criminal justice policies and penal judgements with a veneer of neutrality. Critical here is the declining emphasis on recidivism and a focus instead on offender management within the penal system. A number of examples of detainment, surveillance and tracking are cited as symptomatic of the drive to protect society through the management of populations. For Feeley and Simon (1992; 1994) the new penology is indicative of a rebalancing of the criminal justice system towards the safety of the public rather than the rehabilitation of the offender. New penological strategies typically deploy methods of risk assessment which have at their heart not so much the punishment and/or treatment of the offender as the reduction of risk for (potential) victims. The identification of new types of penology is not so much concerned with the punitive tendencies identified by Garland (2001), nor the rehabilitative model that it may have replaced. Instead, Feeley and Simon (1992) highlight the emergence and cementation of risk management of 'unruly groups' through the co-ordination of information and data. Distancing itself from potentially emotive questions of blame, responsibility and rehabilitation, the new penology is instead 'concerned with techniques to identify, classify and manage groupings sorted by dangerousness. The task is managerial not transformative' (Feeley and Simon, 1992: 452). New modes of penology are thus theoretically dispassionate about reforming offenders and concerned instead with managing risk to populations. Through techniques of assessment, individuals are sifted and categorized according to risk. On the basis of formal classification and grouping, criminal interventions can be scientifically directed and resources of crime control used efficiently. Alongside the evolution of an abstract scientific approach to crime control, discourses around criminality revert from the moral to the actuarial, as groups within the population become classified according to the risk that they pose. The evolution of new penological strategies also represents an attempt to improve cost effectiveness, as resources are focussed on peoples and areas subjected to most harm, with new technologies such as electronic tags and global positioning systems being used to monitor those defined as dangerous. Bearing out Feeley and Simon's (1992; 1994) observations, the use of actuarial risk-based measures has became evident in some Western nations across a range of criminal justice processes and practices, including sentencing, detention and offender management (see Hudson, 2000; Kemshall, 2002; Mythen et al., 2012; Zedner, 2009). In the punishment of serious offenders – for example, those committing murder or planning large-scale terrorist attacks – sentencing has been impacted by efforts to reduce risks to the public through the administration of lengthy prison sentences designed to deter potential offenders. Similarly, post hoc regulation of violent criminals has been informed by and subject to the logic of actuarial risk. One stand out example in this regard has been the monitoring and surveillance of post release sex offenders. The sinister image of the predatory paedophile has long been used as a powerful symbol in raising public awareness of issues around child protection, as typified in 'stranger, danger' campaigns in the United Kingdom, Australia and the United States. Those convicted of sex offences against minors have typically been issued lengthy prison sentences and been subject to continued monitoring after being released from prison. In the United Kingdom convicted paedophiles have been formally tracked since 1997 through the sex offenders register which they are obliged to sign in order to inform police of their whereabouts.

In the United States, 'Megan's Law', first introduced under the Sexual Offenders Act in 1994, exemplifies the use of risk reduction strategies to enforce regulation and surveillance of offenders in the present while simultaneously seeking to prohibit future offending (see Simon, 2000). Currently in operation in the majority of States in America, Megan's Law legally binds convicted child sex offenders to notify local law enforcement authorities of place of abode and subsequent changes of address after release from custody. Megan's Law came into being after the tragic rape and murder of seven-year-old Megan Kanka. In this notorious case, it transpired that the offender, Jesse Timmendequas, had two previous convictions for sex offences against young girls. After her death, the victims bereaved parents publically stated that it should have been their right to be informed about a dangerous offender such as Timmendequas living in proximity. The Kanka's argued that had they known about their neighbours criminal history, the procedures of risk management they implemented with their daughter would have been very different. In terms of the balance of risk in society, what is enshrined in Megan's Law is the very transformation of rights and responsibilities advocated in the Floud and Greenwood reports. Instead of the rights of the released offender being upheld through post sentence anonymity, the rights of future victims are prioritized. This transformation facilitates the burden of risk shifting from parents of minors who may be unaware of the vulnerability of their children to attack, to previously protected sex offenders whose identities and locations become publically disclosed on posters, bulletin boards and distributed flyers. Aside from the risk of inaccurate information being published, the knock on consequences for exposed child convicted sex offenders include eviction, job loss, threats, harassment and damage to property (see Levenson and Cotter, 2005). In a similar case to that of Megan Kanka, in England in 2000 the family of a murdered eight-year-old girl Sarah Payne, campaigned for tighter regulation of child sex offenders after Roy Whiting was sentenced to life in prison for her murder, having previously abducted and assaulted another girl. Although the campaign for 'Sarah's Law' – led by her mother Sara Payne – did not initially result in the legislative changes demanded by its supporters, public and media pressure eventually led to the State sanctioning a range of preventative procedures. These included known offenders being subject to routine risk assessments, required to sign a sex offenders register and legally bound to declare their locations to crime control authorities. A series of pilot schemes were set up in 2008 whereby parents were permitted to check with the police if a named individual in contact with their child had a record of sex offences and these procedures were rolled out in all 39 police forces in England and Wales in 2011.

The debate about the utility, ethics and limits of the child sex offender disclosure scheme notwithstanding (see Levenson and Cotter, 2005; Travis, 2010a), the actuarial logic of risk and the overriding goal of public safety very much underpin these forms of legislation. Striking a chord with Feeley and Simon's (1992; 1994) new penology thesis, the prime assumption being made is that the implementation of predictive and preventative measures can reduce the occurrence of future abuse and better protect vulnerable members of society. Integral to actualizing this goal at a policy level, new technologies of risk regulation have emerged in recent years, including geographical logging, tagging, tracking and community posting (see Hebenton and Thomas, 1996). In other contexts in which the threat of harm is of low probability but high consequence – for example aviation security – advanced forms of risk-based actuarial assessment and profiling have been developed (see Amoore, 2011; Salter, 2008). Since the 9/11 attacks there have been several failed attempts to detonate explosives on planes, including a plot to co-ordinate the explosion of liquid nitrate on a number of intercontinental flights between the United States and the United Kingdom, the small explosion caused by the so called 'shoe-bomber' Richard Reid and the attempt by Umar Faruk Abdulmulmatallab to detonate explosives sown into his undergarments with a syringe onboard a plane from Amsterdam bound for Detroit. Each incident has been followed thrift upon by calls in the media for tighter security measures to be introduced alongside 'common sense' risk profiling techniques necessary to identify travellers that pose the greatest threat (see Bauman and Lyon, 2013: 14; Blackwood et al., 2012). Such incidents have led to the intensification of processes of aviation security such as the banning of liquids being taken through security clearance, the removal of footwear at scanning points and the use of iris recognition hardware. Nevertheless, it is perhaps behind the scenes that the actuarial scales are being put to work most vigorously to separate out the safe from the dangerous. As we shall see in Chapter 5, one of the consequences of risk regulation in the context of national security has been a locking of the surveillant lens on non-White people of Asian descent (see Abbas, 2011; Mythen et al., 2009). As Hudson (2003) reasons, such blanket attempts to define and distinguish for differential treatment 'safe' and 'risky' groups are fraught with difficulties and provoke thorny questions about the impartiality of policing methods and associated criminal justice procedures. It is worth noting that those that support the use of racial profiling often draw on an actuarial rationale to justify their position. After the 7/7 attacks in London the Chief of Transport Police Sir Ian Johnston sought to justify dragnet policing that had resulted in a disproportionate number of Black and Asian people being targeted for stop and searches with reference to a common-sense narrative of actuarialism: 'intelligence-led stop and searches have got to be the way ... we should not waste time searching old white ladies. It is going to be disproportionate. It is going to be young men, not exclusively, but it may be disproportionate when it comes to ethnic groups' (see Dodd, 2005). Despite such arresting examples, it would be erroneous to assume that an actuarial trend has colonized either policing, criminal justice policy making or punishment across the piece. As O'Malley (2006: 47) reasons:

> While risk has become much more pervasive in criminal justice, it has not developed into anything resembling actuarial justice. Risk plays only a minor role in sentencing. While incapacitation may be a major rationale of imprisonment in some jurisdictions this is not necessarily attributable to risk. Indeed, where risk has been explicitly involved in the shaping of sanctions it has been linked with expert therapeutic and correctional knowledge. In some respects this is also what has happened in crime prevention.

Contra Feeley and Simon (1992; 1994), O'Malley correctly observes non linear patterns of crime governance and stresses the existence of a messier mix of actuarial risk-based legislation, corrective measures and punitive sanctions that exists in Western nations. Taking a rather different but parallel view on the rising presence of risk, criminologists such as Zedner (2007; 2009) and McCulloch and Pickering (2010), have sought to illuminate the trend towards early intervention in certain areas of crime control. Such motions towards pre-emptive crime regulation or 'pre-crime' are increasingly common in certain sections of criminal justice legislation and policing, such as counter-terrorism and the management of youth offenders (see Mythen and Walklate, 2010; Squires and Stephen, 2012). The idea of 'pre-crime' originates in the science fiction writing of Phillip K. Dick (1956) and alludes to anticipatory modes of crime control that involve intervention before crime materializes (see Zedner, 2007). In Dick's short story, *The Minority Report* (1956), predictions of crimes taking place in the future are delivered by three mutant creatures with pre-cognitive abilities. These 'pre-cogs' provide visions of forthcoming crimes taking place which are then used by law enforcement agents to intercede ahead of their occurrence. While Dick's novel provides an uncannily perceptive insight into future–present aspects of crime control, in the real world the barbed question it raises is exactly why it is that pre-crime interventions have been advanced in some areas – such as countering terrorism and anti-social behaviour – but are palpably absent in others such as financial embezzlement, tax evasion and environmental crime. This patchiness of application further indicates that we should be circumspect about hailing general shifts such as those forwarded by Feeley and Simon. While aspects of the 'new penology' can be discerned in some areas of crime control and criminal justice, we would do well to keep a trained eye on evidence of continuities as well as changes. What is certain is that questions of power and privilege appear to underscore the uneven appearance of pre-emptive regulatory measures. Following on from the calculated malpractices of some major banks and trading houses that took place prior to the manifestation of the financial crisis in 2008, such as rate fixing, reckless lending and short-selling of stocks, one might expect a raft of preventative legislation to be introduced to prevent such behaviour from occurring in future. Yet, after the Libor scandal in which up to 16 banks were involved in manipulating global interest rates to the tune of upward of $500 trillion, a series of further cases of widespread price fixing and corruption have emerged (see Taibbi, 2013). Since the economic bubble officially burst in 2008 many banks have been forced to pay out in multimillion-dollar settlements for anti-competitive practices. Similarly, after the widespread misuse of the expenses system among British MPs was revealed in 2009, it would be logical to expect the enforcement of a regime of pre-emptive surveillance to ensure that public monies were not being filtered through a laxly regulated expenses system to top up politician's already fulsome salaries. In both of these cases, the appetite of the Government to implement pre-emptive measures was noticeably lacking.

Returning to the broader issue of the viability of the new penology thesis, there is a suspicion that the novelty of the processes it describes is somewhat overplayed, with many 'new' trends being traceable over several decades. As Garland (1997) points out, the assessment of crime and deviance across populations and the segregation of dangerous classes were also common features of crime governance at the beginning of the twentieth century. Insofar as the new penology emphasizes a somewhat detached use of risk as a modern technology for crime management, it remains the case that most countries are characterized by messy blends of pre-emptive and post hoc crime control: punitive penalties exist alongside rehabilitative programmes for offenders and direct coercive interventions sit beside policies to incentivize problem groups. Clearly, trends in crime control are themselves affected by changes in political tenure, public opinion and the prevailing economic climate. To give one example of this, while the Conservative Party in the United Kingdom have traditionally assumed a hard line on criminality and favoured long prison sentences to deter offenders, the dual problems of prison overcrowding and a huge fiscal deficit have led to an apparent change in policy, externally badged as a 'rehabilitation revolution' (see Fox and Albertson, 2011). In such circumstances, the extent of public exposure to risk and indeed the risk of reoffending plays second fiddle to economic priorities. In the United Kingdom at least, one can discern in recent appeals for the development of a 'Big Society' a risk-shift in responsibility from State agencies towards citizens, community groups and the third sector in areas of security, crime control and offender management (see Mythen et al., 2012). The success or otherwise of such regime changes remains to be seen, but suffice it to say that crime regulation has become increasingly decentralized as the State seeks to further devolve accountability and responsibility to the local level through private companies, NGOs and charitable bodies.

Harnessing risk? Crime, control and governance

While Feeley and Simon's thesis is theoretically influenced by both risk society and governmentality perspectives (see Newburn, 2009), the work of the Scottish criminologist David Garland can be more firmly associated with the development of governmentality theory. Garland's writing has been extremely influential within criminology and his notion of a 'culture of control' is seen as a major breakthrough in conceptualizing the relationship between risk, governance and social control. Developing a panoramic overview of the changing landscape of crime control in the United States and Britain, Garland (2001) contends that a combination of practices and policies have come together to form a 'crime complex', in and through which the aspirations of dominant economic, political, military and cultural groups articulate. In Garland's opinion, a general shift has occurred from modernist notions of crime regulation towards a new model of crime control. In *The Culture of Control* (2001), Garland documents what he sees as fundamental changes in crime control strategy and the broader management of the criminal justice system. Assembling a range of evidence, Garland reasons that punitive sanctions have re-emerged with force, with an emphasis being placed on retributive justice through which offenders must be seen to have publicly paid their penalty for offending. In his eyes, the return to incarceration and the trend towards incapacitation are emblematic of an ideological motion away from the ideal of rehabilitation through which offenders might be reformed in the course of serving their sentences, towards punitive populism in which political parties seek to maintain public trust by administering disciplinary sanctions and coercive measures of control. For Garland, forms of retributive justice are bound up with the increasing presence and visibility of the victim in decisions about punishment, sentencing and crime control. As such, law-making is structured around the principle of defending the rights of future victims. In a renewed project of crime control, the State has to demonstrate its attempts to protect the public against crime, with various methods of incapacitation emerging under the auspices of improving public safety.

Resonating with Garland's thesis, multi-agency approaches designed to enhance community safety have become very much *en vogue* in the West (see Hughes et al., 2002; Welsh and Farrington, 1999). Further, such crime prevention initiatives are geared towards harm reduction and improving security within the community rather than the enactment of criminal justice per se. Alongside the increasing involvement of communities in the regulation of crime, a range of private security bodies and charitable organizations have been invited in to work in partnership with the police and the public in the management of crime. For Garland (2001), the myriad operations and functions of the new crime control complex are defined with recourse to adaptive and expressive strategies. Adaptive policies are designed to pragmatically deal with the problem of crime through attending primarily to the effects of crime, rather than addressing their root causes. Expressive strategies seek to publicly disgrace and vilify offenders and, in so doing, simultaneously create binaries by identifying insiders and outsiders, dangerous and safe groups. Concurring with Garland's viewpoint, there have undoubtedly been changes in the tone and manner in which crime and security discourses are articulated in the media and in politics. As we shall see, emotive appeals to the sensibilities and fears of members of the public have become stock features of the persuasive armoury for politicians (see Newburn, 1997: 331). Although his thesis does share some similarities with the work of Feeley and Simon, the capacity of Garland's approach to capture divergent trends adds a deeper layer of sophistication to understandings of risk governance in the context of crime control.

While both Feeley and Simon and Garland seek to reveal macro shifts in the governance of crime, Pat O'Malley draws attention to the micro level effects of risk-based forms of regulation on individuals. Extending Foucault's work on the 'conduct of conduct', O'Malley's (1992; 1998; 2010) historically informed contribution illuminates the drift towards prudentialism through which individuals are encouraged to act for themselves in organizing safety rather than relying on the State to act on their behalf. O'Malley focusses in detail on crime prevention policies and practices, noting the diverse ways in which citizens have become practised in managing their own security risks. There are obvious parallels to be drawn between O'Malley's work on prudentialism and Garland's (2001) notion of responsibilization. For Garland (2001), responsibilization involves the techniques and practices of 'indirect action' through which the State invites the individual to perform risk regulation via security choices. The privatization of security transfers responsibility from public crime control agencies to individuals who are induced to manage their own safety by installing burglar alarms, fitting CCTV cameras, placing tracking devices in vehicles and phones and carrying personal emergency alarms. Importantly, the processes of inclusion and exclusion noted by Garland are not limited to the spheres of politics, criminal justice and crime control. As Young (1999; 2007) reasons, there has been a distinct motion from an inclusive society to a more exclusive culture, characterized by side-taking and vindictiveness. To cite one example of who is 'in' and who is 'out', we might consider mainstream media coverage of Muslim 'problems' since 7/7, ranging from religious extremism and radicalized youth to violent families and disputes about the wearing of the veil in public (see Meer et al., 2010; Abbas, 2011). In ostracizing Muslims and rendering them 'other', sections of the Western media have clumsily grouped together diverse ethnic groups, reinforcing stereotypes and cementing imagined divides (see Flood et al., 2012; Nickels et al., 2012). Mediated security cues give out indicators of which groups are victims and which are to be considered aggressors. As we shall see in Chapter 5, these cues are not simply ideological media constructions thrown out into the ether. Rather, they possess material weight, being connected to and played out in domestic crime control measures and international foreign and military policy. Beneath the veneer of the formally democratic neo-liberal State that guarantees the freedoms of all, we can see the emergence and consolidation of a State of 'partial securities' in which rights are conditional and retractable (see Mythen et al., 2013). To return to the example of targeted policing, the number of Asian and Black males stopped and searched in London under section 44 of the Terrorism Act 2000 rose more than 12 fold after the 7th July bombings (Dodd, 2006). What is, in effect, the bald implementation of upstream racial profiling has, for those caught downstream, become an unpalatable security peril of the risk society. As Hudson (2006) warns, in a persecutory climate, the normalization of prejudicial forms of 'White man's justice' loom large, both inside and outside the court room.

Casing risk: Chasing the Foucauldian shadows – policing, data and surveillance

Having considered the ways in which risk has been used as a tool for predicting crime, a driver for regulation and a mechanism of governance, it is time to turn to our first application of theory to practice. In this case study, I wish to consider the possibilities of Ericson and Haggerty's (1997) neo-Foucauldian approach to understanding transitions in the occupational culture and practices of policing. As noted earlier, in the period directly after the publication of the Floud and Greenwood Reports, the tenor of party political voice in support of preventative techniques of crime control became raised. One important aspect of discourses supportive of the introduction of preventative measures relates to policing and the quest to shore up social order through tighter legislation and prohibitive punishment. In the United Kingdom, following on from episodes of urban unrest in several English cities in the early 1980s, a drift to the right in British politics took shape, characterized by authoritarian forms of social control, punitive treatment of offenders and coercive policing methods (see Hillyard and Percy-Smith, 1988). By the late 1980s, signs of a change in preference from penal modernism to interventionism was discernible among the major political parties. Underpinning this consensus was the view that *post hoc* punishment acted as a necessary but poor relation to *pre hoc* crime management. As Feeley and Simon observe, central to this shift in approach was the roll out and championing of processes of risk assessment and evaluation. In order to prevent crimes from materializing in the future, the logic of actuarial risk involved the use of extant data to identify criminals, the types of crimes they may commit and under what conditions crime might occur. Notwithstanding the hyper-realist gist of such a logic – plus the tendency of risk scales and models to flatten ambiguities – economic and political priorities encouraged the need to be tough on crime and its causes in many countries in the 1980s. Yet, in the United Kingdom at least, while the long and socially divisive period in office of Margaret Thatcher accelerated a policy drift to the right – exemplified by an intensification of law and order measures, hard-line policing, aggressive individualism and a rolling back of the State to reduce health and welfare costs – crime rates were largely unaffected (see Hillyard and Percy-Smith, 1988; Lodziak, 1995). By the early 1990s it had become apparent that stringent law and order measures and punitive sentencing had had little or no direct positive effect on crime reduction. Indeed, the statistics detailed in British Crime Surveys in the 1980s – contemporaneously known as the Crime Survey of England and Wales (CSEW) – show that crime was trending in the opposite direction. In many urban areas, such as London, Liverpool and Birmingham, relations between the police and minority groups had completely broken down. Following the shift from marginal Conservative control to a large Labour majority Government in 1997, several things changed in policing and crime control, but many stayed the same. In some respects, the incoming Prime Minister Tony Blair delivered old wine in new bottles, continuing an established tradition of populist punitiveness that was: 'tough on crime, tough on the causes of crime' (BBC News Online, 2004). Yet changing perspectives and approaches towards policing can be evidenced in the 1990s among think tank researchers, policy analysts and senior politicians. As economic and social conditions improved and greater resources were put into welfare initiatives and public services, the crime rate steadily dropped. With changing attitudes towards criminality and punishment came new public expectations of the police and the day-to-day practices and processes of policing. Although these are perhaps but two sides of the same coin, at the level of institutional presentation a shift has become apparent over time from emphasizing the upholding of law and order and the apprehension of perpetrators, to protecting the public and proactively reducing crime. The galvanizing mantra embossed on modern police vehicles in England and Wales is emblematic of this reconfigured occupational objective: 'fighting crime, protecting the public'. However, while an appetite for preventative interventions driven by risk assessment and profiling can be discerned from the late 1980s into the 1990s and beyond, the extent and depth of the institutional commitment to pro-active policy remains debatable. For O'Malley (2006), the early trend towards prevention was largely constituted by the police seeking to engage other actors, communities and institutions and to involve them in the process of crime prevention. For example, through the instigation of *Neighbourhood Watch* schemes, invitations to the public to report suspicious activity, citizen's panels and various campaigns directed at securing property and belongings. These examples are arguably early signs of the gestation of a much broader incorporation of technologies of risk into the policing process that became consolidated – albeit in a disparate fashion – alongside other aspects of the new penology in the 1990s. All of this provides the neccessary context in which to understand the argument outlined by Richard Ericson and Kevin Haggerty (1997) in their influential book *Policing the Risk Society*. This text represents an attempt to grasp both the drivers involved in and the nature of transformations in policing. Inspired by the networked conception of power advanced by Foucault, Ericson and Haggerty (1997: 3) argue that both policing – and the society in which policing is performed – need to be understood in terms of risk: 'our point is that policing consists of the public police coordinating their activities with policing agents in all other institutions to provide a society-wide basis for risk management (governance) and security (guarantees against loss)'.

While policing had previously been oriented towards combating crime as it broke out and attempting to keep the peace, Ericson and Haggerty (1997) suggest that, during the mid to late 1980s, risk management became an elemental goal, stimulating both a modification of and an expansion of policing activities. The extension of police procedures included greater networking and information exchange with other public and private bodies, including insurance companies, private security firms, local government, vehicle licensing agencies and community support groups. This is significant for Ericson and Haggerty (1997) in that it is illustrative of an extension of the surveillant tendencies of neo-liberal States, but also in that it symbolizes the diffusion and sharing of the burden of crime risks between different institutions and agencies. Based on an extensive ethnographic study in Canada which included interviews with 155 police officers and administrative personnel, participant observation and archival analysis, Ericson and Haggerty illuminate the burgeoning array of external contacts that have become fused to the police and the inclination towards exchanging information as a commodity. They posit that the links established between the police and external agencies are not only informational, they are also corporate and financial, with private companies sponsoring various police projects. For Ericson and Haggerty (1997: 338) such changes are indicative of the ways in which technologization and associated informational networks alter the structure of police institutions: 'by levelling hierarchies, blurring traditional divisions of labour, dispersing supervisory capacities, and limiting individual discretion'. In their view, the demands for risk information are such that the police have become central to a vortex of data circulated between institutions and agencies. Further, the boundaries between different agencies become permeable and are not contingent on capacity to be directly involved in crime control. The key example which Ericson and Haggerty use to illustrate this trend is the practice of community policing. They argue that the combined initiatives that crystallize under the banner of community policing, reduce the autonomy of police officers, unhelpfully muddy the boundaries of responsibility for crime control and lead to invasive forms of surveillance. Importantly, a key shift is said to have taken place in the dynamics of policing strategy, from coercion to compliance:

> While they have considerable coercive power to produce knowledge of risk, the police mainly distribute the knowledge so obtained through risk communication systems of other institutions that govern in terms of a compliance mode. Coercive control gives way to contingent categorization. Policing is effected not only through territorial surveillance but also at the extra-territorial level of abstract knowledge of risk.

> (Ericson and Haggerty, 1997: 5)

While the title of the book may indicate an affiliation with Beck's risk society thesis, Ericson and Haggerty's approach is primarily informed by the governmentality perspective. The echoes of Foucault are most voluble in the networked account of power and Ericson and Haggerty's conception of the police force as a hub of data used to inform classification, monitoring and surveillance of populations. Foucault's appreciation of the knowledge/power dialectic is writ large through the thesis which rests on the proposition that knowledge acquired through data gathering and surveillance is fundamental to the operation of soft power facilitated by the police. Recognizing the diffusion of power from the State to other active organizations in civil society, Ericson and Haggerty argue that security is now co-produced by a range of actors and agencies. Further, the dispersal of information into the public realm via discourses about crime and security becomes consolidated in policy and practice. In such a way, Foucault's conduct of conduct occurs through the rationalization of power through risk-based forms of governance and control. It is important to note that Ericson and Haggerty's approach is sensitive to the wider milieu in which the transformations they describe are situated. The broader rise in awareness of risk and risk issues that emerged in the mid to late 1980s and the process of bureaucratic and governmental decentralization that characterized the rolling back of the State are clearly important factors in propelling changes in policing. Nonetheless, there are some notable gaps and flaws in the argument too. In their desire to supplant traditional coercion-based explanations of police practices with a new networked occupational paradigm based around knowledge production, Ericson and Haggerty (1997) arguably over-emphasize change and underplay continuities. In the first instance, the limited geographical zone in which the research was undertaken invokes doubts about the generalizability of the findings. Further, their presentation of everyday working practices is somewhat generic and oriented towards office rather than street-based policing. The narrative presented is partial in that it does not account for divergent policing practices across continents, countries or regions, nor indeed the capacity of police forces to switch up and down between aggressive militaristic tactics and hands-off data-gathering and observational approaches (see Punch, 2007). The various tactics used in the policing of protest and urban unrest in the United Kingdom illustrate this point well. During the 2011 spree of riots there are strategic and operational reasons why the initial police response in London, Birmingham, Liverpool and Salford was to document and record rather than intervene with force. These tactics can be contrasted with the militaristic interventionist tactics used against anti-violence demonstrators campaigning in London against attacks by the Israeli State on Gaza (see Gilmore, 2010). As Ferret and Spenlehauer (2009: 160) point out in their empirical application of Ericson and Haggerty's thesis: 'analysis of the implementation of projects designed to transform police forces into panoptic bodies shows that these projects are always paralleled by contradictory, traditional law enforcement projects targeting the risk to be dealt with'. Once more we find that the realities of risk regulation on the ground are more labile and diffuse than the theoretical frames of reference suggest.

In summary, Ericson and Haggerty can be praised for highlighting the motion towards risk-based policing and crime management that has become a pillar in the architecture of contemporary policing, even if their approach is ultimately fractional and somewhat risk centric. Ericson and Haggerty's observations of a ground-shift in policing away from direct and coercive hands on approaches towards 'panoptical', knowledge-based work, does capture a broadening out of agencies involved in policing and a trend towards data gathering and surveillance. Yet it is true to say that their intervention captures some aspects of a bumpy transition rather than a visible sea change (see Ferret and Spenlehauer, 2009).

Criminal motives and motivations: Risk-taking, culture and pleasure

So far in the chapter we have examined the place of risk in the institutional regulation of crime, focussing primarily on prediction, prevention, policing and punishment. In Chapter 4 we will move on to consider more fully the social construction of crime risks, focussing on shifting approaches towards victims and the critical role of the media and politics in setting the agenda for public debates about crime and punishment. As we shall see, the dominant gaze of research around fear and risk within the social sciences has been one that has both twinned the two concepts and linked them strongly to harm. Risks are things to be staved off, avoided and minimized. Meanwhile, fears are negative emotions that may destabilize our ontological security and threaten our well-being. While the theoretical perspectives on risk we have considered suggest several reasons for this slant – among them the institutional proclivity towards using risk as a tool for social control and the increasing scale and volatility of the threats that we face – there are good reasons to see exposure to risk – and, perhaps, to a more limited extent, feelings of fear – as human experiences that are commonplace and can, in certain circumstances, be deployed positively. Insofar as the preponderance of social science research has been directed by the idea of risk as threat, within criminology and cultural studies, a small number of inquiries have drawn attention to the positive dimensions of risk-taking in particular contexts. The 'pleasures of risk' have been observed by researchers observing a range of activities on the margins, including drug consumption (Measham and Moore, 2008; Reith, 2005), base jumping (Lyng, 2005) and urban free running (Saville, 2008). What is perhaps missing from our specific discussion of crime and regulation so far is the role that risk might play in motivating the actions of perpetrators. We need to be aware that, alongside theoretical work that has sought to examine the institutional regulation and management of crime through risk, other longstanding currents of research have sought to bring to the surface the role of risk-taking in explaining criminal behaviour, albeit without specifically using risk as a foundational organizing principle. One such approach is rational choice theory, first advance by the American Nobel Prize winning economist Gary Becker (1976) and popularized by the sociologist James Coleman (1990). In the context of criminal behaviour, rational choice theory has been used to explain the risk factors considered by perpetrators when considering whether or not to commit a crime. Followers of the rational choice model see offenders as conscious risk assessors, setting the possible losses of liberty that may result from being apprehended against the gains of criminal activity. It is fair to say that rational choice theory has received something of a mixed response within sociology, social policy and criminology. Those advocating the model have sought to demonstrate how the principles of rational choice can be used to predict criminal behaviour and thus can be utilized in policy making that designs out or reduces opportunities for crime (Cornish and Clarke, 1987). If we choose to follow rational choice theory we are able to track the potential choices that perpetrators may make and, on the basis of this, make modifications to security procedures and building design to deter criminals. Yet critics of rational choice theory have quibbled with such an assertion, arguing that it can only assist as an explanation with regards to a limited number of offences, rather than being used to explain or predict criminal behaviour in the round. One could see, for example, how the weighing of risk versus reward might apply in the context of domestic burglary or tax evasion, but it may be limited in accounting for offender behaviour in more emotive and compulsive crimes such as physical or sexual assault. Disregarding the fact that rational choice theory is more applicable to some crimes and some criminals than others, it does need to be remembered that offenders are in some senses risk-takers, whether this is actively cognized at a conscious level or not.

Pre-dating the emergence of rational choice theory, the relationship between criminal behaviour and risk also features in the classic research of the Chicago School, albeit again in a way which is implied, rather than focal. The Chicago School were pioneers of the ethnographic approach and sought to connect the lifestyles of various groups living in urban areas to wider structural processes of unemployment, inequality and deprivation. The research undertaken by Shaw and McKay (1942) typifies the Chicago School approach, emphasizing the strong connection between social structure and human agency. Their research demonstrates that capitalist urbanization tends to undo traditional tight-knit communities and to loosen value systems, resulting in transient communities with alternative value systems. Chiming with the research of other Chicago School researchers such as Burgess and Park (1921), Shaw and McKay argue that human beings are moulded by the social, cultural and economic context in which they are raised and live. In their research of 'juvenile delinquents' Shaw and Mackay claimed that delinquent behaviour did not materialize at an individual level as an outcome of abnormal psychology or cognitive dysfunction. Rather, they stated that structural factors such as abnormal living conditions, poor housing, social problems and poverty were contributory factors in criminal behaviour among young people. Alongside the early contributions of the Chicago School, subcultural theory – emerging from Albert Cohen's (1955) work on youth gangs – also focusses on the formation of alternate value systems which encourage individuals in certain cultures to interpret crime risks in ways which diverge from the dominant worldview reproduced by the State and social institutions. In *Delinquent Boys: The Culture of the Gang* (1955), Cohen advanced the notion of sub-cultures to describe the formation of cohesive sets of values and rituals among those that are economically and culturally situated outside the mainstream. Cohen proposes that delinquent youths who are unable to acquire social worth through the prescribed socially sanctioned routes and goals – such as education, employment, conspicuous consumption and housing – experience 'status frustration'. As a result, these marginal-ized young people often respond to their inability to meet society's expectations and demands by creating their own structures of meaning within gangs. The gang setting suspends – and sometimes negates – conventional rules and expectations about status and identity. Thus, while it may be seen externally as problematic for young people to play truant from school, steal and engage in violence, within the gang context such actions may function as mechanisms of achieving status. In effect, gangs switch dom-inant norms and values with their own systems of identity, hierarchy and esteem. For Cohen, deviant behaviour in gangs is symptomatic of the strains experienced in every-day life by young men and acts as a symbolic rejection of dominant norms and values and the assertion of an alternate model of status. Rather than one's degree certificate symbolizing social standing, in a gang setting vandalism, stealing or joyriding may act as parallel markers of prestige. This process of replacing society's norms and values with alternative ones is referred to by Cohen as 'reaction formation'. Similar findings on the link between risk-taking, identity and status were reported in the United Kingdom by John Barron Mays (1958). His ethnographic study in an economically deprived area of Liverpool reported that apparently dangerous and 'delinquent' behaviour could be understood as a response of socially excluded young people to situations in which they have little opportunity for self-expression and autonomy. Willmott's (1966) subsequent study conducted in Bethnall Green in East London challenged Cohen's notion of 'status frustration' and instead linked delinquent behaviour to thrill seeking and the adrenalin rush of transgression. In many respects this study is the marker for more contemporary approaches to crime and risk-taking within cultural criminology, particularly those that subscribe to Stephen Lyng's (1990) theory of 'edgework'. Cohen's original findings are reinforced by Walter Miller's (1958) ethnographic study of the attitudes and values of young gang members in Boston which similarly emphasized the role of substitute values within gangs, with risky behaviour serving as a means of achieving respect and status. Miller (1958) explored the positive values attributed to 'getting in to trouble' linking this to expressions of autonomy and masculinity. He argued that risk seeking behaviour exhibited through criminality, sexual exploration and excessive alcohol consumption acted as a both a form of social lubrication within the group as well as a compen-satory valve for relieving some of the tensions caused by the mundanity of everyday life. As the old adage goes, when all you have is a hammer you tend to treat everything as a nail. Willmott's (1966) Bethnall Green study also linked delinquent behaviour to thrill seeking and the adrenalin rush of transgression. Echoing Cohen's (1955) benchmark study of the formation of delinquent subcultures and also the findings of Miller's (1958) study, Willmott's research acknowledges that young men in particular may seek out dangerous situations and actively engage in criminality to gain excitement and to play out displays of masculine bravado. While the emphasis on class in such work serves as a reminder of the strong associations between inequality and risk, the danger is that, collectively read, we are inadvertently encouraged towards pathologizing the working classes (see O'Malley, 2006). One might, for instance, make the riposte that the middle and upper classes have fair histories of excessive alcohol consumption, sexual 'deviance' and recreational drug consumption, but that this behaviour has, by and large, not taken place in spaces and places in which they are likely to be criminalized, such as inner city streets, public parks and city centre bars and clubs.

Whatever one's moral viewpoint, the urban studies of the Chicago School and its followers have acted as a marker for more contemporary approaches to crime and risk-taking within cultural criminology that have utilized Lyng's (1990; 2005) concept of 'edgework'. Edgework essentially describes activities in and through which individuals and subcultures probe the boundaries of order and disorder and safety and danger. A small but robust body of work in this tradition has sought to illuminate the way in which risk-taking can be used positively by those seeking sensual thrills, existential fulfilment and the development of autonomy (Lyng, 2005). As a counterpoise to conceptual takes on risk which stress harms, Lyng seeks to theoretically develop a 'sociology of risk-taking'. In so doing, he borrows the term 'edgework' from the literary and journalistic work of the controversial American writer and self-proclaimed 'gonzo journalist' Hunter S. Thompson. In the autobiographical novel *Fear and Loathing in Las Vegas* (1972), Thompson narrates in graphic detail his drink and drug fuelled dalliances on two assignments across the United States in the company of the Samoan attorney Oscar Acosta. Describing a series of scrapes and altercations the two encountered along the way, the author defines edgework as a practice of pushing the boundaries of risk and control in order to find self-fulfilment and pleasure. Thompson describes the practice of getting as close as one can to the 'edge' or point where danger turns into chaos. Broadening out this idea, Lyng (1990: 877) believes that edgework affords the possibility of sensual pleasure, self-fulfilment, and creative determination, reasoning that the practice of voluntarily and autonomously searching activities on the 'edge' of control is manifested across a range of diverse lifestyles, including stock trading, sadomasochism, street anarchism and extreme sports. Further, the desire to express oneself through risk-taking activity is not exclusive to certain ethnicities or sexes. Rather, Lyng (1990) is keen to stress the universality of engagements on and with the edge: 'skydiving, for example, may offer a transcendent experience, but it is unlikely to be available to many young black members of the urban underclass. Crack, on the other hand, may provide a similarly transcending experience, but unlike skydiving is available to all, rich and poor' (Lyng, 2005: 209). Lyng's work has been highly successful in widening the sociological lens of risk and promoting valuable research into the embodied, sensuous texture of risk-taking. Further, in its appeal to the general pleasures of risk across the social spectrum, the theory of edgework hastens a positive shift away from attributing risky behaviour to discrete classes and groups. Although Lyng is keen to point up the breadth of activities and pursuits in which voluntary risk-taking arises, his work has been seized upon by academics working in the area of cultural criminology to explain the motivations of individuals operating on 'the edge'. In this genre, ethnographic studies into drug consumption (Hutton, 2006), shoplifting (Katz, 1998), scavenging (Ferrell, 2006) and violent crime (Presdee, 2000) have highlighted the positive dimensions of risk-taking in terms of stimulating the somatic senses or, in Measham and Moore's (2008) terms, of affording 'experiential intensity'. These studies recount the positive possibilities of risk for those transgressing law in different contexts, whether these be related to existential needs, material gain, self-affirming practices, personal resourcefulness or power. Thus, attention is justly drawn to the experience and performance of crime and the ways in which criminal acts are made sense of and occasionally enjoyed by those that commit them. Rejecting both rational choice theory models and stratification-based approaches as incomplete explanations for criminality, Katz (1988: 9) points up the 'seductive pleasures' that may make certain crimes attractive. Describing shoplifting as a 'sneaky thrill' for young people, Katz (1988: 9) believes that such crimes involve asserting individual skill and act as a means of secretly expressing power over present adults that are unaware a criminal act is taking place. The edgework tradition of research acts as a useful rejoinder to the dominant trajectory in risk research towards cataloguing risk as harm. Yet, while recognition that the drive to take risks is a universal feature of human life that transcends class, gender, age and ethnicity, the social acceptability or otherwise of risk-taking is affected by these factors. As Measham and Moore (2008: 284) eloquently argue, the site of risk-taking is also an important determinant of the types of regulation pursued: 'impermissible pleasures generated by transgressive leisure activities and identities become subject to regulation, surveillance and control'. Insofar as we may all experience compulsions to take risks at various intervals, the kinds of risks we take, how these are viewed in society and the regulatory sanctions imposed upon risk-taking behaviour remain connected to forms of stratification and the locus of power.

A final note of caution might also be sounded regarding the relationship between researchers and those that they research. Amidst the magnetic draw of the criminal underworld for social researchers, there is, of course, the danger that law breaking and harm causing behaviours are glossed over and transgressive behaviour becomes valorized. Aside from the potential buzz of breaking the law for those involved in crime, social researchers themselves run the risk of being allured by those whose – potentially morally dubious behaviour – they observe. Thus we need to be alert to the possibility of the researcher becoming seduced by a risky world of players, chancers and opportunists. The danger is that danger itself becomes glamorized and a balanced view relinquished. Stan Cohen's (1979) cautionary tale of 'The Last Seminar' bottoms out this issue with aplomb. Cohen recounts an imaginary situation in which problematic behaviours sometimes explained away at a distance by social scientists come home. In 'The Last Seminar' some of the focal subjects of social science research – criminals, prisoners, people who are mentally ill, the economically excluded – begin to congregate on campus and start attending classes. The newcomers become unruly and eventually resort to using coercion, violence and eventually arson to take over the University. Cohen's provocative fable acts invites us to think seriously about our relationships with the subjects of our research and to be reflexive in thinking through the processes and practices we are exposed to as researchers, as well as the perceptions and actions of research participants.

Conclusion

Although there has been a distinct movement within sociology and criminology towards more critical takes on the analytic capacity of risk, it is evident from the applications considered in this chapter that forms and uses of risk vary considerably across time, space and place. Rather than typecasting the concept of risk as an *enfant terrible* which has produced divisive effects in terms of crime prevention and regulation, we are perhaps better served reminding ourselves of the value of a critical, but open approach. Rather than avowing that modes of risk regulation are an inherently good or bad thing in and of themselves, we should begin by looking at the context of their introduction and consider both the potential benefits and the possible drawbacks. To be clear, adopting such a position does not involve benignly acting as an apologist for neo-liberal forms of social engineering that seek to harness or exploit risk in order to mask inequalities and perpetuate privileges. Rather, the cultivation of an open critical perspective permits an appreciation of the ways in which risk can and has been progressively used in relation to crime management or drug rehabilitation, while retaining a critical eye that interrogates institutional uses of risk across the piece. Developing a more dialogic stance that encourages rather than closes down conversation and debate is the key to developing a context sensitive approach that differentiates between technologies and manifestations of risk and treats each according to its evidential merits and limits. Such an approach will serve us well as we negotiate the complex and multi-layered relationship between the media, victimization and crime in Chapter 4.

4 Fear, Victimization and the Media

Introduction

In Chapter 3 we focussed primarily on the application of risk as a technology for the measurement, assessment and control of crime. Our inquiry featured an analysis of interventions that have utilized risk in the interconnected spheres of policing, sentencing and punishment. We also examined the utility of neo-Foucauldian criminological theories – such as the new penology and the culture of control – which have mobilized risk as a prism to view changing patterns of social and legal regulation. In the final quarter of the chapter, our discussion moved from discussing the macro institutional uses of risk towards a more micro level examination of explanations for individual risk-taking in the context of criminal behaviour. Although the place of risk in institutional forms of regulation remains important in this chapter, the emphasis will shift from methods of determining and managing crime towards the impacts of representations of danger on specific groups and individuals. Therefore, we will be retaining our emphasis on crime, but focussing more sharply on the social construction of criminality, motivations for criminal behaviour and the impacts of crime on victims. To make a crude distinction, while the focus in Chapter 3 was broadly oriented towards the 'objective' – that is, the way in which institutions have sought to construct, incorporate and mobilize risk – our discussion of risk-taking behaviours towards the end of the chapter provides a bridge to the more 'subjective' side of risk. Thus, in this chapter we centre on the individual, both as perpetrator, victim and witness of crime. Central to this shift in emphasis will be a thorough engagement with the omnipresent issue of 'fear of crime'. I intend firstly to provide an overview of criminological uses of the concept of fear in relation to crime, risk and criminal victimization and, secondly, to evaluate research and literatures that have investigated public fears about crime. Here the significance of the media in constructing representations of criminal behaviour and circulating discourses of crime is vital. The role of various media portals – both professional and social – in the transmission of notions of criminality is arguably more pronounced in modern society than at any previous point in history. Insofar as research in the social sciences has historically focussed on traditional media forms such as television, radio and newspapers, it is evident that changing patterns of media consumption – particularly among the under thirties – are yet to be properly understood (see Lievrouw, 2012). While media research has historically been nation focussed and concerned with the outputs of large-scale conglomerations, the globalization of the media, new technological platforms and increasingly stratified consumption of products changes the contextual terrain in which sense making takes place in ways that are yet to be fully appreciated within the social sciences (see Anderson, 2009; Bauman, 2012; Mythen, 2010). I will argue here that a complex and differentiated media environment means that there are a greater range of constructions – and indeed interpretations – of crime and criminality in circulation than in preceding epochs. Furthermore, the *quality* of media representations of crime has altered dramatically in recent years with real time news, blogging, tweeting and growing use of social media sites. Keeping sight of theoretical vistas, towards the end of the chapter I wish to put Furedi's culture of fear perspective to work, highlighting the ways in which political and media disquiet around 'knife-crime' has served to incite anxieties that are out of kilter with the magnitude and frequency of harm.

Victimization, risk and rights

As the contributions reviewed in the last chapter indicate, until the last two decades of the twentieth century, the economic and political thrust of crime control in the majority of Western nations had been geared towards combating law-breaking and punishing offenders, rather than directly addressing the needs of victims of crime. It is only relatively recently that victims of crime have received systematic legal redress, economic compensation and access to psycho-social support (see Davis et al., 2007; Williams, 2005: 493). These transformations have formed part of a wider formal commitment by the State to 'rebalance' the criminal justice system to give greater rights to victims of crime, rather than to focus on protecting the rights of perpetrators (Hall, 2009; Walklate, 2007a). In the United Kingdom, in the late 1970s and early 1980s, crime rates rose sharply, promoting rising interest in victims of crime in the mass media and institutional concerns within criminal justice and welfare agencies about the plight of victims. In the last two decades, the 'victim' has steadily moved from the margins to the centre in public debates around crime regulation, offender management and punishment (see Davis et al., 2013; Walklate, 2007b). During this period, assorted politicians, media outlets, charities and NGOs have all sought to champion the rights of victims across a range of contexts. In addition, legal professionals have taken on high-profile cases in which the criminal justice system has previously been seen to fail victims, as exemplified by Michael Mansfield's successful prosecution on behalf of the Lawrence family which finally brought to justice those involved in the racist murder of Stephen Lawrence. In tandem, media professionals and cultural producers have shown a keener interest in the narratives and biographies of victims. More concentrated attention on those that have been abused has not, however, produced a chorus of views, either in terms of political viewpoint, media representation or public opinion. Rather, rival ways of thinking about victimization, responsibility and culpability have emerged, sculpted by the life histories, political persuasions and the moral values of involved parties (see Mythen, 2007a). Indeed, a range of pejorative terms have materialized in common parlance, such as 'victim mentality', 'victim prone' 'playing the victim' and 'victim culture'. While people's views on the robustness and resilience of others is clearly something of a mixed and messy bag, what is clear in terms of criminal justice is that it is no longer sufficient for the police to simply seek out offenders nor is it considered enough to have a court system that solely punishes offenders. Rather a spectrum of attendant processes that give due credence to the perspectives, needs and feelings of victims are now integral to the workings of the criminal justice system (see Hall, 2009; Karmen, 2009). In order to understand the processes that underscore such a transformation it is worth considering the shifting cultural meanings attributed to victims and the institutional networks that have emerged to support victims of crime. In the 1980s and 1990s governments of all persuasions, State agencies and policy researchers in Western nations became progressively interested in the perspectives and experiences of victims, both as identifiable individual parties and collective groups (Furedi, 2002: 102; Walklate, 2007b). Since this time, the rights of the victim have been advanced to such an extent that the impacts of criminal justice decisions on victims now serves as a key factor in policy formation around punishment and penality (see Garland, 2001; Rock, 2002). A number of developments serve as evidence of a crystallization of interest in the feelings and experiences of victims. The victim has become more visible in political decisions about crime control, victim's rights have assumed a pivotal role in public policy making and, mirroring the recommendations of the Floud and Greenwood reports, offenders have increasingly been punished and rehabilitated according to their relationship with the victim and their probability of reoffending (see Hudson, 2003: 87; Williams, 2005: 89). At the same time, methods of restorative justice that allow victims to articulate their views directly to offenders have become increasingly popular and there has been a net rise in the number of victim support networks and organizations (Zedner, 2002: 420). The State has also been pressed by the public to instigate a range of educative programmes designed to raise awareness of victims and to improve remuneration schemes for victims of harm through compensation schemes. To cite one example, in the United Kingdom in 1979 around 22,000 claims were received by the UK Criminal Injuries Compensation Authority. Twenty years later the annual number of applications had risen to 79,049 and a total of 234.6 million pounds was paid out to victims of violent crime (see Criminal Injuries Compensation Authority, 2010). The move towards defending the rights of victims has also been advanced through various forms of legislation such as the 1998 Human Rights Act. In 2007 the UK Government established a Commission for Equality and Human Rights (CEHR) with a mission to protect those victimized by gender, ethnicity, disability, sexual orientation, age and religion. Although such moves are positive in setting down ethical and moral markers, they do stretch out the concept of victimization. As Green (2006: 6) calculates, in the quest to extend and defend the rights of marginalized groups, the combined total of groups potentially 'victimized' in the CEHR definition amounts to almost three-quarters of the UK population. Such a situation does run the risk of normalizing victimization and raises the question of whether gradations of harm and injury are being lost amidst the miasma of political correctness. As there are different types and classes of offender, so too there are different kinds of victims. What is more, who or what counts in the attribution of victimization is critical – and this itself is influenced by processes of institutional definition and labelling. In the routine course of their duties, professionals employed within the media, politics, the police force and the criminal justice system construct multiple types of victims: those that are innocent; those that are feckless, even those that are considered as 'deserving' of harm by dint of amoral behaviour or previous transgressions. Insofar as cases in which children are abused by adults justifiably illicit widespread sympathy, it is fair to say that there is little public appetite for vocalizing the rights of victims who are injured by home-owners in the course of undertaking domestic burglaries. As Carrabine et al. (2004) show, the acquisition of victim status is vitally connected to moral judgements, power relations and extant ideologies, making it possible to talk about a 'hierarchy of victimi-sation'. It is clear that public expressions of sympathy for crime victims are not absolute but stretch along a continuum from home-owning elderly ladies at the apex down to homeless young males with drug addictions at the foot.

A sharper focus on the victim within and outside of the criminal justice system is, of course, connected to tectonic sociocultural transformations. As we shall see, the work of various thinkers such as O'Malley, Garland, Beck and Furedi has been instructive in pointing up the salience of broader macro-social changes, such as the spread of individ-ualization, the rise of the so-called 'compensation culture' and the surveillant incursions of the State into what was once considered to be private life. For O'Malley (2006: 52), the growing visibility of the victim can be connected to the extension of risk as a tech-nology for categorizing and understanding human behaviour and the wider ideological project of neo-liberal governance: 'the victim . . . became a new subject of risk, to be worked with and upon in order to correct ignorance, vulnerability and misunderstand-ing'. For Garland (2001), the very idea of the victim can be – and has been – mobilized as a powerful symbol in the management of crime. In his view, protection of those harmed by crime constitutes an important component of the culture of control. As individu-als comply with institutional exhortations to responsibilize themselves around crime to avoid victimization, so too do they bear more of the burden of managing their own crime risks. For his part, Furedi (2002) speaks of the factors involved in the evolu-tion of a 'culture of victimhood' within which 'victim identities' are cultivated. Furedi (2002: 96) is critical of the public valorization of victimization which, in his view, 'has become a highly prized cultural artefact'. Underlying this shift, experts from all profes-sions – medics, academics, securocats, writers and journalists – have been responsible for encouraging people to see themselves as 'at risk' and to define themselves as vic-tims. Beck (2009) – writing very much from a sociological rather than a criminological standpoint – declares the dubious achievement of the risk society to be one of render-ing us all victims, albeit victims that are imperilled not so much by exposure to crime but by uncontrollable nuclear, genetic and environmental risks. Despite pursuing diver-gent routes of inquiry, Furedi, Garland, Beck and O'Malley all agree that heightened awareness of victims and victimization within neo-liberal capitalist countries needs to be understood in relation to underlying political, economic and cultural processes. While these theoretical interventions have been advantageous in capturing the mood music of the zeitgeist, the implications of the residual victimological complexities are yet to be fully hollowed out. It needs to remembered that being labelled as and/or or being treated as a victim is not a neat or unconditional journey (see Mythen, 2007a; Tulloch, 2006). To be given the status of victim involves the individual being exposed to and involved in a range of interactions and processes, including identification, categoriza-tion and recognition. Exactly who is cast as a victim and under which conditions are questions that are subject to shaping by a range of social forces. As Hudson (2003: 65) reminds us: 'suspect people do not have (actually) to commit crimes to be identified as criminal, nor do respectable people have to experience crime to identify themselves as (potential) victims'. In discussions around the nature and status of the victim in society, the issue of plasticity again emerges and the diffuse and ambivalent social effects of risk once more come to the surface. Institutional technologies of risk can be used to increase public safety, but so too can they be used to fit political agendas and to buttress social control. In making claims about the democratization of victimization in the light of global manufactured risks, the risk society perspective ironically articulates with many of the regulatory regimes pursued by government, law enforcers and legislators. There are several reasons to be wary of narratives that suggest that we are all in the same boat, whether it be sailing against the tide of violent crime, facing the storm of environmental apocalypse or keeping ourselves materially anchored amidst the billowing winds of the economic downturn. Perhaps we need instead to redirect attention to the tight relationship between risk and social stratification in terms of which groups tend to avoid victimization and which routinely become victims. For example, empirical studies show that young people have the highest rate of committing crimes, but are also at the greatest risk of being a victim of a crime (see Fattah, 1991; Muncie, 2003). Alongside age, social class, gender and ethnicity remain important indicators of risk exposure in general and crime victimization in particular. In my view the creeping tendency towards identifying and talking in terms of a generalized culture of victimhood inhibits our capacity to differentiate between gradations of harm and leads to muddled political priorities (see Mythen, 2007a). When the generality of crime risks becomes accepted, the inference for patterns of victimization is the same as it is for risk distribution. If we have all collectively become victims of crime, then the voice of the individual victim becomes muted.

There are clearly degrees of risk involved in criminal victimization and these can be indexed to patterns of inequality, social exclusion and geographical location. What is more, in cases of individual harm and abuse, primary victimization serves as a firm predictor of future victimization (Shaw and Pease, 2000). The weight of empirical evidence shows that individuals have different levels of vulnerability and different degrees of exposure to different types of crime (see Davis et al., 2013; Pantazis, 2000). Empirical research on the victim-offender overlap indicates a strong association between offending and victimization, with individuals with criminal histories having a higher rate of victimization than those that do not (see Pauwels and Svensson, 2011). As Williams (2004: 92) points out: 'the general risks of victimization disguise the greater real risks for some groups. Individuals within certain groups may fall victim to many offences in a year whereas others in different subgroups may never, or only very rarely, experience a crime'. Even if one were to disregard these findings and mistakenly assume that crime risks manifest themselves generally rather than sectorally, at the level of the victimization, equivalent crimes are *experienced* differently by victims who respond in markedly different ways (Zedner, 2002: 429). As the work of Murray Lee (2001; 2007) demonstrates, anxieties about the risk of victimization are impacted by social structures, shaped by lived experience and indexed to specific cultural milieu. To understand both general anxieties about victimization and individuated cognitive processes of victim positioning we need to attend to the matrix of cultural forms involved in the construction of fear. Tudor (2003: 249) obligingly elaborates the creative role of institutions in the construction of risks, noting the potential effects of social reinforcement on public attitudes towards danger:

> If our cultures repeatedly warn us that this kind of activity is dangerous ... then this provides the soil in which fearfulness may grow. Indeed, the very constitution of the ways in which we experience and articulate fear is significantly dependent

upon the channels of expression made available to us by our cultures. That is particularly apparent where 'new' fears emerge and become widespread in relatively short periods of time.

Stitching this point about the construction of fear to differential patterns of victimization might lead one to conclude that the specificities of Anglophone countries are being projected as general and universal. While there may be good reasons for some citizens in the Europe and North America to be concerned about violent crime, in other parts of the globe such problems are justifiably magnified. If we compare rates of knife-crime in the United Kingdom with countries such as Mexico, for example, the relative risk of victimization becomes readily apparent. Beyond Mexico there are other areas of South America which receive little publicity but are sites of even graver violent crime. The murder rate in Guatemala of 39 per 100,000 is more than twice the Mexican rate of 18 per 100,000. In Guatemala City there have been a total of 22,021 murders between 2008 and 2012 alone. Marta, a resident of Peronia, Guatemala City, describes her feelings after being subjected to a hold up by an armed gang on a bus: 'I cannot explain what it is to experience a single moment that decides your whole life . . . they decide whether you live or die. You are so fragile, but this is life in Peronia' (Storr, 2013: 18). We will return to the problem of violent crime in the context of the propagation of 'new' fears in the case study, but let us now delve a little deeper into the phenomenon of public anxieties about criminal victimization.

Surveying crime: (Mis)calculating risk and anxiety?

Questions of risk and the changing context of rights for victims form an important backdrop to parallel developments around what has been generically called 'fear of crime'. Like risk, fear of crime has assumed cultural prominence in a relatively short time, been applied to a range of security problems and is a highly contested phenomenon. 'Fear of crime' has become both a commonly used descriptor and a well worn metaphor in contemporary society, invoking a spectrum of emotions, opinions, sets of evidence, claims and counterclaims. Within sociology, psychology and criminology, fear of crime research has branched out in many directions, taking in areas as varied as the relationship between probability and fear of victimization (Chadee et al., 2007); psycho-social drivers of fear of crime (Gabriel and Greve, 2003); the salience of vulnerability; poverty as an indicator of fear (Pantazis, 2000); the frequency of public anxieties (Farrall and Gadd, 2004) and the expressive aspects of fear of crime (Jackson, 2004). As Farrall et al. (2000: 399) posit: 'fear of crime is now one of the most researched topics in contemporary criminology . . . it appears that the fear of crime is a social phenomenon of truly striking dimensions'. While this statement is well founded, Farrall's use of the word 'appears' perhaps gives away something of a healthy scepticism. As we shall see, despite the ubiquity of the topic in academic circles, some of the assumptions underpinning research into fear of crime are questionable and notable methodological shortcomings remain.

Although it may have achieved near doctrinal status in political rhetoric, 'fear of crime' should not be considered as either a uniform phenomenon or an omnipresent social fact. As Lee (2001: 467) explains, it is, instead, the product of a 'contingent category born of a set of very particular discursive arrangements and shifts'. Although now is not the place to elaborate a genealogy of fear of crime, I do wish to draw attention to key trends in the empirical research as they pertain to changing conceptions of risk. In Britain, the issue of fear of crime was given impetus in the late 1970s by exhaustive and sensationalist media coverage of the increase in street robberies, captured under the clumsily applied banner heading of 'mugging' (see Hall et al., 1978). Around this time the first large-scale criminal victimization survey to be conducted in England and Wales by Richard Sparks et al. (1977) informed the survey methodology initiated in the first *British Crime Survey* commissioned by the Home Office in 1982, later to be replaced by the *Crime Survey of England and Wales* (CSEW). On the back of these developments, the fear of crime debate took shape in Britain in the early 1980s and gained momentum throughout the decade. As Garside (2013) explains, the methodology used in the BCS and the CSEW has changed over time. The number of participants in the BCS rose from approximately 5,000 people at its inception to a larger scale survey of around 50,000. Although a broader range of crimes are now included in the replacement of the BCS, the CSEW still covers a smaller number of crimes than the statistics recorded by the police service. Murder is excluded from the CSEW as are sexual offences, although these are now recorded in a linked report.

So, what do crime surveys such as the BCS/CSEW tell us about fear of crime? One of the most historically salient findings is that estimations of personal vulnerability are out of kilter with both levels of crime and the mathematical probability of victimization. The most recent survey shows, for example, that 60 per cent of adults aged 16 and over in England and Wales thought that crime had risen at the national level, while both the CSEW (2012) and the police recorded data indicate the contrary. In more specific categories such as burglary, car crime and violent crime – a sizeable majority of respondents overestimated their chances of being a victim. Notwithstanding the methodological shortcomings, there may well be some value in such studies as a rough barometer of levels of crime or a dip-stick test of public perceptions. Yet, what is wrongly extrapolated from them – oft from the sanctity of the leafy suburbs – is firstly the myth of an amorphous public that is uniformly affected by crime and secondly the assumption that collated data sets are reflective of tangible realities. As we shall see, both of these assumptions are flawed. Unfortunately there has been a degree of sloppiness among those studying fear of crime, that has led to the simplistic postulation that 'objective' measurements of crime risk and 'subjective' feelings of anxiety are misaligned. Despite a range of critical questions being levelled at the methods used to extract information about fear of crime and the representativeness of studies (see Lee and Farrall, 2009; Walklate, 2007a), the annual publication of crime statistics remains for some administrative criminologists an irresistible opportunity to feign surprise about the void between falling crime rates and rising public fears about crime and to repeat the condescending message that the public really ought to stop worrying quite so much about crime. Indeed, at the time of writing, an *Institute for Economics and Peace* Report (2013) indicating that two-thirds of people think crime is on rise – while statistics indicate that it is at the lowest level for 30 years – has been dutifully seized upon by journalists (see Travis, 2013). Amidst the furore over public fears about crime, what is apparently less open to media discussion and debate is the potential limits of official statistics and the policy uses to which they are put. The quantitative chasm between the figures generated by self-report surveys and crime as recorded by the police – is one obvious indicator of the restricted exploratory power of crime statistics. In the United Kingdom in 2011–12 for instance, the police recorded crime figure of 3.8 million crimes occurring in the year ending September 2012 can be contrasted with the 8.9 million crimes reported in the *Crime Survey of England and Wales*. If it is the case that crime – and perceptions of it – cannot be accurately recorded then the centrepiece production of discourses which counterpoise the relatively low annual probability of being a victim of crime with the 'irrational' fears of the public are fabricated on shaky foundations. This observation raises questions about the methodological auspices under which public fears about crime emerges as a problem.

In the first instance, despite being a relatively novel concept, both government funded surveys and academic inquiries have tended to assume that 'fear of crime' exists as an entity which is 'out there' and can be reliably measured and recorded via surveys and questionnaires (see Walklate and Mythen, 2008). We need not dwell too long on this point, but suffice it to say that the standard method of directly asking participants about their fears of crime is not only methodologically questionable, it has also yielded unreliable findings, soon translated into accepted 'truths'. The dominant method of calibration both differentiates between and pairs up fear (understood as subjective anxiety) and risk (understood as probability of victimization) in a fashion that has encouraged a decidedly narrow debate about whether or not individual and, construed as an aggregate, public fears about crime are rational when set against the statistical risk of being a victim of crime. In response to comparisons between 'crime risks' and 'public fears' that accentuated knowledge deficits, Left Realist thinkers began in the 1980s to develop an alternative research design which drew on local crime surveys that were geographically sensitive and structurally informed (see Young, 1988). Following this trajectory Lea and Young (1984) reported findings which emphasized the crime risks faced by disadvantaged communities as opposed to the population at large. In seeking to provide a more 'democratic measurement' of crime, Lea and Young (1984) set the tone for a tradition of theoretically anchored empirical work within criminology (see Newburn, 2009: 268). What is more, it is quite probable that Lea and Young's (1984) focus on the experience of victimization – as well as the statistical frequency of crime – informed the subsequent structure of later crime surveys commissioned in the 1990s by the Home Office.

As well as recognizing the methodological limitations that have historically plagued fear of crime research, we also need to be alert to the possibility that the findings of surveys into fear of crime can be manipulated to fit particular economic, political, cultural and academic agendas. Without doubt, conducting criminal victimization surveys has become a lucrative business and a vocation-making occupation for some criminologists. The fear of crime industry has tangible social effects and attracts heavy media and political coverage. As Furedi (2007b: 3) observes, frenetic media reporting of fear of crime surveys may actually serve to increase rather than decrease public anxiety: 'this process of trying to quantify a cultural mood means that the fear of crime becomes objectified, and thus can acquire a force of its own. Its objectification may turn it into a fact of life, and this can help to legitimate, if not even encourage the fear response'. In the light of such observations, we might want to ask some searching questions about just what it is that survey questions seeking to gauge public anxieties about crime can actually tell us. Statistical surveys that claim to reveal the extent of fear of crime are not objective artefacts and they may tell us more about people's perceptions of the local environment, quality of life and their discomfort with the adverse effects of social flux (see Lee, 2007). Although it remains patchily recognized in the literature, 'fear of crime' can act as outlet vent for wider concerns about community cohesion, social order and the uncertainties of everyday life (see Kearon and Leach, 2000; Pantazis, 2000: 417).

Before going on to suggest some ways out of the cul-de-sac that debates about fear of crime appear to have meandered into, it may first be worth pausing to ask what we can glean from victim surveys in the round and crime statistics more generally. Putting aside methodological quandaries for the moment, if we are to suppose that UK crime statistics offer us a rough and ready indication of crime levels, some clear trends have arisen over the last three decades. Using Police Recorded Crime (PRC) measures, total recorded crime rose steadily from 1981 to 2003, after which crime rates have been consistently falling. The data gathered in the BSC/CSEW shows crime rising more sharply in the 1980s and early 1990s, reaching an apex in 1995 and declining thereafter. Over the nine years between 2002/03 and 2011/12 the PRC statistics show crime dropping by 33 per cent, while the comparable figures for the BSC/CSWEW suggest a fall of 28 per cent (see Garside, 2013). Thus, the statistical probability of being a victim of crime in the United Kingdom is, at present, relatively low. Nevertheless, averaging everything towards the middle and talking in terms of 'overall' crime rates gives a rather crude and potentially unrepresentative picture of key trends and the mediating role of age, class, gender and location. For example, according to the CSEW (2012) the average risk of being a victim of burglary is 2.5 per cent (1.5 per cent of these involving entry and 1 per cent attempted entry). However, once one begins to break the statistics down by demographic group, the risk of victimization for the average person begins to look like something of an unhelpful measure. For individuals aged between 16 and 24 years the rate of victimization is relatively high (7.2 per cent) as it is for single adults with children (6.8 per cent). However, for elderly people aged over 74 the rate is way below the average, standing at just 0.9 per cent. So far as the hierarchy of victimization alluded to early is concerned, it would seem that those afforded the highest rates of public sympathy are also often those that are the least likely to become victims.

According to statistics produced by the *Institute for Economics and Peace* (2013), the violent crime rate in the United Kingdom has fallen by about a quarter in the last decade, from 1,255 per 100,000 people in 2003, to 933 in 2012. Yet if we are thinking about risk of victimization, we need to look beyond the headline findings into the more detailed nuances within the data sets. Again, where one lives in the United Kingdom is a firm indicator of probability of exposure to violent crime. Broadlands in Norfolk was statistically determined to be the most peaceful place to live, while Lewisham had a homicide rate of 2.5 in 2012 – two-and-a-half times the national average. All five of the least peaceful local authority areas were London boroughs – the others being Lambeth, Hackney, Newham and Tower Hamlets. In addition to being aware of the uneven geographical layering of crime, forms of criminal behaviour spike and recede over time. While the risk of being a victim of crime 'overall' might well have fallen over the last 20 years, different types of crime have experienced peaks and troughs. For instance, the annual homicide rate (including murders, manslaughter and infanticide) has halved in a decade from

2002 and 2012, with PRC statistics showing 549 homicides in the year ending September 2012. Such peaks and troughs do not just reflect the successes or failures of policing and law and order policy, they are indexed to wealth and prosperity, technological developments, consumer behaviour and safety precautions. Putting himself in the shoes of a felon – and inching, in this instance, towards a rational choice explanation for criminal behaviour – Garside (2013) explains why robbery, theft from the person and bicycle theft have either remained steady or risen in recent years while burglary and vehicle crime have fallen: 'Why go through the risk and hassle of breaking into a house when you can steal a smart-phone or a laptop or pinch a bike with a cheap pair of bolt cutters?' In all of this we need to appreciate that even the most methodologically rigorous measurements of crime can only offer us lightening rods of what is happening in the real world. Despite often being assumed as objective facts by sections of the broadcast and print media, we should note that such forms of statistical risk information are imperfect and incomplete. How else would we be able to explain the huge gulf between the police recorded figures on crime and criminal victimization surveys? As Garside (2013) reasons, both data sets have their limitations:

> Though in some ways more reliable as an insight into certain crime victimisations, CSEW is also a fairly partial measure, covering a relatively narrow range of crime incidents. It does not, for instance, cover homicide or death from dangerous driving, nor does it cover sexual offences in the main dataset. PRC data, on the other hand, covers a wide range of crime types, albeit in a partial manner as it is highly dependent on what the police chose to record, or on what offences come to their attention.

Beyond the public deficit model of 'Fear of Crime'

The steady growth in interest in public perceptions of crime in the media, politics and policy can be plotted quite tightly against the turn to risk. Indeed, from a point of view it could be argued that fear of crime is actually one – albeit pronounced – element of the more general turn to risk. It should be acknowledged that the increasingly frequent appearance of 'fear of crime' in public and policy debates in the last two decades must be considered against the backdrop of a motion from offender centric to victim-oriented approaches to crime management documented previously. Certainly, the historical proliferation of criminal victimization surveys and the surfeit of studies which have indicated anomalous matches between public fears of crime and the 'actual' probability of victimization have proven to be attractive to the broadcast media and acted as annual fodder for political jousting and vacuous point-scoring. Within all this, the 'fear–victimization paradox' (Lindquist and Duke, 1982) has been used as a foundation stone for those wishing to argue that public fearfulness is ill founded and irrational. If we were to suspend our disbelief and place our trust in the validity of State generated crime statistics, it is young men whose risk of being a victim of crime is relatively high that appear to be breezily unaware of their potentially perilous future plight, while elderly ladies are apparently unduly anxious about crime given the comparatively low levels of offences committed against them (see Goodey, 2005). This 'victimization–fear paradox' – also commonly referred to as the 'risk–fear paradox' – has generated a raft of studies oriented towards determining exactly why such 'ignorance' has emerged and how the 'irrationality' of certain groups could be addressed and re-aligned such that public fears of crime can be matched with rates of victimization (see Gottfredson, 1984). Despite its shaky evidence base and ripeness for misuse, the risk–fear paradox does, at least, flag up the importance of cultural differences in perceptions of crime risks and the ways in which anxieties about crime – however they are construed – are gendered, both in relation to their social and political construction and the ways in which they are cognized, articulated and negotiated (see Stanko, 1990; Walklate, 2002). Casting back to theory, in many respects, some of the macro perspectives recounted in Chapter 2 may seem insufficiently attuned to cultural differences that arise in *exposure* to victimization and *experience* of crime risks according to gender and other forms of stratification such as class, sexuality and ethnicity. The historical tendency towards victim blaming is palpably gendered, most notably via notions of 'victim precipitation', through which those at the receiving end of criminality are seen to have rendered themselves vulnerable through lax behaviour, recklessness or a lack of vigilance. The grotesque suggestion by the former English Circuit Judge James Pickles that girls who wore short skirts were effectively 'asking for it' serves as a case in point (see Thomas, 2007). Political adoptions of diluted versions of this grim assumption shrink the problem of managing crime risks from the societal/governmental to the personal/local (see also Hale, 1996). Tracking the line marked out by Garland (2001), both fear of crime and repeat victimization are thus transposed as individual problems and pathologies to be attended to by more cautious forms of personal risk management. O'Malley (2006: 52) sets up the fallacious logic neatly: 'since statistical risks of experiencing serious crime are very low (for example, there is less than one per cent probability of being a victim of assault resulting in injury in any given year) then those who do experience crime – especially repeat experiences – are in some sense contributing to their victimization'.

Alongside the methodological critiques offered by Foucauldians (Lee, 2007) and Left Realists (Lea and Young, 1984), feminist criminologists have challenged both the underpinning assumptions and the findings of standard victimization surveys. Stanko (1990; 1997) dismisses the view that women's expressed fears about crime are irrational and attempts instead to situate women's anxieties within the context of the patriarchal flows of everyday life, including experiences of male violence and sexual harassment. Walklate's (2007a) work both concords with and augments this position. She demonstrates that the faulty presumption of males as innately risk seeking and females as risk averse has wrongly reduced both fear and risk to items that can be quantitatively calibrated. In response to these critical interventions, some elements of criminal victimization surveys have been redesigned and the debate about gender and fear has thankfully moved on from the condescending focus on women as either victim precipitators and/or possessors of faulty risk thermostats, to concentrate on the important issue of how women's safety might be enhanced by structural and institutional changes. Although the grounds for the critique of fear of crime research from within Left Realist, Feminist and Foucauldian traditions are concrete, it is worth noting that some studies which remain within the fear of crime tradition have produced nuanced views of perceptions of crime risks that are culturally situated and do account for structural dynamics. The work conducted Ian Taylor (1996; 1999) into the relationship between fear, locale and ontological security is exemplary in this regard. Drawing on Raymond Williams's concept of 'structures of feeling', Taylor (1999) locates anxieties about crime within a situated cultural context enabling him to tap into lived experiences of crime and attitudes towards criminality in the round. In arguing that individual structures of feeling are constructed by a combination of perceptions, myths and narratives about crime in particular places, Taylor demonstrated what was being dubbed elsewhere as 'fear of crime', was actually serving as a much broader vent through which people were expressing of a range of localized concerns, such as a lack of community integration, high unemployment rates and falling house prices (see Taylor, 1996).

In an alternate vein, Hollway and Jefferson (1997) approached the fear of crime issue by looking at how people mobilize individual solutions to structural problems. Drawing theoretically on the risk society thesis and using a psycho-social method, Hollway and Jefferson (1997) mapped the extent to which a person's expressed fear of crime articulates or jars with the way in which they cognitively mobilize defence mechanisms against anxiety. They conclude that the mobilization of personal defence mechanisms will vary according to forms of stratification such as class and gender. Such findings illustrate well that the 'risk society' will be experienced, perceived and navigated differently according to social position and cultural place. So far as 'fear of crime' is concerned, Hollway and Jefferson's studies illustrate that we are not all equally nor evenly exposed to the crimogenic bads of the 'global' risk society.

It is evident that, although there is still much room for development, fear of crime research has become more sophisticated over the course of the last three decades. It is now widely accepted that forms of social stratification influence one's risk of becoming a victim of crime and that specific crimes will affect some groups and classes more than others (see Goodey, 2005). People of Black and Asian ethnicities for example are more prone than White people to suffer repeat victimization, prolonged exposure to crime and racial harassment (Hesse et al., 1992; Bowling, 1998). There remains then a palpable need for a deeper understanding of both the differential constitution of experiences of victimization and the extent of fear of crime alongside the wider factors that it may signal or stand in for. In my work with Sandra Walklate (Walklate and Mythen, 2008; 2010), I have sought to advance an admittedly messy but nonetheless more encompassing approach to the risk/fear couplet than has typically been cultivated within mainstream criminology. If we are to assume that the concept of fear has greater breadth than simple calibration of public anxieties about crime via the production of State sponsored survey data, common approaches towards fear of crime have rather crudely sequestered anxieties about crime from everyday life-worlds. Other social scientists have made similar observations, arguing that fears about crime are themselves located within the wider tapestry of 'risk biographies', and comingle with a range of anxieties about local community, relationships, employment and money troubles (see Taylor, 1996; Tulloch and Lupton, 2003: 63). Adding positively to this body of research requires de-centring conventional understandings of crime and risk that have become stock features of the fear-of-crime debate. To address the misunderstandings and problems that have surrounded fear of crime research, it is necessary to adopt sensitive research methodologies that are able to capture the place of worries about crime in an everyday context and, importantly, locate them amidst a range of other pressures and concerns that individuals may have in their day-to-day lives. I would question the extent to which fear of crime research in general and criminological research in particular has historically accounted for the interplay of global and local that is central to the dynamic between social structure and human agency in the contemporary world. Despite the useful interventions made by Gadd and Jefferson (2007), there remains work to be done if we are to properly understand the everyday spectrum of fears within which anxieties about crime are located. The problem of the *prioritization* of fear of crime research remains. The issue of prioritization is significant as it feeds directly into the process of knowledge generation. As Turner (2013: 157) notes, in the broader context of crime discourses and criminal justice policy:

> One might also consider how governments themselves smother inconvenient truths with the alternate truths provided by more compliant experts; or how the skewed research agenda of the Home Office can produce truths focused on particular areas of research that then drown out truths concentrated on less congenial topics; and how narrow criminological genres (e.g. administrative criminology and crime science) can dominate and squeeze out other ways of knowing from the competitive criminological marketplace.

These remarks illuminate some important general aspects of the relationship between academic research, discourse and power that we will return to in Chapter 7.

The media, crime and moral panic

Our discussion of the public fears about crime indicates that media platforms are crucial vehicles through which crime risks are discursively constructed, visually represented, communicated and shared between individuals and social groups. The mass media is indubitably a significant source of information about crime and a technology through which notions of criminality, victimization, punishment and justice are circulated. Given the omnipresence of the media within contemporary culture, media products are an important factor in the formation of perceptions of crime (see Banks, 2005; Greer, 2009). It is apparent that the media at once represents and influences the range and the narrowness of meanings of crime. Further, through assorted representations of crime victims the media not only sets the agenda, but also creates symbolic identities for sufferers of crime (see Farrall and Gadd, 2004: 149; Tulloch, 2006). Far from acting as a simple mirror to crime realities in the contemporary world, the political economy in which the mass media is embedded, the proclivities of media moguls and the temporal and technical dynamics of the production process mean that news making about crime is a filtered and selective process. Mass media outlets operating in the private sector are governed by the need to meet financial imperatives such as achieving market share and attracting advertising revenue. The need to meet profit margins can lead to exaggerated coverage of crime issues which are designed to pander to the apparent fascination about crime among media audiences (see Greer, 2007). In as much as it is important to account for the role of traditional media technologies such as newspapers, radio, TV and film on perceptions of crime and attitudes towards rehabilitation and punishment, we need to acknowledge that the media environment has changed dramatically in recent years. As we shall see, the advent of hand held media technologies which facilitate instantaneity and the increasingly niche choices of consumers are producing profound effects on media consumption patterns that are yet to be fully embraced by academic research. While we will be returning to this point later, it is first necessary to detail the dominant framework within which the relationship between risk, the media and crime has been approached: the moral panic model.

The term 'moral panic' is widely used to describe a situation in which the core values of society are seen to have been transcended, leading to a climate of generalized anxiety. This usage connects to the model first developed by the late Stanley Cohen (1972) in his seminal book *Folk Devils and Moral Panics*. Cohen initially used the term to describe the exaggerated media response to a relatively small set of disturbances in 1964 involving Mods and Rockers in the seaside resort of Clacton in the South East of England. On Easter Sunday the two rival groups had battled with one another and caused damage to beach huts and shop windows, with 97 arrests being made. The following day the incident was widely reported by national newspapers such as *The Mirror* and *The Daily Telegraph* who ran bold headlines such as 'Wild One's Invade the Seaside' and 'Day of Terror by Scooter Groups'. Cohen argued that such sensational press coverage exaggerated the scale of the incident and sought to arouse public fears through the use of emotive descriptions of the events as a 'riot' and a 'siege'. The classic moral panic cycle is described by Cohen (1972: 9) as:

> a condition, episode, person or group of persons emerges to become defined as a threat to societal values and interests; its nature is presented in a stylized and stereotypical fashion by the mass media; the moral barricades are manned by editors, bishops, politicians and other right thinking people; socially accredited experts pronounce their diagnoses and solutions, ways of coping are evolved.

In his study, Cohen (1972) tracked media reaction to what transpired to be relatively minor breaches of the peace and low level incivilities. Cohen argued that the media headlines describing of a 'day of terror' exaggerated the severity of the disturbances and served to fuel public concerns about a lack of decency and morality among young people which threatened the wider social fabric (see Mooney et al., 2004). This 'deviancy amplification spiral' details the route through which a specific incident can invoke inordinate media coverage, leading to public calls for stronger law and order measures, increased arrests and greater public concern. The 'control culture' invoked in response to perceived transgressions entails intense monitoring and surveillance of the deviant group and harsh punishments for transgressions (see also Lyon, 2013). It is important to note those that those have been cast as 'folk devils' over time have largely emerged from within youth culture, from Teddy Boys and Mods and Rockers to Skinheads, Clubbers and Ravers. All of these subcultures have been associated with amoral and/or violent behaviour and represented as a threat to society by sabre rattling civil servants and vote-conscious cabinet ministers. As an aside, we can plot some parallel lines between the moral panic model and Douglas's anthropological perspective. Both theories seek to identify the ways and means by which outsiders are determined as threats to the social order and how labelling acts to not only cast out 'others', but also to reinforce dominant norms and values. Cohen's groundbreaking research had a major impact in Sociology and Criminology, and was extended by Hall et al. (1978) in relation to street robbery or 'mugging'. Hall et al. (1978) recount the cycle through which intense media coverage of isolated criminal acts can extend into labelling of law breaking sub-cultures and 'moral panics' about deviant groups. As Goode and Ben-Yehuda (1994: 57) note, a number of different characteristics are present in situations in which moral panics emerge, including initial concern about the behaviour of a particular group, suspicion or hostility towards that group and Establishment consensus regarding the risk in question. The presence of these three characteristics is likely to produce heavy handed regulatory interventions where the measures introduced are disproportionate to the magnitude of the risk. It is indisputable that both government and the media have pillared particular 'folk devils', honing in on symbolic displays to reinforce deviance attachments. Following on from the moral panics around Mods and Rockers in the 1960s and mugging in the late 1970s and 1980s, a series of lower frequency moral panics have occurred, including those focussed on satanic abuse, violent films, video games and consumption of ecstasy (MDMA). Indeed, Cohen (1972: 204) himself correctly proph-esized that the moral panic is a condition that surfaces sporadically but with historical regularity:

> More moral panics will be generated and other, as yet nameless, folk devils will be created. This is not because such developments have an inexorable inner logic, but because our society as presently structured will continue to generate problems for some of its members . . . and then condemn whatever solution these groups find.

As Cohen infers, much more is being socially and publically expressed in an episode of moral panic than simply anxiety about crime. This point is taken up by the social his-torian Geoffrey Pearson (1983), who believes that moral panics are connected to social nostalgia and the recurrent notion that society is somehow not what it once was. Embed-ding his argument with reference to various cases, Pearson (1983) reasons that moral panics are in part a consequence of middle aged generations harking back to the 'good old days' of an imagined 'golden age' of morality that is set against the apparent moral bankruptcy of the present and the anomie of contemporary youth. This view is founded on the idea that society is going through a phase of social fragmentation and demor-alization in which previous structures that provided discipline and order, such as the family and education have become fractured, leading to egotism, irresponsibility and a lack of respect for authority. As Mooney et al. (2004: 11) note, in such circumstances 'respectable fears' are aroused and can become sustained over time: 'against the waves of crime and unrest the law enforcement agencies of the era, whatever era it is, are increasingly impotent, powerless to defend people and their property from the criminal hordes'.

So, does the moral panic model serve as a useful model to understand the con-struction and regulation of lawlessness in contemporary society? In my view, yes and no. To explain my ambivalence, it may be useful to latch onto a particular example: the period of urban unrest which began in Tottenham in the summer of 2011. At the time, following the fatal shooting of Mark Duggan by police, disorder broke out firstly in London and subsequently in other areas in the United Kingdom. In many ways the British riots bore some of the classic hallmarks of the moral panic. The media cov-ered the unrest that occurred to the point of saturation and a dominant discourse was established around out of control, anomic youth. While the media focus centred on a narrative of 'youth out of control' – conveniently ignoring the mixed-age range of those involved in the disturbances – the Government maintained that the unrest could be attributed to a problem underclass that had been allowed to abuse the system in the 'broken Britain' established by the former Labour Government. The language used by Prime Minister David Cameron (2011) could not have been starker:

> What we know for sure is that in large parts of the country this was just pure criminality . . . And these riots were not about poverty: that insults the millions of people who, whatever the hardship, would never dream of making others suffer like this. No, this was about behaviour. People showing indifference to right and wrong. People with a twisted moral code. People with a complete absence of self-restraint.

Aside from the overbearing Conservative ideology underpinning such statements, Cameron's remarks are also illustrative of the political practice of not wanting to waste a good crisis. Chiming with the quest to shore up law and order identified by Hall in the late 1970s, post the riots the British Government was quick to float various changes to law, such as the introduction of extraordinary general curfews, all of which are decreed as necessary to 'protect the public' and implemented in the 'public interest'. Nevertheless, although there are recognizable elements of the moral panic model here, it is debatable whether the rioting and looting which erupted in 2011 can be seen as a moral panic within the parameters first described by Cohen. While discrete elements are clearly in evidence – such as media amplification, public calls for tighter law and order controls and political opportunism – there are aspects of the case which do not articulate with the original formulation of the moral panic. One might for instance argue that while the fracas between Mods and Rockers were small scale, localized, led to few serious injuries and produced limited damage, the riots in 2011 were of a larger scale, widespread and produced substantial damage. Five people were killed in the rioting and at least 16 others injured. Over 3,000 people were arrested across the country and an estimated 200 million pounds worth of property damage was caused. While the moral panic model infers a minor threat that is amplified out of all proportion to its magnitude, the urban unrest in 2011 presented a serious law and order problem that confounded criminologists and defeated routine policing strategies. We might also observe that while the dissenting and oppositional voices running contra to the Government's preferred reading of the situation may have had scant opportunity to broadcast their views during the Clacton disturbances in 1964, the same cannot be said of the recent unrest, with a range of academics, social workers and youth workers being able to publically articulate the frustration and alienation felt by frustrated and marginalized young people. What is more, the young people who took part in the rioting have taken the opportunity to explain their actions on various media platforms, such as Twitter, Bebo and Facebook. If we revisit the moral panic model in its initial state, two key groups are active in the construction of deviance: primary and secondary definers. Primary definers are those that are proximate to or arrive at the scene of the incident, such as the emergency services and the police. Secondary definers are agencies such as government and the media who receive information about incidents second-hand and filter and shape this information. This distinction had undoubted utility in outlining the social construction of risk in previous epochs, but it is debatable whether matters are quite as clear cut now. As incidents materialize in contemporary society, members of the public have the capacity not only to witness but also to visually record and post footage of events on the internet or to distribute it to others via mobile phone networks. As such, it might be argued that the capacity of the police to impose primary definition on a situation is stretched by the range of views that can be articulated instantly and uncensored across a range of platforms. As a consequence, the scope for secondary definition is broader and the possibility of a dominant one-dimensional meaning being imposed impossible. In Cohen's (1972) original formulation of the model, groups that were the focus of moral panic were dubbed 'folk devils', while those that initiate and amplify concerns about folk devils were referred to as 'moral entrepreneurs'. In contemporary society, a much broader range of players are involved in the construction and of deviant or criminal acts and in influencing public interpretations of such events. Thus, in order to grasp the process of social construction today we might also want to add in other prominent stakeholders that act as event and meaning shapers, such as 'visual witnesses' and 'oppositional actors'. While the moral panic model provides a robust historical lens for viewing instances of constructed anxiety and the temerarious implementation of law and order, there are limits to its reach. Putting interpretative disputes about what might constitute a moral panic, and indeed questions about whether the term 'panic' is an overstated description of the conditions elaborated, a number of factors have increased the possibility that potential moral panics may be interrupted or dissipated in the early stages of formation. In the national media environment that prevailed in the mid to late twentieth century, the range of media portals was smaller and the relationship with government closer. In such a context, greater control could be exercised over the communication of threats to the public and the possibility of the State playing an important role in the shaping these messages was high. In contrast, in the twenty-first century, information about incidents and events is gathered from multiple media sources, many of which are directly transmitted by members of the public rather than shaped by professional journalists media or filtered by the State. In addition, modern citizens are considered to be sophisticated and critical users of media products, with the simplistic hypodermic model of media effects having long since been rubbished (see Lodziak, 1995). When one adds to this reportedly high level of public distrust in information disseminated by both government and the mainstream media, the opportunity for the occurrence of a full blown moral panic is arguably reduced. All of this is not to dispute that a strong relationship still exists between State agencies and mass media outlets, nor that the police, government and media attempt to set the agenda and frame incidents in ways which support their interests, whether those be economic imperatives of selling copy, aspirations to crack down on 'problem groups' or the imperative of maintaining law and order. Nonetheless, it needs to be recognized that the rapid pace of technological development, cultural globalization and changing patterns of media consumption have reformed the relationship between the media and the public. This is most evident in the media preferences of young people. Just two decades ago the daily media diet of the average British citizen – should he or she exist – might have included a newspaper, the nine o'clock news on TV and a couple of soap operas or radio programmes. Today such forms of national, mass consumption can no longer be seen as the norm. Young people in particular cultivate active and bespoke media practices, seamlessly streaming together different technologies and platforms. Advances in mobile phone technology mean that people are immediately able to surf social news sites for information, catch up with events taking place on Twitter and watch TV and listen to radio programmes on demand from across the globe. Further, the capacity of citizens to record incidents as they evolve and to disseminate these to others via the internet adds a further layer of complexity to traditional processes of media representation. While technophiles might well have over-celebrated the emergence of 'citizen-journalists' the way in which risk incidents were made to mean by the mass media has been interrupted by a greater volume and range of inputs by members of the public (see Mythen, 2010).

In all of this, the dangers of media-centrism loom large and it is important to keep hold of the many processes, factors and filters that feed into our perceptions of crime. Attitudes towards crime and punishment are effectively multi-factorial. Considered crudely as a monolithic block, 'the media' can inform but does not singularly determine people's perspectives on criminality and victimization. In modern society, reflexive individuals think critically about their experience and are not willing to passively accept the communiqués of experts (see Bauman, 2000; Beck et al., 1994). People's perceptions of crime are influenced not only by levels of risk but also by ingrained assumptions, political values and prevalent worldviews. As we shall see, in our case study of 'knife-crime', it is important to scrutinize the way in which victims – and indeed offenders – are institutionally labelled, represented in the media and treated by agencies responsible for crime and security.

Casing risk: 'Knife-Crime' and the culture of fear

As a means of sweeping up some of the problems and issues raised in the chapter around crime, victimization, the media and public anxieties, we will return to one of the key theoretical perspectives on risk, the culture of fear approach. Furedi's thesis has contemporary resonance and is useful in highlighting both the institutional construction of deviance and the political harnessing of public anxieties around crime. In his analysis of the relationship between the media and crime, Furedi echoes Garland's (1990) view that fear of crime has become a more widespread social problem than criminal acts themselves. Acknowledging the value of the moral panic model, Furedi (2007b: 3) focusses on the proclivity of the mass media to generate sensationalist coverage of rare but shocking incidents, and, in so doing, incite public anxieties about spectacular but relatively rare violent crimes. Paedophilia and terrorism are the prime examples discussed by Furedi, but we can also demonstrate the explanatory value of the culture of fear thesis by applying it to the case of 'knife-crime'.

Violent assaults involving knifes have a long history in many countries and are far from a modern phenomenon. Nevertheless, amidst growing concern regarding the problem of 'knife-crime', particularly among teenage gangs, the British Government instructed researchers undertaking the British Crime Survey in 2008 to take measurements across their sample of the population. The first survey reported an estimated 22,000 criminal incidents involving the use of knifes. Putting aside the questions of reliability and representativeness discussed earlier, these figures do indicate that criminal acts involving knives are a legitimate cause for concern, especially in inner city communities where the highest levels were recorded. Yet, without belittling the size and scale of the problem, other socially prevalent crimes have not been thrust into the full glare of the media spotlight, nor seized upon quite as readily by politicians. Laying the theoretical template of the culture of fear perspective over the problem of 'knife-crime', it is perhaps the degree of fervour with which the issue has been taken up by senior politicians and the extent of media coverage which is striking. Following on from the public announcement of the first British Crime Survey figures, tabloid newspapers and TV news programmes gorged on the issue, unfurling a steady flow of media coverage. In the height of the panic, one national newspaper dubbed the country 'Knife-Crime Britain', the Lord Chief Justice diagnosed Britain as suffering from an 'epidemic' and the Mayor of London referred to knife-crime as a 'scourge' (see Leach, 2008). The epidemic metaphor was developed by right of centre newspapers to describe the apparent diffusion of knife-crime from the cities – where the dangerous and unruly live and where it is presumably expectable and tolerable – into British towns and villages occupied by middle class newspaper readers. Overlooking anything as trifling as evidence, such sensationalist responses falsely presented a statistically rare and geographically clustered problem as endemic and universal. Without making light of the tragedy experienced by the families of victims of knife-crime, there has been a distinct tendency to amplify the problem in the media and a clamour to denounce knife-crime as symptomatic of moral malaise among politicians keen to press home punitive positions on law and order. Again, the familiar narrative of 'youth out of control' unspooled during the 2011 urban unrest resurfaces.

For followers of the culture of fear perspective, the media furore regarding 'knife-crime' and the associated political rhetoric elides proper contextualization of the problem and proportionality of response. Although the statistics should be treated with caution due to the small numbers of cases involved, in 2009/2010, police recorded 35, 666 offences involving knives. This represents a fall of 7 per cent on the previous year's figures. In 2009/10, there were 262 attempted murders involving a knife, a fall from the 275 recorded the previous year. Furthermore, the British Crime Survey, indicates that the majority of knife crime occurs in urban areas, with the Metropolitan Police, Greater Manchester and the West Midlands forces reporting a large proportion of total knife-crimes. The 2009/10 British Crime Survey estimates that knives were utilized in 5 per cent of violent incidents, down from 8 per cent in 2008/09. This, in effect, returns the level of knife-crime to a level similar to that estimated 2007/08 (6 per cent). If these statistics are accurate, they reveal several important things so far as the justification for generalized fears about knife-crime are concerned. First, the evidence suggests that knife-crime is rare, both in comparison with other types of crime and also in terms of its general frequency. Second, it is apparent that the risk of being a victim of knife-crime is higher for those living in inner city areas and, in particular, among young people who are involved in gangs. Third, rather than escalating, the rate of knife crime incidents has kept relatively stable, remaining between 5 and 8 per cent since 1996. Fourth, it needs to be recognized that knife-crime is a broad-ranging term that covers many acts, ranging from stabbing to simply buying or carrying an illegal knife. Despite the available evidence, it is probable that the political fixation with knife-crime – itself stitched to a media narrative of unruly youth – has encouraged an unnecessary degree of fearfulness among some members of the general public. Although it is difficult to measure, it is most probable that public anxieties about knife-crime have been heightened and that this itself may have fuelled distorted perceptions of its frequency. Rendering this point concrete, despite a small fall in knife crime over the preceding 12 months, 90 per cent of respondents in the 2009/10 survey believed that there had been a national increase in knife-crime (British Crime Survey, 2011: 27). Through the culture of fear prism we can begin to identify some of the important contextual details that may allow us to develop a more rounded picture of the problem. For instance, more than half of 'knife-crimes' reported in the United Kingdom occur in just three cities, with a significant number of fatal incidents involving knives being gang-related (see Stewart, 2008). What goes missing as the media vie for public attention and politicians attempt to gain public approval via punitive policies is a reasonable social concern that is commensurate with the scale of the risk. If we consider issues of risk perception and risk management, it could be argued that institutional responses to 'public fears' about 'knife-crime' are not aligned with the degree of threat. As the criminologist Richard Garside (2008) remarks of media coverage of 'knife-crime': 'reporting has been out of all proportion to the scale of the problem and has distracted attention from where the real harm to young people lies. Far more young people kill themselves than are killed by others, for instance'. In Furedi's view, perceptions of risk have less to do with available evidence and are instead reflective of dominant political and cultural assumptions and assertions. As such, it is notions of human vulnerability and often unfounded fears about the future that may well be driving the formation of a culture of fear. By applying Furedi's thesis to the problem of 'knife-crime' we can draw attention to the role of the media, politicians and the security industries in the social construction of fear and also reveal some of the vested interests that may inform and sculpt such constructions. In a climate of anxiety about violent crime, the opportunity presents itself for Government to trade on fear in an attempt to secure public endorsement for new law and order and security measures. Further, public concerns about crime can also be exploited by what Furedi (2007b: 3) refers to as 'fear entrepreneurs' – those private sector companies that trade on insecurity and anxiety in pursuit of profit, 'touting a dilating array of security wares to keep the public "safe" from crime'. As we have seen, there is a fair degree of crossover between Cohen's (1972) moral panic model and the culture of fear perspective. Both approaches foreground the social construction of risks and detail the central role of the media and politicians in attenuating concerns about particular incidents and episodes. Further, both describe social situations in which the extent of the risk is exaggerated when considered against the potential degree of harm. However, there are differences too. Insofar as Cohen sought to draw attention to the process of labelling through which stigma is attached to particular folk devils, Furedi is more inclined to unravel the discrete incidents that cause panic, such as terrorist attacks and child abuse. Moreover, while Cohen (1972) drew attention to the episodic nature of moral panics, Furedi believes that a culture of fear has become generalized and pervades all aspects of our lives.

Conclusion

Over the last two chapters we have utilized governmentality and culture of fear perspectives to illuminate processes of criminality, victimization and regulation. In attempting to grapple with the multiple forces that affect crime, victimization and policing I have not advocated subscription to either perspective. Insofar as macro theories of risk have value in affording us the opportunity to interpret discrete events and processes, they do not unveil the complete workings of the world. As always, the dangers of presenting one part of the picture as the whole loom large. What has become clear is that the relationship between 'risk' and 'fear' requires further research, especially at the empirical level (see Chadee et al., 2007: 142; Walklate and Mythen, 2008). More specifically, our discussion has several implications for future research into the media, fear of crime and victimization. So far as fear of crime is concerned, it would appear that the concept is both ubiquitous and overstated. As Lee (2007) notes, the expansion of the 'fear-of-crime' industry has led to artificial production of conceptual binaries of the fearing subject and the criminal to be feared. Not only does this binarism trade on existing notions of the dangerous other, it misses the ambiguities that arise in situated environments. For instance, as we shall see in Chapter 5, in some inner city areas young Asian males are open to classification as either fearful subjects or feared victims as they face higher risk of being victimized by racial hatred while simultaneously being cast as suspect under the cloud of 'home-grown' terrorism. While those working in the area of fear of crime would doubtless point to advances in research methods and more sophistication modes of data gathering, greater attention still needs to be directed to the wider question of the composition of fear (see Burkitt, 2005; Chadee and Ditton, 2005: 330). As Gabriel and Greve (2003: 601) justly note, the bulk of criminological research has rather tidily focussed on fear as a quantifiable entity and sought to relate this to the specific concept of crime. If we accept that fear is a complex cultural and psychological phenomena, it appears short-sighted to hive off one dimension for analysis and close off other interesting connections which may emerge through more subtle and detailed probing of the range of articulations of fear. This being the case, the persistent finding that fear of crime is widespread may actually tell us more about methods of calibration than extant social realities (see Dolan and Peasgood, 2007: 122). An honest appraisal of the methodological drawbacks that have dogged fear of crime research, alongside the experiential angles that it fails to capture gives us a more contingent picture of established 'facts' about public anxieties about crime and also steers us into thinking about how people's fear of crime is situated in relation to a shifting palette of worries and concerns.

Following the method established in Tulloch and Lupton's qualitative inquiries (2003: 102), there is much room for research that seeks to identify different types of risk – financial, intimate, labour market, environmental – and seeks to trace the ways in which they impinge upon and influence ontological (in)security. Research exploring the extent to which parallel typologies of fear exist would be similarly useful. To what extent do quotidian fears about family, work and relationships mesh with global anxieties around global warming and terrorism, for instance? As noted in our discussion of risk-taking subcultures, fear has been treated almost exclusively as a negative entity. In addition to the positive deployments of fear documented previously, there is insufficient research into the cognitive and cultural strategies that people use to manage and ward off fear. Stealing Tillich's (1952) wonderful phrase, which everyday tactics and psychological processes do people deploy to prevent their minds becoming 'factories of fear'? It may also be conceptually valuable to extend research that deconstructs fears sister concepts of safety and protection. Following the trajectory of critical feminism, moving away from the criminologically hackneyed debate about fear towards an analysis of safety – particularly so far as women's experience of intimidation and male violence is concerned – remains a positive vein of inquiry and an important mode of oppositional thought and resistance to taken for granted, gendered assumptions about fear of crime (see Stanko, 1997; Walklate, 2002).

If we assume that Furedi (2002; 2007a; 2007b) is correct in his assertion that in the modern Western world we have become inured to engaging with a burgeoning number of social issues through the lens of fear, then this implies that imagining that fear of crime exists in isolation from other worries and concerns is a particularly limited way of understanding social experience. Thus, those working in the interstice between sociology and criminology might profitably direct their attentions on fleshing out the fits and gaps between the feeling of fear in different types of contexts and focus on how the local and the global dynamic is played out in such negotiations and (dis)articulations. For example, might there be a case for seeking to chart a continuum of sources of anxiety, relating to both the fears and the risks that inform these processes? In relation to victimization, the 'place sensitive', subjective aspects of what it feels like to be a victim is worthy of continued exploration (see Banks, 2005; O'Malley, 2006: 51; Walklate, 2007a). We cannot assume either that we are all victims, nor that victims of similar crimes attribute the same meanings to their victimization. The risks and fears associated with being or feeling like a victim are not simply a result of being located at the sharp end of criminality. While the experiential aspects of victimization can be addressed by ramping up micro level empirical forays, it is important that victimologists are alert to the macro structural effects of victim-centric forms of regulation and punishment. The ongoing politicization of victims and the tendency for media organizations to pay lip-service to the idea that we are all victims indicates that a critical and inquisitive criminological imagination is required to interrupt efforts to manufacture consent. Although disparately conceived, the contributions of Garland and Furedi, lead us to re-examine the constitution of victimization and to ask whether the opening up of the category of the victim ultimately serves to obscure important gradations of suffering and harm. At present, there is a very real possibility that ubiquitous historical happenings – such as terrorism and violent attacks involving knives – are being manipulated for political ends. Echoing Furedi's sentiments, it should be remembered that politicians are not averse to hue and cry in the media in pursuit of party aspirations or professional advancement. Despite the diversity and multiplicity of media forms in contemporary society, the sources that people use most frequently for information about crime and violence – such as daily newspaper, national broadcasts and news websites – continue to disproportionately focus on extreme but statistically rare crimes, such as knife attacks, murder and paedophilia.

5 Terrorism, Risk and Regulation

Introduction

In Chapters 3 and 4 our focus was directed towards the relationship between risk and crime. In Chapter 3 we broached various aspects of the association between risk and crime, considering the ways in which regulatory institutions and agencies have assessed and deployed risk in relation to criminal behaviour, deterrent and punishment. In addition to governance through risk, we also touched upon the significance of risk in explaining offender behaviour, drawing upon the early work of the Chicago School and more contemporary contributions that extend this tradition from within cultural criminology. We then turned in Chapter 4 to address the problem of criminal victim-ization, noting both the changing rights of victims and the impact of victims' views on the shaping of criminal justice policy. Following on from this, we examined the related topic of fear of crime and developed a critical analysis of modes and methods of research in this area. Finally, we accounted for the role of the media in representing the crime problem and communicating crime risks to the public.

In Chapter 5 we will move on to fix on one of the central security issues of our time that, in its enactment, fundamentally challenges criminal, legal and political forms of regulation: terrorism. While the inter-relationship between terrorism and risk is multi-textured, in this section of the book we will be prioritizing four of the most salient connectors, namely: the changing level of threat, the representation and communication of danger, the restructuring of counter-terrorism strategies and the trend towards pre-emptive forms of legal sanction. At each of these points of articulation I will be adopting a critical view on the ways in which the terrorist risk has been constructed, managed and policed in the West since 9/11. I will begin by flagging up some of the problems that arise when security experts, academics, lawyers, politicians and media commentators attempt to define terrorism. From here, we consider the changing nature of the terror-ist threat, outlining the features of the 'new terrorism thesis' (see Burnett and Whyte, 2005). In elucidating the inconsistencies in the social construction of the terrorist threat I wish to draw attention to the consolidation of a set of security discourses promoted by the State which seek to sanction historically exceptional law and order measures. I will demonstrate that the discourses underpinning the new terrorism thesis and the wider 'war against terrorism' (United Kingdom)/'war on terror' (United States) both rely on and facilitate an ideational shift in the management of security by the State.

The view that 'the world changed' after 9/11 has endured in political circles (see Dawdy, 2010: 766; Gardner, 2009: 2; Worcester, 2001) and this assumption has been instrumental in the development of counter-terrorism and security policy over the last decade. Although political violence is a historically prevalent phenomenon, the 9/11 attacks have been defined by media and political commentators as both momentous and iconic (see Beck, 2002; Kellner, 2002). Whether one subscribes to such a view or not, there can be little doubt that 9/11 prompted the leaders of Western nation states to sharpen their focus on national security and to devise new operational methods of tackling terrorism. Furthermore, such methods have utilized a future-centric calculus of risk which is focussed on the catastrophic impacts of upcoming threats (Amoore and de Goede, 2008: 156). Drawing on discrete examples, it will be argued here that method-ological tools of imagining future risks – such as horizon scanning, scenario testing and disaster simulation – have not only proliferated in the last decade but have taken on wider social and political significance (see Grusin, 2004). In our case study, we will explain why Ulrich Beck (2009: 10) views political violence as an archetypal risk soci-ety threat, comparing some of the foundational principles of his thesis to the practices that have been associated with new terrorism. In conclusion, we will collect up some of the contradictions and dilemmas that arise around security and justice when politicians, legislators and securocrats attempt to mobilize pre-emptive forms of risk regulation to ostensibly reduce threat levels.

Since the 9/11 attacks on America by followers of the Islamic fundamentalist net-work Al-Qaeda, the terrorist threat has become a focal social concern (see Gilbert, 2003; Goodin, 2006; Ould Mohamedou, 2007). Although many countries – including the United Kingdom, Germany and Spain – have been party to episodes of political vio-lence in the latter half of the twentieth century, the events of 11 September 2001 have been considered exceptional, stimulating the reconfiguration of security practices in Western nations. Following on from 9/11, a series of attacks have been undertaken by individ-uals and groups inspired by radical Islamist philosophy in various locations around the world, including London, Madrid, Istanbul, Bali and Mumbai. The repercussions of such terrorist attacks have extended far beyond the nation state and have set in train global geopolitical processes of violence and retribution. While the hyperbolic discourse of the war against terrorism/war on terror popularized by George W. Bush and Tony Blair has receded as a result of changes in political administration and a waning public appetite for international military incursions, over a decade on from the 9/11 attacks, death, punishment and civil unrest remain daily features of life for many people living in Afghanistan and Iraq. The centrality of the terrorist threat in contemporary society is indicated not only by its omnipresence in political and media debates but also by the extensive amount of State expenditure directed towards national and international counter-terrorism measures. In the wake of 9/11, nations in Europe and North America directed unprecedented expenditures on border patrols and new levels of policing and surveillance (Borger, 2006; Monahan, 2006). Less than a decade on from 9/11 the total amount spent by the American government on the war on terror had exceeded a tril-lion dollars (see Belasco, 2009). On a smaller scale, in the United Kingdom the amount allocated to fund domestic counter-terrorism measures in 2010–11 alone amounted to £38 million (Travis, 2010b). The unusual modus operandi of the 9/11 attacks – hijack-ing airplanes and appropriating them as a self-detonating weapons – encouraged many security experts and academics to subscribe to the idea that violence enacted by groups such as Al-Qaeda should be regarded as a distinct form of 'new terrorism'. It is evident that a range of areas of policy making and social regulation have been influenced by the discourse of new terrorism, including immigration, welfare, education and religion.

Despite general acceptance of the narrative of 'new terrorism' in politics and the media, I wish to stress that it is important that a sense of perspective is maintained, both in relation to the *extent* of the terrorist threat and the appropriate *means* of regulating the risk to reduce the possibility of future attacks. Challenging the pervasive view that everything changed on 9/11 2001, I will instead be drawing attention to the ways in which the inconsistent discourse of 'new terrorism' sets an exaggerated threat level that has been used as an ideological prop for draconian countermeasures.

Defining the terrorist risk

Like crime and risk, terrorism is a contested and fluid concept (see Law, 2009; Maras, 2013; Saul, 2006). In many respects, terrorism needs to be understood as a culturally determined category, rather than an immutable historical fact. From the outset, we need to recognize that there are competing interests, ideological conflicts and power struggles at stake in the process of labelling a specific act or group as terroristic. As Rehn (2003: 57) remarks, one nation's freedom-fighter can be another nation's terrorist. With this caveat in mind, we should proceed to seek some definitional clarity. The etymological roots of terrorism emerge in French language and can be traced back to the 1790s when the term 'la terreur' was first used to describe the violent conflict waged between Girondin and Jacobin factions in France. During what became known as the 'reign of terror', the Jacobin government put tens of thousands of citizens opposed to their rule to death, generating widespread fear among the population (see Ayto, 1990: 524). These bloody origins give us some interesting clues as to the competing values and claims that are made about terrorism and its contested nature. In contemporary Western society, the meaning of terrorism diverges from its initial usage to describe organized violence wielded by Government against citizens. In sharp contrast to the violence enacted by the infamous Revolutionary Tribunal in eighteenth century France, modern Western definitions of terrorism allude to situations in which both the State and its citizens are under threat of attack by external non State groups (see Jackson, 2005). Insofar as we might justly ask why it is that contemporary Western States see the politically sanctioned violence they are sporadically involved in as somehow beyond the categorical arc of terrorism, there can be no doubt that addressing the problem of political violence has become a focal concern for government. As we shall see, the fixing of terrorism as an axial problem can be accounted for in a number of ways. Nevertheless, disputes persist about the nature, extent and the most effective means of regulating terrorism. To this end, the full gamut of positions have been assumed in the public sphere, from Right-wing cultural commentators that herald the terrorist risk as the greatest threat to humanity (see Amis, 2008), to Left leaning academics who believe that Western Government's have opportunistically presented leaders of terrorist groups – such as Osama bin Laden and Abu Qatada – as bogey-men that act as a convenient repository for a range of social fears (see Burkitt, 2005; Steinert, 2003). While proponents of the former position postulate that extensive and pro-active measures are necessary to combat the magnitude of the threat, proponents of the latter argue that public fears have been harnessed to grease the path for legislation and forms of social control that reinforce the power of the State (see Loader and Walker, 2007: 3). Whatever the political angle assumed, it is easy to see why terrorism has become a fundamental concern for the State in Western capitalist cultures. The terrorist attack effectively undermines the neo-liberal promise that the nation state is capable of securing the safety of its citizens (see Garland, 1997: 448). Furthermore, the polarization of views regarding appropriate countermeasures to reduce the terrorist threat lay bare the competing standpoints on what security is and how best to achieve it.

Before we engage fully with the new terrorism thesis, let us try and seek some definitional clarity. What do we actually *mean* by terrorism? How can we define terrorism? Given the disagreement surrounding what constitutes a terroristic act, it is unsurprising that there has been little agreement on these questions (see Hoeksema and ter Laak, 2003; Law, 2009; Laqueur, 1997; 2003; Martin, 2006). Despite the hermeneutic complexities involved, terrorism is commonly understood to involve the use of violence and intimidation to disrupt or coerce a government and/or an identifiable community. Following this broad descriptor, the United Nations defines terrorism as: 'essentially a political act. It is meant to inflict dramatic and deadly injury on civilians and to create an atmosphere of fear, generally for a political or ideological purpose. Terrorism is a criminal act, but it is more than mere criminality' (cited in Schmid, 2011: 56). In legal terms, British law distinguishes terrorism as exceptional from other forms of criminal violence as it is deemed to be motivated by political and/or religious beliefs. There are other aspects of the terrorist act which mark it out from non premeditated criminal forms of violence, such as the targeting of civilian casualties and the desire to create damage to public buildings and infrastructure (see Rehn, 2003: 55). Although the UK Government has no formal definition of terrorism, Section 1 of the Terrorism Act (2000) states that terroristic activity describes conditions in which:

> The use or threat is designed to influence the government or an international governmental organisation or to intimidate the public or a section of the public, and the use or threat is made for the purpose of advancing a political, religious or ideological cause.

This definition is enshrined in law and thus appears to confer something of an 'objective' status on acts of violence deemed to be terroristic. Yet it remains the case that subjectivity and political values are present when decisions are made both about what constitutes terrorism and which actions fall outside its definitional ambit (see Saul, 2006; Vertigans, 2011). Those writing in the zemiological tradition for instance, have pointed out that definitions of terrorism determined by government obscure the fact that the State is capable of conducting terrible atrocities and engaging in reckless military actions with huge human costs (see Green and Ward, 2004; Hillyard, 2009). Indeed, this observation has spurred critical criminologists to deploy the term 'State terrorism' to describe instances of government sanctioned violence and murder (see Morgan and Poynting, 2012; Poynting and Whyte, 2012). It is evident that it is often not so much the extent and type of violence, nor indeed the human consequences that determine classification as the perceived underlying motivation and the moral and political position adopted by those passing judgement. As Maras (2013: 4) points out, despite using bombs and threatening to use chemical and biological weapons, those using violence to campaign against abortion in the United States have been classified as activists rather than terrorists. Aside from producing conflicting perceptions, it is clear that views about the legitimacy or otherwise of organized groups can shift over time, as demonstrated in prevailing attitudes towards the IRA and its party political wing Sinn Féin demonstrate. In the after-light of the Northern Irish peace process that brought the decommissioning of arms and the cessation of violence by what were formerly identified as 'terrorist groups', the ambiguities involved in being allocated or shedding terroristic status are conspicuous.

The discursive construction of 'New Terrorism': Politics, media and the state

In contemporary geopolitics the ascendance of the terrorist threat since 9/11 has been quite extraordinary. Despite the relatively low frequency of terrorist attacks in Western countries, the idea that terrorism is an existential threat has been omnipresent in the language of political leaders. Considering the rarity of terrorist attacks – the United Kingdom for instance, has suffered just two serious attacks in the last two decades – the belief that terrorism is the principal threat to national security is often repeated: 'we know that terrorist groups like Al-Qaeda are determined to exploit our openness to attack us, and plot to kill as many of our citizens as possible or to inflict a crushing blow to our economy. It is the most pressing threat we face today' (National Security Strategy, 2010: 3). Notwithstanding the curious reference to the economy at a time in which the State's mismanagement of the budget deficit has plunged the country into a period of elongated depression, such observations have been routinely restated. These pronouncements intertwine with information about changing threat levels and leaked details about 'foiled plots' to remind the public of the constancy of the terrorist threat. Such risk communications are at once an exhortation for public vigilance and a reminder that the State is doing all it can to maintain the security of the nation. One of the most noticeable elements of post 9/11 security discourses has been the extent to which they are reliant upon the assumption that 9/11 acted as an inflection point in terms of the management of risk (see Gilbert, 2003). The predominant perspective in political and security circles has been that the severity and scale of the atrocities signalled the need for radical reforms in security policy. Such a view has been writ large in the speeches of political leaders. George W. Bush's inflammatory description of the war on terror as a 'crusade' ran parallel to the more temperate but similarly misguided views of Tony Blair, who opined after the 7/7 bombings in London that a 'new war' had begun, in which the 'rules of the game' had changed (see Jeffrey, 2005). Although the language used by their successors has been more moderate, the underlying assumptions regarding the nature and the scale of the terrorist threat is consistent (see National Security Strategy, 2010). In the case of the United States, while the appetite for military forays into countries thought to be supportive of or sympathetic to terrorist groups has waned, the killing of both suspected terrorists and innocent civilians continues, most notably through the use of drones. Described in military terms as 'targeted killing', it is estimated that in the period from June 2004 through mid-September 2012 predator drone strikes killed 2,562–3,325 people in Pakistan alone. Between 474 and 881 of these are thought to be innocent civilians, including 176 children (see Stanford International Human Rights and Conflict

Resolution Clinic/Global Justice Clinic, 2012: 2). Notwithstanding, the spectre of state terrorism, the assumption that terrorism is the single biggest risk facing the West has been reinforced by senior figures representing the Secret service and intelligence agencies (see Sawer, 2010). In commonly expressed logics, the scale and omnipresence of the terrorist threat post 9/11 demands a 'new paradigm of resistance' (Bourke, 2005: 28). While we will pause to consider the contentious content of this 'resistance' in due course, it is first necessary to consider the particular elements of transformation as described in the 'new terrorism thesis'.

It should be pointed out from the outset that academic debates about the formation of 'new terrorism' predate 9/11. In the 1990s, security studies analysts such as Laqueur (1996) and Lesser et al. (1999) postulated that underlying shifts in the constitution and the modus operandi of terrorist groups was suggestive of a new form of political violence. Nevertheless, from September 11 forth, the term 'new terrorism' steadily gained currency among military strategists, security agents and politicians. The discourse of 'new terrorism' has commonly been mobilized as a coda to separate out the activities of extreme Islamic groups from those of traditional 'terrorist' organizations such as ETA and the IRA. Taken as an ensemble, the discourse of new terrorism invokes a cluster of arguable, but nonetheless commonly articulated factors through which 'new' and 'old' terrorism are separated out. The new terrorism thesis suggests that due to a combination of geographical reach, fluid organizational formation and extensive weapons capability, groups such as Al-Qaeda, Lashkar-e-Taiba and Jemaah Islamiyah are practicing highly lethal forms of political violence (see de Dijn, 2004; Laqueur, 1997; Martin, 2006: 206). Understood in these terms, the contemporary terrorist threat 'has no limits, no inside or outside: it is transnational, truly global, highly mobile and cellular' (Peters, 2004: 4). While traditional terrorist organizations such as the IRA and ETA acted within predictable geographical parameters, under united ideological objectives and through tangible formational hierarchies, new terrorist groups are defined by their scattered aims, disparate organizational structure and capacity to launch attacks in countries across the globe (Morgan, 2004). For proponents of the new terrorism thesis, ideologically motivated and radicalized individuals are preparing in organized cells to launch 'spectacular high-lethality' attacks which directly target civilian populations (see Hoffman, 2006: 9; Lesser et al., 1999: 42). In planning future attacks, new terrorist groups seek to use weapons capability specifically designed to cause mass destruction and maximize on human casualties, such as chemical, radiological or nuclear bombs (see Barnaby, 2002). Further, rather than drawing on local sources for economic support, new terrorist groups receive donations from an expansive range of benefactors around the globe, including private financiers, charities and non-governmental organizations (see Levi, 2010; 9/11 Commission Report, 2004: 57). The global structure of terrorist networks means that they are favourably positioned to exploit new media technologies in order to analyse data, disseminate information and to recruit new members (see Leitzinger, 2004; Vertigans, 2010: 79). For Peters (2004: 4), this infers that the new terrorist group is essentially telegenic: 'it is aware that wars and terrorism must use the media in all its forms to shape the subjectivities of the viewing public'. The destruction of landmark United States buildings in the 9/11 attacks is an indication of the desire of terrorist groups to strike targets of symbolic importance. As the postmodern theorist Jean Baudrillard (2003) points out, the spectacle of terrorism has become a crucial factor in shaping the meanings that are attributed to political violence. In Baudrillard's (2003) view, global symbolic events like 9/11 have the capacity to fix as markers in consciousness, promoting a 'terroristic imagination'. Baudrillard (2003: 4) links visual and ideational representations of terrorism in the media with broader shifts in the assessment and management of security: 'the whole play of history and power are disrupted by this event, but so too, are the conditions of analysis'.

Casing risk: Situating terrorism in the risk society

While I shall return to challenge both the ideas underpinning the new terrorism thesis and its role in the reconfiguration of security practices in due course, it may be instructive to show how the risk society thesis provides a theoretical framework in which the shift from old to new terrorism can be situated. In this section I wish to elaborate on the ways in which the specific claims Beck makes about the changing nature, topology, distribution and effects of risk can be aligned with the claims made by proponents of the new terrorism thesis. First, terrorism can be classified as a 'manufactured risk' both in terms of the human volition involved in its execution and the propensity of terrorists to utilize man-made technologies and weapons. It is, in effect, scientific and technological advances that have enabled terrorists to produce mass casualties through the use of remote detonating devices and sophisticated weapons involving chemical, biological and radiological agents. Second, in common with the manufactured risks of the second modernity, the terrorist threat transcends nation state boundaries and is international in its geographical scope (see Beck and Sznaider, 2006: 11). Al-Qaeda, for instance, has followers in scores of nations around the world (see Barnaby, 2002: 131; Burke, 2005). Third, the unpredictable global distribution of the terrorist threat mirrors Beck's claims about the universality of manufactured risks. While the patterning of risk in the first modernity follows hierarchical class-based grooves, the types of new terrorism which threaten the second modernity follow a circular motion that transcends the filters of social status, affluence and power: 'acts of terror are (potentially) directed against everybody, and everybody becomes a potential or actual witness to the horror' (Beck, 2006: 152). Given that one of the stated objectives of new terrorist groups is to indiscriminately target civilians, no-one can feel safe and the security of all citizens is at threat. Fourth, there are undoubted echoes of the risk society's 'boomerang effect' in the way in which new terrorist groups are able to turn the fruits of globalization against Western nations through the use of mobile technologies and activities such as cyber-attacks, phishing and money laundering (see Meikle, 2011).

Beck is certainly no advocate of the new terrorism thesis, yet these conceptual parallels invite us to ask some more searching questions. Although there can be little doubt that the idea of new terrorism has been an integral ideational component in the restructuring of terrorism management – through law, intelligence, policing and policy – we should treat its suppositions with caution. As Burnett and Whyte (2005) forcefully argue, the new terrorism thesis both exaggerates and distorts historical differences in the nature and incidence of political violence. Echoing Burnett and Whyte's concerns, Field (2009) notes that 'many of the supposed hallmarks of the new terrorism have been seen in the past', while Hammond (2004: 4) disputes the hazy boundaries between actual and imagined threat that courses through the new terrorism thesis. In the first instance, if we consider the evolving use of weaponry, there is no reason to presume that serious terrorist groups would want to do other than make use of whatever technological means were at their disposal at any given moment. The methods of attack used by traditional terrorist groups were doubtless very different to those prevailing during *la terreur*. As the guillotine gave way to guns, we can expect nail bombs to be supplanted by dirty bombs. As technological artefacts, weaponry and technical knowledge evolve, so too do the selected modes of violence used by both terrorist groups and the State. These transformations do not occur suddenly, but evolve recursively over time, meaning that we should be sceptical about narratives that emphasize sudden change (see Copeland, 2001). Although there are differences in the use of political violence in the last half a century there are also continuities. The IRA, for instance, made use of new technologies, operated a cell system and targeted areas of civilian use, as the bombs detonated in public houses and shopping centres in Birmingham, Manchester and Warrington attest. While the global aspirations of specific Islamic fundamentalist groups to establish a caliphate may be novel, many of the general assumptions of the new terrorism thesis are exaggerated or distorted. As Sprinzak (2006: 3) reasons: 'there is neither empirical evidence nor logical support for the growing belief that a new postmodern age of terrorism is about to dawn, an era afflicted by a large number of anonymous mass murderers toting chemical and biological weapons'. Two factors are critical here. First, the descriptors of the new terrorism thesis are in part real and in part fictive. They do capture aspects of the present activities of terrorist groups, but they also factor in a hefty dose of anticipation about future modes of attack. It is this hypothetical aspect of the discourse of new terrorism that has been emboldened at the level of political and cultural regulation. The oft used 'ticking bomb scenario' has become a well worn metaphor used not only in security drills but has also been embedded in cultural products, such as the popular British and American TV dramas *Spooks* and *24*. It has been relatively common for Government ministers to issue warnings to the public to remain vigilant against the threat of a terrorist attack lurking on the horizon. Demonstrating more than a hint of the opportunistic use of fear for instrumental ends, the pronouncements of the former Security Minister Tony McNulty (cited in Roberts, 2008) the day before the British Government presented plans to extend the period of detention without charge in the 2008 Terrorism Bill are revealing: 'imagine two or three 9/11s. Imagine two 7/7s. Given the evidence we've got such scenarios aren't fanciful'. In such exhortations, the emphasis placed on the novelty and uniqueness of the threat drives the demand for more extensive legislative responses. Thus, although there is a undoubtedly a modicum of truth amidst the hyperbole, the discourse of 'new terrorism' draws an arbitrary historical demarcation between forms of violence that gives a warped reflection of reality and dissembles strategic political motives. Not only does the 'new terrorism thesis' involve the piecing together of a sequence of contestable knowledge claims, these claims have themselves been used to justify both the international war against terrorism and the undermining of domestic civil liberties through anti-democratic counter-terrorism legislation. Stripped down, the popular discourse of 'new terrorism' represents an ideological effort to solidify a set of common characteristics in order to reproduce social control through the placing of subjects, populations and objects under intensified surveillance. For such control to operate effectively, both 'terrorism' and the 'terrorist' must be discursively constructed as items and entities that are recognizable, actionable and potentially controllable by the State. Returning to Foucault's governmentality thesis, one of the most important aspects of discourses is their capacity to represent dominant groups as the safe 'norm' and subordinate groups as unruly, dangerous 'others'. In the case of the discourse of 'new terrorism', binary risk assessments have extended way beyond the individual/local and encompassed entire countries and regions. George W. Bush's allusions to – and illusions of – 'rogue States' comprising an 'axis of evil' are but one obvious case in point. Despite its conceptual shortcomings and dubious effects, the new terrorism thesis has gained an ideational foothold and remains the prevalent way of understanding non State political violence against the West among political, military and media elites.

Envisaging terrorism: What if questions and risk imaginaries

To be clear, none of the arguments raised in this chapter suggest that the terrorist threat in contemporary society is either insignificant or fabricated. Rather, what I have been arguing is firstly that a future-centric calculus of risk has become prevalent in threat assessments around national security and, secondly, that this focus on upcoming harms introduces highly speculative forms of prediction that draw on possible rather than probable happenings. The shift from a calculus of risk steered by past occurrences to one directed by hypothetical dangers is signalled in the UK Government's recent counter-terrorism strategy: 'our National Security Strategy needs to position us for the future as well as the present. We must scan the horizon, identify possible future developments and prepare for them' (National Security Strategy, 2010: 15). Connected to this accent on futurity has been the emergence of forms of speculative prediction that seek to envisage worst case scenarios. On this issue, I have argued elsewhere that the terrorist risk has been politically and culturally fictionalized, such that the line between the real and the imagined has become somewhat blurred (see Mythen, 2010; Mythen and Walklate, 2006b). In addition to risk communications that have some basis in reality, there has been an appeal to the public imagination in the governance and policing of terrorism in recent years. Constructions of violent futures have involved a decreasing emphasis on the past and/or present threats as a driver of risk assessment and a stronger accent on upcoming threats (Amoore, 2007; Ewald, 2002; Gibbs van Brunschot and Kennedy, 2008: 3; Vedby-Rasmussen, 2004). Reduced to a sound-bite, a shift has taken place in the assessment of national security from asking questions of 'What was?' and 'What is?' to posing the question 'What if?' (Mythen and Walklate, 2008). Such a line of imagining inevitably conjures up an assortment of dystopic occurrences, from mass contamination of water supplies to airplanes ploughing into nuclear facilities. In terms of evidence required for intervention, the threshold under a calculus of risk which focusses primarily on the 'What if?' question is lowered. As Durodie (2006: 2) surmises: 'over the past few years a precautionary approach has come to dominate police and other security operations. This holds, at its heart, the notion that officials have to act in advance of conclusive evidence, before it is too late'. Such policing practices and forms of legislation have helped to cement a pattern of future oriented thinking that permits a range of pre-emptive forms of social control. In seeking to maintain national security, a calculus of risk based on past events has effectively been trumped by future led risk judgements in which worst case scenarios serve as a motor for action. Doubtless spurred on by the 9/11 Commission's (2004) reporting of a 'failure of imagination' on behalf of the intelligence services, securocrats, media professionals and politicians involved in countering terrorism have placed 'more emphasis on spotting emerging risks and dealing with them before they become crises' (National Security Strategy, 2010: 5).

The 'What if?' question has not remained ensconced as a mode of risk assessment within the judicial, intelligence and security communities. Rather, it has become engrained in media and political rhetoric about the terrorist risk. Such 'pre-mediations' are diffuse, ranging from visual cultural representations of terrorist attacks in popular television dramas to incitements by politicians for the public to envisage worst case scenarios (see McMillan, 2004). What is interesting from an analytical point of view is the decidedly blurred lines between the real, the imaginary and the rumoured in constructions on new terrorism. Specific stories have appeared in the media as examples of 'near-misses' in which diligent intelligence operations prevented a catastrophic attack. In the United Kingdom these include a failed aircraft attack on Canary Wharf Tower, explosive strikes on the Houses of Parliament, plans to plant a bomb in a Manchester shopping centre and a plot to set off an explosive device during a football match at Old Trafford. Critically, these 'near-misses' have been reported in the media as fact, despite being largely unsupported by concrete evidence (see Mythen and Kamruzzaman, 2011; Mythen and Walklate, 2006b). All of this serves to fuel a climate of uncertainty and may illicit unnecessary anxiety for those that accept such media reporting at face value. Returning to questions around the construction of victims, as Joanna Bourke (2005) suggests, the amplification of the terrorist risk, can invoke a 'national identity of victimhood' that is both unwarranted and socially corrosive. It is interesting too to note broadcast media treatment of attacks that do not fit the customized norm of the fanatical Islamist terror network. A case in point is the politically motivated attacks in Norway in July 2011 committed by Anders Behring-Brevik, an individual holding extreme right-wing Christian Fundamentalist views (see Tietze et al., 2012). Although early eyewitness reports indicated that the gunman indiscriminately shooting people on the island of Utoya acted alone and was a Norwegian-speaking Caucasian male, in Britain broadsheet and tabloid newspapers initially framed the attacks as being perpetrated by Islamic extremists, dutifully presenting the views of a range of 'security experts' hypothesizing that the attacks were most likely to have been undertaken by Jihadi terrorists (see Siddique and Godfrey, 2011). What is of further interest is the way in which post the arrest of Behring-Brevik, the original emphasis on the assaults as politically motivated acts of terrorism receded to be replaced by an explanatory discourse of the psychotic 'lone-wolf'. Despite Behring-Brevik being declared sane after psychiatric assessments, the terroristic nature of the attacks diminished at the level of media and political representation. Yet acts of violence barely come more politically motivated than that undertaken by Breivik. Prior to his attacks, he outlined in manifesto his opposition to Marxism, Feminism and most vehemently policies of multiculturalism which he claimed pandered to Islamists bent on establishing a caliphate across Europe (see Tietze, 2012). It would seem that the discourse of new terrorism does not allow in anomalous cases. Suffice it to say that right-wing Christian groups – and, moreover, Christians in general – are unlikely to be subjected to the high levels of surveillance and interrogation experienced by Muslims following on from the attacks committed by Islamic fundamentalists in America and the United Kingdom. Returning to the dominant mode of constructing the terrorist threat, it is important to recognize that the invitation to focus on possible terrorist attacks constitutes much more than a symbolic exercise in vigilance. Following Furedi's argument, the prevailing discourse of insecurity adds fuel to a wider 'culture of fear' that can be exploited for the purposes of political decision making and the reassertion of social control. As Curtis (2004: 6) reasons:

> Politicians have found in fear a way of restoring their power and authority and recreating a sense of legitimacy . . . put simply, they have found a grand, dark force to protect people against and they can use the power of the State to do this. It is a mirror image of the positive future they used to promise us. But now it is a frightening future they promise to protect us from.

Although the case may be somewhat overstated by Curtis, it is apparent that fears about the terrorist threat have been operationalized by the State as an ideological persuader for the introduction of stringent counter-terrorism legislation. In this way, the playing out of possible future threats contributes towards a fearful climate in which members of the public may become more receptive – or at least less oppositional to – the implementation of pre-emptive procedures. There are, of course, historical precedents to bear in mind so far as the mobilization of fear is concerned, such as the extensive propaganda in the West surrounding the threat from Russia during the Cold War. However, as we shall see, contemporary ideational strategies of risk control can be understood as examples of a burgeoning trend of 'pre-crime' (see Wall, 2010). We will go on to consider some of the impacts and effects of pre-crime in the context of counter-terrorism policy, but before we do so, I should issue the caveat that the focus below is chiefly on the impacts and effects of processes of securitization emerging post 9/11 in the West and in North America. With this in mind, it is worth keeping hold of the observation made by Bauman and Lyon (2013: 16) that the 9/11 attacks were received and interpreted very differently across regions around the world. One man's terrorist is indeed another's freedom fighter.

Counter-terrorism and risk: The pre-emptive drift

To connect together the dots of the argument so far in the chapter, since the events of 9/11 a pervasive case has been made that the magnitude of the contemporary terrorist threat requires that nation states rethink their security policies and develop a broader range of horizon scanning techniques to identify upcoming terrorist attacks. As we shall see, attempts by the State to invoke future harms as a basis for present action have been subject to widespread criticism (Bigo, 2002; McCulloch and Pickering, 2009; Zedner, 2009). The sheer amount of counter-terrorism legislation passed through in the United Kingdom in the first decade of the twentieth century was historically unprecedented and included the introduction of a range of preventative powers, such as extensions to the period of detention without charge, more intense forms of data gathering and surveillance and an expansion in pre-emptive powers available to the police (see Thiel, 2009: 31; Walker, 2008). It should be noted that, prior to 9/11, the United Kingdom already had a comparatively weighty set of legislative measures in place to combat terrorism as a result of the conflict between the IRA, the UVF and the British State that lasted from the late 1960s to the brokering of the Good Friday peace agreement in 2008 (see Hillyard, 2005; McGovern, 2010). The pre-existing legislation on the statute books included exceptional countermeasures such as powers of mass arrest and the internment of suspected terrorists rendered permissible under the authority of the Special Powers Act and the Detention of Terrorists Order. Being layered over the top of already advanced anti-terrorism legislation, the wide ranging measures introduced in Britain in the first decade of the twenty-first century were quite remarkable (see Hanman, 2009). During this period, the New Labour government implemented five substantial Acts: the Terrorism Act (2000); the Anti-Terrorism, Crime and Security Act (2001); the Prevention of Terrorism Act (2005); the Terrorism Act (2006); and the Counter-Terrorism Act (2008). Other related forms of legislation that involved measures to combat terrorism include the Criminal Justice (Terrorism and Conspiracy) Act (1998) and the Regulation of Investigatory Powers Act (2000). While proponents of legal activism have argued that such extensive measures were a necessary response to the unprecedented threat level, many new powers sanctioned to combat terrorism have courted political controversy and been challenged by civil rights groups (see Gill, 2009: 145; Mythen, 2012b).

As Walker and Bulent (2003) have noted, exceptional security measures are commonly justified with recourse to a narrative which constructs the nation as at threat from an emergency situation that necessitates dramatic and swift action. Yet the haste with which some counter-terrorism measures have been introduced has led to protracted disputes between legal specialists about offences that have proved difficult to prove in a court of law – such as 'acts preparatory to terrorism' and the 'glorification of terrorism'. While it is beyond the scope of this book to consider the effects of the full latitude of legislation introduced to combat terrorism in recent years, I wish to concentrate on those measures that rely on projective risk assessments and embody the 'preventative turn' in crime control (see Hughes, 1998; 2007). Insofar as 'risk-preventive' approaches have also been applied in some areas of crime control, including domestic abuse, drug and alcohol harm reduction and youth justice (see O'Malley, 2008; Squires and Stephen, 2012), pre-emptive methods of regulation and policing have become increasingly pronounced in counter-terrorism (see McCulloch and Pickering, 2010; Mythen and Walklate, 2010; Zedner, 2010: 25). Further, given the expressed logics underpinning the UK involvement in the invasions of Afghanistan and Iraq – respectively the 'safe-housing' of Al-Qaeda and Saddam Hussain's WMD 'capability' – it is apparent that domestic pre-emptive measures introduced in the criminal justice system have been developed in tandem with international military policies (see Martin, 2012: 236). The UK National Security Strategy (2010: 13), for example, explicitly states: 'our Armed Forces are fighting in Afghanistan because of this threat. We and our allies are supporting the Government of Afghanistan to prevent Afghan territory from again being used by Al Qaeda as a secure base from which to plan attacks on the UK or our allies'. Connected to the unilateral use of military force, I wish to discuss three controversial domestic powers implemented by the New Labour government which serve as notable historical markers in the use of risk in law making by the State. These are stop and search powers permitted under Section 44 of the Terrorism Act (2000), the introduction of Control Orders via the Prevention of Terrorism Act (2005) and the extension of the period of detention without charge brought in under the Terrorism Act (2006). Our examination of these cases has both a consolidatory and a developmental purpose. First, I wish to connect the new terrorism thesis and the political harnessing of fear described earlier to practical examples of exceptional legal measures. Second, I intend to raise concerns about the impacts of particular forms of counter-terrorism legislation on the constitution of democracy in general and the rights and freedoms of ethnic minority groups in particular.

The extension of stop and search powers under Section 44 of the Terrorism Act (2000) has proven to be politically controversial and produced discriminatory practices in application. Stop and search powers introduced under Section 44 allowed police to stop and search vehicles, people in vehicles and pedestrians for articles that could be used for terrorism without the requirement of 'reasonable suspicion' that an offence was being planned or had been committed. In theory such preventative measures were designed to deter terrorists in the planning phases of attacks and to pre-empt future threats by intervening early in the cycle. Disregarding questions of efficacy, Section 44 powers have been implemented unevenly by police across different ethnic groups. Statistics gathered categorically show that the application of Section 44 powers has produced a demographic skew in relation to the ethnicity of those subjected to stop and search (see Thiel, 2009: 32). In 2007/08 alone police figures showed a 322 per cent rise in Black people and a 277 per cent rise in Asian people stopped and searched under Section 44 powers (see Ford, 2009: 1). Making a conservative assessment of the aggregated statistics, British Asians are between five and seven times more likely to be stopped under Section 44 than White British people (Liberty, 2011). Given the removal of the need for 'reasonable suspicion', in making decisions about intervention aggregate characteristics such as skin colour, age and religious faith have erroneously functioned as indicators of dangerousness. As a result, thousands of innocent Black and Asian youths have found themselves party to questioning and interrogation about their behaviour, movements and plans (see Mythen et al., 2009). It is unsurprising then that Section 44 powers have ratcheted up the list of grievances for minority groups and exacerbated the *froidieur* between Black and Asian communities and the police, particularly in urban areas (see Lambert and Spalek, 2008; McGhee, 2010). In addition to these iatrogenic effects in local communities, the unjust and arbitrary nature of the powers have led to legal challenges being made. In January 2010, The European Court ruled under article eight of the European Convention on Human Rights that the powers were insufficiently circumscribed and did not provide adequate legal safeguards against abuse. As a consequence of this decision, in July 2010 the UK Government announced the suspension of Section 44.

While the use of stop and search powers has caused much consternation among civil rights campaigners, Control Orders which were introduced in the Terrorism Act (2005) are perhaps the archetypal example of pre-emptive counter-terrorism regulation. Control Orders were originally deployed in circumstances in which a person is suspected of being involved with terrorism but where the evidence may be uncertain or incomplete. Individuals subject to Control Orders were subjected to a range of measures including electronic tagging, constant surveillance and restrictions to freedom of movement. Enacted without formal charges being brought, in some cases suspects were placed under house arrest for up to 16 hours per day with basic legal rights such as privacy, asylum and freedom of association being denied (see Saner, 2009: 28). Unsurprisingly, many Control Orders previously sanctioned by the Home Secretary were deemed to infringe basic human rights by the European Commission for Human Rights and judged to be illegal by the House of Lords. In addition to Section 44 stop and search laws and the use of control orders, the preventative turn in counter-terrorism legislation in the United Kingdom has involved extensions being granted to the period of time in which terrorism suspects can be legally detained without charges being brought. In less than ten years, the permissible period for detaining terrorist suspects rose from seven to 28 days. Directly after the 7/7 bombings, Tony Blair campaigned for the period of detention without charge to be advanced to a total of 90 days. The commonly cited rationale for such an extraordinary extension was twofold. Firstly, the 'ticking bomb scenario', in which a detainee may know the details of an imminent terrorist attack but may be wilfully withholding that information has been used to justify the need for extraordinary legal measures. Secondly, it has been claimed that the complexity of terrorism plots involving individuals based in many countries may take long periods of time to unravel. In both circumstances the line of reasoning followed is that greater time available to question suspects may yield the valuable information that can be acted on to prevent an attack. These examples usher in some pressing material questions. Do media technologies such as computers and mobile phones not leave a deeper evidence trail and thus make gathering primary evidence required to charge easier? If it were already possible for the police to hold a suspect for 28 days and charge them with a low threshold terrorism offence, was such an extensive period of detention without charge reasonable? Disregarding these rhetorical questions, a convincing case is yet to be made as to why the United Kingdom should require a period of detention that is out of kilter with that imposed by other nations similarly threatened by political violence. The maximum permissible period of detention without charge in the United States is 48 hours, in Spain it is 72 hours and in Italy 24 hours. It is in the gaps between these disparate forms of regulation that we begin to see just how significant the social construction of risk is in shaping counter-terrorism legislation and wider national security policies. Both complex plot and ticking bomb vindications for legislative transformation are offered without historical precedent and are, in effect, hypothetical scenarios. Contorting Jessop's (2004: 168) notion of 'economic imaginaries', I would argue that such 'risk imaginaries' are vital elements in the process of meaning making around terrorism. Operating in a similar way to Jessop's economic imaginaries, they feed into and develop dominant discourses that serve to frame certain conflicts and processes and become inscribed as fact in policy making.

The examples discussed above are but some of the remnants of a denser legacy of securitization around the terrorist threat which has involved the ramping up of pre-emptive policing measures, the expansion of data gathering practices and invasive modes of surveillance (see Biglino, 2002). To summarize, there are a range of spiky issues that arise out of the penchant for preventative and pre-emptive counter-terrorism policing. First, the evidential basis on which decisions to monitor, intervene and regulate has diminished dramatically, raising vital questions about law, due process and justice (Moss, 2011). Second, the tendency to construct suspect populations and communities has led to ethnic minority groups being subjected to undue and unjust surveillance and scrutiny (see Edmunds, 2011; Lyon, 2013). In effect, the increasing reliance on pre-emptive measures solidifies the process of 'social sorting', where dangerous classes are separated out from safe groups and subjected to the intense focus of the surveillant lens (see Bauman and Lyon, 2013: 13; Kibbe, 2012; Wall, 2010). Third, there is little practical evidence to suggest that pre-emptive counter-terrorism measures are actually effective in reducing the terrorist threat. Insofar as proponents of 'stamp hard, stamp fast' (Gill, 2009: 152) would point towards the thwarting by security services of attacks in the planning stages, the wide casting of the net based on dubious risk profiling across populations appears to have retarded rather than enhanced security. This said, it would be naive and misleading to infer that the desire for punitive responses and stricter legislation remains the solitary catch-cry of flinty-hearted ministers and intelligence supremos. Recent statecraft in the realm of counter-terrorism needs to be understood in the context of the wider trend of authoritarian populism discussed in previous chapters which has characterized crime control in the Anglo-North American world. In the United Kingdom, there has been a steady drift towards authoritarian modes of law and order, regardless of party political tenure (see Hudson, 2003: 63; Sparks, 2001). We need too, to appreciate that this trend of authoritarian populism has at least in part reflected the desires and proclivities of voters. As Garland (2001) observes, public opinions about criminality in general have hardened as people have become more intolerant of crime and more amenable to the use of punitive measures. There is a fair degree of public support for the introduction of stricter counter-terrorism measures, even if it transpires that these measures may reduce rights and freedoms for some. It needs to be conceded that – if public opinion polls are reflective of anything – there is considerable support for stricter law and order policies to regulate terrorism. In the United Kingdom an ICM poll which random sampled 1,006 adults reported that almost three quarters of respondents believed that it was right to give up civil liberties to improve security against terrorist attacks (Branigan, 2006: 1). When asked whether foreign nationals with radical Islamist views should be returned to countries known to use torture, 62 per cent of respondents were in favour, while 68 per cent supported the implementation of powers to hold terror suspects for three months without charge. Across the Atlantic, a *New York Times* poll reported that 62 per cent of respondents believed there were circumstances in which torture is justifiable (Toner, 2006: 28). It would seem that the ticking bomb scenario may be having effects beyond the armchairs of aficionados of *Spooks* and *24*. The methodological problems affecting opinion polls notwithstanding, a degree of consent for the relinquishing of freedoms of some under the auspices of the protection of the many clearly exists. This presents a messy problem that social scientists ought not to sweep under the carpet. Nevertheless, the defence that there is public taste for punitive measures does not in itself render exceptional measures desirable nor justifiable. As Stenson (2000: 17) cautions:

> Giving the people (or at least large constituencies with clout) what they want can mean tossing them the red meat of revenge with liberal values of justice the principal casualties. There are serious concerns that the hyperbole surrounding the identification of individuals and groups as representing 'high risk' criminal threats can be a warrant for and a prelude to withdrawing from them the rights to rigorous due process of law and a fair trial.

Conclusion

In the course of this chapter we have scrutinized the synergistic relationship between the logic of anticipatory risk, political attempts to harness fear and the pre-emptive turn in counter-terrorism regulation. Both the State and the mass media have been cast as complicit in the reproduction of a flawed discourse of 'new terrorism' that exaggerates the magnitude of the present threat and conceals historical continuities in forms of political violence. It has been argued that the shadow of the worst imaginable accident has been etched into specific counter-terrorism policies and the trend for visually and verbally rehearsing future attacks has been instrumental in the wider drive to seek public consent for what has been an unprecedented wave of securitization. In this respect dominant political discourses around the terrorist threat can be seen as intervallic, occurring in the space between material attacks and public knowledge about the terrorist threat. I have demonstrated that the appeal to public fear resounds at a higher pitch and is cranked up at times when governments are seeking public support for law and order measures designed to enhance social control. The problem is, however, much deeper than simply challenging the hue and cry around terrorism. As Bourke (2005; 2006) asserts, it would seem that fear itself is being manipulated and utilized to silence and foreclose political discussion. In a climate of political manipulation and anxiety around national security, it is incumbent on critical social scientists to ask what it is that is 'new' about 'new terrorism' and to question the extent to which attempts to regulate political violence by Western nation states have been either socially just and materially effective (see Kibbe, 2012; Sciullo, 2012). The discourse of 'new terrorism' has acted as an ideological lever for the vortex of measures and interventions that have emerged nationally and globally under the rubric of the 'war on terror'. The erroneous use of the term 'war' in this context notwithstanding, the military excursions in Afghanistan and Iraq and the multiple forms of national counter-terrorism legislation have led to the deaths of tens of thousands of civilians in the first instance and the reduction of basic rights and liberties in the second. The use of this kind of 'terror against terror' (Baudrillard, 2003: 15) is counterproductive to long-term security, morally improper and legally dubious. As Peters (2004: 6) argues, the war on terror has 'resulted in the curtailing of liberties at home and the suspension of the international rule of law and human rights'. Meshing together the domestic and international aspirations of the hegemonic State, Poynting and Whyte (2012: 7) refer to the strategic use of political violence by Western Governments to pursue cultural and economic interests as 'empire terrorism'.

As discussed in Chapter 3, criminologists such as Feeley and Simon (1995) have described the transformations in both the language and the practices of security and social control as indicative of a 'new penology'. There are clear shades in the regulation of terrorism of a motion away from an individual centric penology based around moral or psychological deficiencies, towards methods of crime control that function through the actuarial language of risk calculation and attempts to categorize and group offenders by dangerousness. For the police and intelligence services, closer monitoring of threatening people, places and situations then becomes the 'logical' route to reducing the risk of victimization and eventually bringing fear of crime down to a reasonable level. Such risk-based policies of social control implicitly accept that the rights of some groups will have to be forfeited to protect the rights of others (Hudson, 2003: 65). In a context in which lines have been drawn in the sand between risk/safe individual, groups, nations and regions based on partial and/or inaccurate evidence, the warning issued by Peelo and Soothill (2000: 131) resounds:

> Perhaps it says something about the aetiology of injustice if we can recognize how we may use fictive accounts which, once the marginal status of the accused has been well established, enable us to satisfy and placate our need for revenge and then the re-establishment of a sense of order and safety. The dangers need to be recognized. In brief, it seems that once the bad elements are in place, then one has no need of evidence.

It is evident that the turn towards precaution and pre-emption has become an entrenched feature of institutional attempts to monitor and regulate the terrorist threat (see Durodie, 2004; Martin, 2012: 211; Vertigans, 2011). I have argued, qua Squires and Stephen (2010), that the logic of 'precautionary criminalisation' written in to pre-emptive counter-terrorism legislation is studded with problems that imperil racial equality, human rights and social justice. What is most disquieting about the pre-emptive turn in counter-terrorism regulation is both the haste with which draconian measures have been ushered in and the extent to which the 'states of exception' identified by Agamben (2005) have become routinized and standardized as legitimate modes of risk regulation. These states of exception sanctioned both domestically and internationally under the umbrella of the war on terror have seriously disrupted the balance between liberty and security and, more importantly, made these conditions sectoral rather than universal. For a safe and righteous 'us' security and liberty are all but givens. For suspect populations defined as 'them', such conditions are contingent, partial and subject to temporary and/or permanent removal (see Mythen et al., 2013). Given that risk is infinite and elastic, laws that are based upon it need to be very tightly defined. Despite its flaws, the new terrorism semantic has permitted political elites to pursue a coercive military agenda and to reduce human rights while reinforcing governmental power. To manipulate Simon's (1997) maxim, we might argue that neo-liberal States are not so much contemporarily seeking to 'govern through crime' than attempting to 'govern through terrorism'.

6 The Environment, Risk and Harm

Introduction

Over the course of the last three chapters, we have considered the role that risk has played in changing understandings of victimization, revamped methods of policing, the regulation of criminal behaviour and the development of countermeasures against terrorism. In so far as these issues are undoubtedly at the centre of political and academic debates about risk in the contemporary world, it is also the case that our future security very much depends on the way in which we interact with the natural habitat, the resources we choose to extract from it and the regulatory policies we implement to maintain a clean and healthy environment. Accordingly, in Chapter 6, our attention is directed towards the risks faced by the ecosystem. While this signals something of a move into fresh fields, the foundational concepts that have acted as a compass for the book remain prescient to our analysis. In as much as crime, security and justice may sometimes be in the background in discussions about environmental harm, I will be emphasizing here their centrality, broaching a bundle of disputed issues about the production, distribution and regulation of environmental risks. In excavating the connections between the manufacture and distribution of environmental risks and negligent or intransigent institutional behaviour, we will interrogate the role of the State as an environmental regulator and also subject the actions of powerful global corporations to scrutiny. Transcending a narrow risk-centric approach, it is my intention to investigate some of the underlying connections between the environment, capitalism and harm. In the first section, I consider debates about the end of nature, brought about by the interlacing of natural environmental processes and human industry. This discussion brings to the surface the central concerns to be tackled in the second section regarding the systemic generation of environmental risks in capitalist economies. As we shall see, these questions themselves are intrinsically bound up with the barbed issues of responsibility, accountability and blame. We broach these issues head-on in the case study section where the Hurricane Katrina disaster is used to illustrate how preconceptions about risky groups can influence institutional practices. Drawing on Douglas's anthropological perspective, we connect together dominant notions of risk with processes of rumour mongering and blame attribution. The final section of the chapter examines the role played by human beings in the production of environmental risk. At this point we consider the avenues of opportunity that exist for restoring the environment and developing more sustainable ways of living. Here we draw on cases of resistance to what may ostensibly seem like impenetrable processes of neo-liberal global governance and intractable organizational practices of multinational corporations.

While mention of 'the environment' in everyday conversation may conjure up visions of lush forests and expansive green meadows, I wish to use the term in the broadest sense to describe the structure and fabric of the world in which we live. Adopting this more expansive definition of the environment as a lived and living habitat allows us to grasp the dynamic character of the relationship between nature and society. While most cultures have historically drawn rigid distinctions between the natural and the social, it is clear that these boundaries are symbolically and physically dissolving. We now accept that what people do has a direct impact on the environment, and also that the quality of that the environment itself affects the health, welfare, prosperousness and security of human beings. What we still refer to inexactly as 'natural hazards' are not simply catastrophes visited on society by the brute force of nature. While floods, drought and hurricanes may be commonly attributed to the destructive forces of nature, how, where and when they impact is also influenced by economic, cultural, social and political factors (see Howes, 2005; Kasperson and Kasperson, 2001; Morton, 2012). The severity of the impacts produced by major incidences of flooding, for instance, are affected by a range of socio-structural factors, such as urban planning, architectural design, water defence systems and contingency strategies (see Klein, 2007b: 49; Krieger, 2012).

Since the time of hunter-gatherer societies, humans have always drawn on the resources provided by the environment for food, shelter and fuel. In circumstances in which ample provision is available and population density is low, the balance between the available natural resources and human demands can be managed without undue strain. Yet the expansion of the processes of industrialization, capitalism and urbanization which characterized the 'Great Transformation' (Polanyi, 1944) engendered not only systemic social conflicts but also contributed towards the development of wider ecological problems. The terrain of the world and its climate have changed dramatically over the last 300 years due to mass production and the burning of fossil fuels, such as gas, coal and oil (Bennett, 2010; Kamppinen and Wilenius, 2001: 312). Further, the increased rapidity of flows of people, capital and goods intensified in the modern age by globalization brings into being serious challenges for environmental management (see Holton, 2011). Dwindling stocks of finite resources, accelerated patterns of climate change and loss of biodiversity are all side effects of the expansion of mass consumption in the West and its extension into parts of Asia, Africa and South America (see Behringher, 2013; Shapiro, 2012). Nevertheless, while it is easy to typecast capitalism as the dastardly villain behind the arras, we need to acknowledge the wide network of parties involved in the generalized production of an unstable and unclean environment. In as much as critical social scientists justly draw attention to the macro environmental problems generated by polluting multinational corporations and the failure of World political leaders to meaningfully intervene to prevent the continuation of environmental harm, at a micro level the consumption choices we make, how much energy we use, how we travel and our efforts to recycle and renew are all factors that impinge upon the quality of the environment (see Newell, 2012). We now know that the capitalist system, functioning as an unregulated market system of traders and merchants seeking profitable opportunities, produces what economists politely term 'external effects'. In the twentieth century, the evolution and diffusion of capitalist systems of economic organization – founded on the principles of profit through mass production and recurrent consumption – allied to unprecedented population growth – contributed to environmental disequilibrium on a large scale (see George, 2011; Miller, 2012). Today Western citizens are well aware that turning a blind eye to the environment and continuing with historically embedded economic and cultural practices will only lead to the destruction of the planet. Although the endgame may yet be some decades away, the global depletion of the environment is manifest, from the melting of the polar ice caps in Antarctica to the swathes of smog that shroud industrial areas in China and the dramatic removal of forest cover in Amazonia. These are not simply lamentable side effects of capitalist industrialization, but processes that palpably threaten the longevity, safety and security of the human race.

For environmental historians, the final three decades of the twentieth century might well be remembered for the acrimonious disputes that rumbled between those that believed environmental problems to be part of a natural cycle and those claiming that ecological disequilibrium was a direct consequence of human activity. In the second decade of the twentieth century, the view that our production and consumption habits cause environmental problems is one which is in no way limited to anti-capitalist activists. Rather, professional communities – lawyers, medics, politicians, journalists, film-makers, scientists and academics – are in agreement that the world is seriously imperilled by anthropogenic risks. Recent history proffers no shortage of examples that provide circumstantial grist for this supposition: the category five Hurricane that hit New Orleans in 2005, the Indian Ocean Tsunami which devastated Banda Aceh in 2004 and the major oil spill caused by British Petroleum in the Gulf of Mexico in 2011. In addition to such conspicuous multi-mediated disasters, the scientific evidence regarding the harmful impacts of carbon emissions, reductions in air quality and the seemingly ceaseless march of global warming mounts day by day (see Lester, 2010; Victor, 2011). While there are dissenting views in the public sphere about the extent and the significance of the environmental harms in contemporary society, few would dispute that human activities are having a degenerative impact on the natural habitat. Acceptance that climate change is a consequence of the escalation of Greenhouse gases in the atmosphere – which itself is a by-product of capitalist-industrial development – is widespread, if not quite universal. The 'greenhouse effect', whereby the earth's temperature increases due to higher levels of carbon in the atmosphere, is taken as a scientific fact by the vast majority of members of the climatological community (see Davidson, 2012: 616; Oreskes, 2004; Wilson, 2000: 203). Alongside relative scientific consensus regarding what may sometimes appear as abstract and distant processes, environmental damage comes to our attention in more visible and visceral ways as a consequence of the huge death tolls arising in the aftermath of disasters. The Kashmiri earthquake took over 75,000 lives and the 2011 Japanese earthquake off the Pacific coast of Tōhoku killed over 15,000 people. Yet large-scale environmental disasters are not *sui generis* to modern capitalism, nor are they caused solely by market activity as historical precedents demonstrate. The tsunami resulting from the volcanic explosion on Krakatoa in 1883, for instance, caused over 36,000 deaths with the shockwaves from the eruption travelling around the earth seven times and lasting for more than two weeks (see Green, 2003: 37; Winchester, 2003).

Capitalism, globalization and the environment: The humanization of nature?

It is important to note that the mounting evidence of the damage caused by anthropogenic activity has been facilitated by three key trends. First, it is the increased sophistication of new scientific and medical technologies enabling the tracking and tracing of harm. Such advances have allowed more accurate assessments of the damage caused to the environment to be made and the detrimental impacts on human health to be more precisely calibrated. Second, the development and dispersal of both new and old media technologies has enabled the distribution of a greater range of information regarding environmental harms in the public sphere (see Lester, 2010). In the last decade of twentieth century, the visual power of the 'village green of television' (Beck, 1992: 133) became augmented by the informational vortex of the World Wide Web, raising awareness of the role of the State, private companies and citizens in managing environmental risks. Third, and in part as a consequence of these two processes, a net rise in interest environmental issues has occurred, particularly in the Western world (see O'Brien, 2012). As we shall see, the articulation of these three processes has served to raise questions about the competence, authority and legitimacy of public institutions charged with maintaining a safe and clean environment. Indeed, certain risk theorists such as Beck (1995; 2009) and Strydom (2002) have posited that the inability of risk regulating institutions to diminish the production of high consequence environmental hazards not only heightens public anxiety about environmental risks but also signifies a crisis of capitalism that cannot be sanded over nor resolved without economic and political upheaval. Both Beck and Strydom believe that industrialization and systems of mass production and consumption have spawned global threats to the natural environment that social institutions are unable to control at a local, national or global level. While we will return to further interrogate aspects of the risk society thesis later, let us first inspect the evidence surrounding anthropogenic environmental risks.

Given that the world's population has almost doubled in the last four decades – from 3.7 billion in 1970 to an estimated 7 billion today – it is no surprise that both energy and product consumption have steepled (World Food Programme, 2011). If we factor in the rapidity with which countries with large and growing populations such as Brazil, China and India are developing as consumer economies, it is probable that energy and consumption management will be a major social problem in the coming years (see Bradshaw, 2013; Shapiro, 2012). The International Energy Agency (2012) currently estimates that world energy usage will double by the year 2050. The population of the planet is predicted to reach about 9.2 billion by this time, suggesting a sharp increase in the number of people who are put at risk of hunger and malnutrition, particularly in areas that are already exposed to food insecurity (World Food Programme, 2011). As life expectancy rises and the population increases, the strain on natural resources is likely to be exacerbated. While the breaking of the perfect storm of population growth, global warming and exhaustion of natural energy sources would produce universal problems, we must remain alert to the unevenness of environmental impacts and the disparities that remain in terms of the production of pollution between the developed and the developing world (see Bukovansky et al., 2012). As Biello (2011) points out:

> The world's richest 500 million people produce half the world's carbon dioxide emissions – the primary greenhouse gas responsible for climate change – whereas the poorest three billion emit just seven per cent. The average American – one of 312.5 million – uses up some 88 kilograms of stuff daily: food, water, plastics, metals and other material goods. Americans consume a full 25 per cent of the world's energy despite representing just 5 per cent of global population, and the band of industrialized nations combine to waste 222 million metric tons of food per year.

It is important to recognize that the view that we live in a habitat plagued by environmental risks is far from new. Four decades ago, the *Report to the Club of Rome* issued by Meadows et al. (1972) drew upon computer models to warn of the limits to growth. Espousing a view that chimes with the evidence of environmental harm in the modern world, the authors argued that untrammeled economic development, the acceleration of population growth and the exhaustion of finite resources raised the spectre of human extinction (see Cooper, 2008: 50). Over 40 years ago, the Declaration of the UN Conference on the Human Environment (1972, para 6) stated:

> a point has been reached in history when we must shape our actions throughout the world with a more prudent care for their environmental consequences. Through ignorance or indifference we can do massive and irreversible harm to the earthly environment on which our life and well being depend . . . to defend and improve the human environment for present and future generations has become an imperative goal for mankind [*sic*].

Although the principles agreed at the 1972 meeting in Stockholm were widely disputed at the time – with critics arguing that claims regarding the warnings of environmental damage were exaggerated and distorted – a wealth of scientific research has since confirmed the extent of environmental harm and proven beyond doubt that human activities are generating endemic and potentially irremediable environmental problems (see Boykoff, 2007). A highly cited study by Naomi Oreskes (2004) which surveyed all peer-reviewed academic journal outputs on the subject of global climate change for a decade between 1993 and 2003 did not reveal a single article that disputed the view that global warming is predominantly anthropogenic. The large-scale production of greenhouse gases such as carbon dioxide (CO_2) is indubitably causing a net rise in the earth's temperature (see Bennett, 2012; Wilson, 2000: 203). Since the industrial revolution, it is estimated that the amount of CO_2 that has been introduced into the atmosphere has multiplied by between five and ten times while the average global temperature has risen by 0.8 degrees Celsius (see Greenpeace International, 2012: 5; Hegerl, et al., 2007). More worryingly, the rate of carbon emissions continues to increase, with figures suggesting that global emissions have risen by 2.6 per cent in the last year alone to a high of 35.6 billion tons (Gray, 2012). In addition, a persuasive body of evidence indicates that the capitalist mode of production and consumption is rapidly depleting finite resources (see Biello, 2011; Hinchliffe, 2004). The world's forests are now less than half their original size and continue to shrink by 65,000 square miles every year (Macionis and Plummer, 1998: 655). Further, the widespread destruction of plant life has a cumulative negative effect on the ecosystem. Given that plants and trees consume CO_2 and exhume oxygen which invigorates the ozone layer, the systematic removal of trees, foliage and plant life leads to cyclical increases in levels of CO_2 and decreases the amount of oxygen in the atmosphere. More worryingly, climatologists concur that global warming is happening at a faster rate than previously estimated, with temperatures set to rise by between 1.4 and 5.8 degrees Celsius over the course of the twenty-first century (IPCC, 2012). Evidence of the magnitude of the problem of global warming continues to mount, with eight of the warmest years on record having occurred in the last decade (British Meteorological Office, 2012). As a direct consequence of global warming the polar ice caps are melting, causing sea levels to rise by tens of centimetres and increasing the risk of flooding in low-lying areas. Disquietingly, scientists reported a record melting rate of Arctic ice in 2012, indicating that the rate of global climate change is greater than many climatologists had previously predicted (see Monbiot, 2012a; Victor, 2011). The overwhelming weight of evidence indicates that the material benefits of capitalism come at an unpalatable environmental cost. Dominant systems of mass production and disposable consumption are yielding an environmental deficit that may prove to be irreversible without radical economic, political and cultural transformation. As the Stern Report (2006) commissioned by the British Government shows, the weight of scientific evidence indicates that continuing with a 'business as usual' approach will lead to serious and irreversible harms from climate change. Making a longer-term business case, Stern (2006) contends that the economic costs of climate change are the equivalent of losing at least 5 per cent of global gross domestic product (GDP) each year, unless at least 1 per cent of global GDP is reinvested in technologies to reduce carbon emissions. Without this, Stern (2006) warns that profound climate changes will severely hamper access to water, food, health services and fertile land.

The opening up of economies, borders, trade and capital through the process of globalization is an entrenched phenomenon. Yet it is clear that neo-liberal economic policies have accelerated considerably over the last decade with the expansion of capitalism in large countries such as Brazil, Russia, China and India (see Newell, 2012). The removal of trade barriers and boundaries and the capacity of multinational corporations to expand and relocate all over the world in search of cheap labour costs and new markets have reconfigured patterns of production and consumption. In some cases, the environmental risks that emerge as unwanted side effects of production have been shipped away from the West to the shores of developing countries. While such countries are cultivating or converting to capitalist practices apace, large disparities remain in terms of the consumption of goods and energy between the West and the rest. The major concern is that as newly emerging capitalist countries develop consumer-based economies, the rate of production will spiral upwards, causing catastrophic environmental problems. Although the effects of environmental harms vary considerably across countries, regions and continents, there can be no doubt that human beings are contributing towards the production of a more polluted, toxic and hazardous environment. It is evident that whether we define the present phase as one of 'late', 'postmodern' or 'turbo' capitalism, the dominant mode of producing and consuming goods and services is stretching the environment beyond its limits. As the Green Criminologist Rob White (2009: 1) puts it: 'most of what is happening is directly attributable to negative human intervention and the systemic imperatives and unilateral consequences of the global capitalist political economy'. The many disasters that have occurred involving corporate negligence indicate that the imperative to generate profit has overridden care for the environment. Antiquated legal frameworks, footloose employees and lax political governance have all contributed towards a situation in which private companies and the State have seemed almost immune from criminal prosecution (see Clifford and Edwards, 2012; Tombs and Whyte, 2007).

Proponents of the risk society thesis have expressed deep concern about the impacts of economic and techno-scientific development on the lived environment: 'our epoch has taken progress so far that a minimal exertion may relieve everyone of all further exertions . . . we have done away with life after death, and placed life itself under permanent threat of extinction' (Beck, 1995: 4). For thinkers such as Beck, Strydom and Giddens, one of the major consequences of technological advances, scientific development and capitalist expansion has been the metaphorical and geo-physical removal of the boundary between the natural and the social. This leads both Beck (1995) and Giddens (1999a: 2) to describe the present epoch as one society that exists 'after nature'. What may previously have been perceived as a separate eco-system has now become thoroughly humanized. In capitalist societies, routine economic growth has engendered a concatenation of environmental 'bads', such as poisonous gas emissions, global warming and acid rain. Beck seeks to draw attention to two distinctive trends that emerge out of the inter-relationship between humans and the environment. First, at a practical level, the geographical span of environmental risks demonstrates that locally generated hazards can produce global consequences. Second, at the level of risk consciousness, the escalating scale and media visibility of environmental problems leads to greater social awareness of the harmful impacts of human practices on the flora and fauna of the planet. These two features indicate that environmental risks are inherently global issues, both in terms of consequence and cognition. Contrasted with hierarchical ladders of poverty that typified class societies, the distribution of environmental harms in the risk society follows a horizontal pattern, meaning that all citizens are threatened: 'reduced to a formula: poverty is hierarchic, smog is democratic' (Beck, 1992: 36). Because 'megahazards' shatter spatial and temporal limits, risks have the capacity to revisit wealthy risk-generating nations. Thus, attempting to insure against exposure to environmental risks is impossible, even for those with status and economic power: 'there are no bystanders anymore' (Beck, 1996: 32). In as much as such statements are somewhat totalizing and doubtless designed to provoke, Beck is keen to point out that the present environmental predicament is a consequence of human actions and (non) decisions. For him, it is not too late for humans to collectively mobilize and turn the tide through active campaigns for stronger environmental regulation and establish limits to market activity. In many respects, Beck's call for more rigorous checks on economic, scientific and technological development and the expansion of the precautionary principle in relation to the environment reflects the musings of the German philosopher Walter Benjamin (1974: 1232) who observed that revolution is not so much a runaway train as the application of an emergency brake.

Regulating environmental risks: Gaps in the system

The issue of environmental regulation is one which is marked by divergent stakes, contrasting viewpoints and different value positions. For dyed-in-the-wool neo-liberal capitalists, the market should be left unregulated, and business decisions should not be affected by environmental considerations. However, Green activists assume the reverse position, urging that businesses should be forced to adopt the precautionary principle and should guarantee that economic activity will not generate environmental harms. Of course, preferences on environmental regulation will be affected by embedded personal and cultural values. Perceptions of environmental risks – and the ways in which they ought to be managed and controlled – are shaped by political worldviews (see Davidson, 2012; Hulme, 2009; Wolf and Moser, 2011: 569). Green activists, for instance, have lambasted 'climate change deniers', who they claim are deliberately attempting to repudiate that climate change exists and erroneously refute that it is impacted by human behaviour. Meanwhile, those who reject that global warming is being accelerated as a result of human activity in turn label Green environmentalists as 'sceptics' and 'alarmists' (see Bruckner, 2013; Giddens, 2009: 18). Although scientific evidence points firmly towards anthropogenic climate change, heated debates continue about the extent of global warming and what needs to be done to reduce it. In a world which has become colonized by media forms and in which multiple messages about environmental pollution are circulated by stakeholders, questions of trust are paramount. As Giddens (1999b: 2) observes, questions of trust are connected to (non) knowledge: 'we don't and we can't know – yet all of us, as consumers, have to respond in some way or another to this unstable and complex framework of scientific claims and counterclaims'. This risk society dilemma makes real the need for personal decision making, as citizens choose who and what to believe (see Macnaghtan, 2006: 134). Both Beck and Giddens are convinced that the world we live in is characterized by a widening gap between the environmental risks we are creating and our capacity to manage it. In particular, focus is directed towards social institutions and their role in risk regulation. For Beck (1995) the 'relations of definition' – namely the institutions and agencies that identify, define and communicate environmental harms – have a crucial responsibility for developing the frameworks within which environmental risks are managed. Yet proponents of the risk society thesis argue that the volatility, magnitude and scope of contemporary environmental risks have led to the systemic disempowering of the relations of definition. Legal, health and political institutions that emerged in the nineteenth century and became consolidated in the early to mid-twentieth century were equipped to deal with relatively predictable and benign environmental risks. By contrast, the large-scale mega-hazards of the risk society obliterate established procedures of risk assessment and management, with determination of blame – and thus mitigation and compensation – being hampered by the indeterminate and multi-causal nature of ecological harms.

> It is obviously impossible to bring individual substances into a direct, causal connection with definite illnesses, which may also be caused or advanced by other factors as well. This is equivalent to the attempt to calculate the mathematical potential of a computer using just five fingers. Anyone who insists on strict causality denies the reality of connections that exist nonetheless.
>
> (Beck, 1992: 63)

According to Beck, the relations of definition are effectively engaged in a form of collective denial. They are powerless to tackle the causes of environmental crisis and proceed instead to deploy systems of regulation that effect a bluff of risk management, worsening rather than reduce harms. Not only does the legal responsibility for establishing damage in cases of environmental harm rest with the victim, cases come to court post hoc and direct causal relationships between personal ill effects and specific polluters are notoriously difficult to prove beyond reasonable doubt in a court of law, particularly if they occur in heavily industrialized areas. Thus, the legal stakes are institutionally loaded in favour of the polluter and responsibility for environmental risk becomes shrouded: 'note the consequence: the pollutants pumped out by everyone are pumped out by no one. The *greater* the pollution, the *less* the pollution' (Beck, 1995: 135). The short-term consequence of guilty parties routinely escaping punishment is somewhat dwarfed by the longer-term problem of unfettered mass pollution. Thus, in the risk society perspective, it is the intransigence and evasion of institutional power holders that is a major stumbling block to environmental change. The incapacity of world leaders to agree on substantive pollution limits and the reluctance within both advanced and newly industrializing countries to adhere to environmental regulations is one of the largest social problems of our time.

In the course of high-profile Earth Summits, hosted at great expense in global cities, leading politicians and lobbying teams congregate ostensibly to try to broker deals that will reduce the effects of climate change and improve the quality of the environment. There have, of course, been some notable advances made in principle as a result of Earth Summit agreements. For instance, the 1992 Rio declaration where principles of sustainability were sanctioned and supported by corporations, governments and NGOs. The declaration comprises 27 principles intended to encourage sustainable development and eradicate unsustainable patterns of production and consumption. Having been signed by representatives of 170 nation states, the Rio treaty formally endorsed the principles of precaution: 'in order to protect the environment, the precautionary approach shall be widely applied by States according to their capabilities. Where there are threats of serious or irreversible damage, lack of full scientific certainty shall not be used as a reason for postponing cost-effective measures to prevent environmental degradation' (Rio Declaration, 1992: Principle 15). The subsequent Kyoto Protocol, agreed in 1997, set out binding obligations on industrialized countries to reduce greenhouse gas emissions. Yet at both summits, several heavily polluting countries – including the United States and China – refused to conform, and many of the countries that did subscribe have thus far failed to meet their targets (see Clark, 2012). Moving from the specific to the general, the language commonly deployed by politicians and media professionals about 'saving the earth' is itself instructive at the level of discourses of risk. Debates about 'controllable emissions' and 'acceptable levels' effectively deny the possibility of radical changes and permit, instead, the continuation of environmental despoliation. As Beck (1992: 65) shrewdly surmises, the very idea of controllable emissions sanctions the process of polluting the air, and setting this pollution at 'acceptable levels' relegates a clean environmental for the sake of profit and capital accumulation. The ideological mystification at play here is pronounced:

> The subject . . . is not the prevention of, but the *permissible extent* of poisoning. *That* it is permissible is no longer an issue on the basis of this decree . . . the really rather obvious demand for non-poisoning is rejected as *utopian*. At the same time, the bit of poisoning set down becomes *normality*. It disappears behind the acceptable

values. Acceptable levels make possible a *permanent ration of collective standardized poisoning*.

For Beck the catatonia of the State and an entrenched reluctance to intervene exacerbate the risks of air pollution and global warming. Provided that the prevalent scientific data is accurate, the dominos are getting bigger and closer together. In many respects, the major hurdle is publically acknowledging that the capitalist system of production and consumption is inherently harmful to the environment (see Miller, 2012; Sutton, 2007). The dream of environmental optimists supportive of capitalism is that human beings will be able to rapidly develop new sustainable technologies that will relieve the present crisis. Yet the materialization of such a scenario seems improbable given the cumulative acceleration of global warming and climate change, set against rapid economic expansion in countries with considerable and growing populations. Although the environmental costs of capitalist systems of production and consumption are evident, it should be noted that socialist and communist regimes – for instance those cultivated in the USSR and the DDR – also left grim legacies of mass pollution and major industrial accidents. Extant versions of free-market capitalism, State-centred communism – and social systems that fall in between – have all failed to balance economic development with environmental stability. Reflecting on the historical failure of present and former systems leads Left utopian thinkers, such as Andre Gorz (1982; 1994), to insist that a radical transformation is required from a wants to a needs-based society.

When we think about possible ways out of the crisis, it is important to note that some countries have already made progress in reducing environmental harms. At present, there are some significant differences between the levels of pollution created by countries around the globe. For example, Norway, Finland and Puerto Rico all produce low levels of CO_2 emissions and have relatively sustainable patterns of energy consumption. In contrast, the United States and China are by far the most heavily polluting countries. The United States emits 5.9 billion tonnes of CO_2 annually which is ten times more than the total amount produced by the whole of sub-Saharan Africa (Greenpeace International, 2012: 7). India is now the fourth biggest environmental polluter and also has a population which is increasing faster than any other country in the world. Australia has the highest per capita energy consumption, annually emitting 20.58 tons of CO_2 per person (see Maplecroft, 2009). As we shall see, it also needs to be recognized that harmful effects are often felt by groups and communities distant from the site of production (see Himmelweit and Simonetti, 2004: 99). Those possessing the lion's share of economic capital and the sharpest elbows are able to swaddle themselves away at safe distance from sites of environmental risk. It would appear that the 'enclave society' described by Turner (2010), or, in Klein's (2007b: 422) terms, a world divided into red and green zones are living realities.

Disaster(ous) capitalism? Markets, crisis and environmental crime

As has been established, one of the central problems with attributing liability for environmental harms relates to the manifold sources and sites of pollution. Processes of despoliation such as deforestation, depletion of the ozone layer and climate change are caused by a multitude of factors. As such, it is difficult to unilaterally attribute blame for environmental risks and to introduce measures that can effectively regulate guilty parties. In particular, corporate responsibility is hard to determine given that law has historically been founded on the principle of individual culpability. Green criminologists have long campaigned for the corporate production of environmental harms to be treated more seriously and for offending parties to meet with graver penalties (see Clifford and Edwards, 2012; Lynch et al., 2008). In addition to the problem of multi-causal pollution chains, questions of ideology and power are paramount, particularly in relation to strategies of risk communication and the maintenance of corporate image. Many companies involved in serious instances of environmental pollution have launched heavily funded marketing campaigns in an attempt to counterbalance negative publicity and to convince the public of their green credentials. These attempts at 'greenwash' involve companies utilizing various media portals to impose favourable narratives of corporate commitment to sustainable principles (see Heckenburg, 2009: 14; Matthiessen, 1999: 12). Without doubt, some firms have seen environmental concern as an advertising opportunity rather than an integral social responsibility, with the rhetoric of environmental commitment not being mirrored by effective corporate policy (see Howes, 2005: 166). British Petroleum's advertising campaign to foreground their commitment to alternative energy projects led *Greenpeace* to ironically award the company an 'emerald paintbrush' (see Walker, 2010). Unfortunately, it would seem that the dominant approach towards profit generation among major multinational companies places short-term human interests above those of future generations and the longer-term restoration of the environment. But do the apparently conflicting goals of economic growth and environmental harmony mean that the driving forces of capitalism are at odds with ecological equilibrium?

For several decades, environmentalists and political campaigners have vocally argued that capitalist free markets and a clean and green environment are fundamentally incompatible. To understand this position it is worth drawing on some of the foundational principles of macro-economics. From the classical theory of Adam Smith (1776) through to modern neo-liberal approaches, the idea of an 'invisible hand' operating in the market accounts for the process by which markets align supply with demand and the self-interested actions of individuals serve to contribute to the common good. Essentially people's demands for goods and provisions in the open market are matched by the private production of consumer items and services. In such a scenario, individual choices exacted by social agents are made according to personal taste and choice rather than external considerations. Equally, the goods and services that companies and service providers offer are determined by the resources they have access to, demand in the marketplace and the technologies available to them. The concept of the price mechanism offers an account of the matching of buyers and sellers needs and wants which operates through incentives and the free flow of information between companies and consumers (see Himmelweit and Simonetti, 2004: 87). Of course, the neo-classical perspective depicts a model of economic efficiency and fair resource distribution that has not and cannot be translated in practice. Despite attempts to produce 'caring' or 'green' forms of capitalism, the drive towards accumulation and profit that capitalism demands to sustain growth is not congruent with either universal welfare needs or a balanced and stable environment. All of this assumes that individuals exhibit self-seeking behaviour through their consumption choices, that the market is unable to find sustainable solutions and that environmental concerns are not factored into decisions to purchase goods and services. As we shall see, these underpinning assumptions about human agency and market behaviour are questionable. To this end, Urry (2011) exhortation to sociologists to actively publicize the damage caused by anthropogenic climate change and to advocate creative solutions to the problem is well justified. Yet if individuals are indeed making self-interested consumption choices then what are the environmental costs of such market preferences and who is responsible for paying for them? If producers and consumers of pollution are not required to factor environmental harms into their decision making then what economic theorists describe as externalities may occur. Externalities arise when individual/private costs and benefits are out of kilter with social costs and gains. Negative externalities arise when both consumers and companies are able to enjoy the benefits of market activity without facing the costs of their actions. For example, when the disposed packaging from goods consumed in the United Kingdom are shipped to China and become an environmental problem for those distant from the site of consumption. Given that capitalist markets rotate around the production of profit, negative externalities such as environmental pollution fall outside of the parameters of corporate decision-making. Further, the immediate need for businesses to accumulate capital means that the longer-term repercussions of environmental side effects for future generations does not appear on the radar. This raises to the fore some rather important questions of environmental justice (see Dominelli, 2012; Gaba, 1999). Do citizens have a collective duty of care to maintain the environment so that those that are not yet born can enjoy clean water and fresh air? Should both producers and consumers have to factor the upcoming social and environmental costs of their actions into market decisions? How can the rights and interests of future generations be properly articulated? These are complex questions to which neo-classical economists do not have answers. What is clear is that the theoretical possibilities captured by Smith's description of the invisible hand have not been achieved in reality. As Michael Jacobs (1991) reasons, we might instead recognize the operation of an 'invisible elbow' through which routine decisions and choices in the market result in serious damage to the environment.

For most companies and public agencies involved in risk-sensitive industries such as nuclear power and food production systems of risk management are designed to reduce threats. Indeed, prevention of harm is the formal objective of the risk management process. Yet despite attempts by some companies to manage risk 'ahead of the curve', environmental harms continue to emerge with regularity and disasters appear at periodic intervals as a consequence of human error or systems failure (see Smith, 2006: 309). The term 'environmental crime' is used to describe a wide range of activities that harm or deplete the environment, ranging from fly tipping to the dumping of toxic waste. Several historical incidents bear testament to the potential potency of environmental crimes. The leaking of methyl isocyanate gas and other chemicals from a plant owned by Union Carbide India Limited (UCIL) in Bhopal in 1984 led to over half a million people suffering toxic exposure. Well over 20,000 citizens died as a direct result of the accident and around six times this number were left with a range of afflictions including blindness and breathing complications (see Newburn, 2009: 384). The subsequent inquiry into the disaster found a range of negligent practices and systems flaws at the plant that compromised both worker and public safety, including storage of hazardous materials in tanks beyond recommended levels, an over dependence on manual operations, poor maintenance of equipment and safety systems being deactivated to save on costs. It later transpired that there had been several serious leaks in the years preceding the disaster. It was not until 2010 that seven former UCIL employees were found guilty of causing death by negligence and imprisoned for a maximum of just two years. In addition to environmental crimes perpetrated by companies, the State and its agencies are also implicated in the production of environmental harms either directly or indirectly. Political and economic parties may collude with corporations to either cover up or downplay the extent of environmental damage caused after major disasters or they may themselves be involved in directly producing environmental risks. At the time of the Bhopal disaster, Union Carbide India Limited was the Indian subsidiary of Union Carbide Corporation, a company in which the Indian Government held a sizeable stake.

In her critique of capitalism, the writer and campaigner Naomi Klein (1997a) has sought to theorize the economic and social functions of disasters, drawing across a range of examples of environmental harm. Klein believes that rather than key incidents such as Chernobyl and Bhopal leading to positive improvements and the installation of rigorous risk management systems, environmental crises can instead act as opportunities for dominant groups to re-assert economic and political power. This is what Klein (2007b: 49) refers to as 'disaster capitalism':

> After each new disaster, it's tempting to imagine that the loss of life and productivity will finally serve as a wake-up call, provoking the political class to launch some kind of new deal. In fact, the opposite is taking place: disasters have become the preferred moments for advancing a vision of a ruthlessly divided world, one in which the very idea of a public sphere has no place at all. Call it disaster capitalism. Every time a new crisis hits even when the crisis itself is the direct by-product of free-market ideology the fear and disorientation that follow are harnessed for radical social and economic re-engineering. Each new shock is midwife to a new course of economic shock therapy. The end result is the same kind of unapologetic partition between the included and the excluded, the protected and the damned.

In Klein's view, the objective of disaster capitalism is to displace the social and economic responsibility of the State and to replace Government funding with private market provision geared towards profit. The aftermath of Hurricane Katrina in New Orleans serves as an archetypal case of the disaster capitalism complex in motion. Pointing to the slew of private contractors drafted in by Government to rebuild parts of the city and the re-consolidation of a two-tier educational system, Klein describes a rupture between affluent well-educated children invited to attend well-resourced charter schools and those from impoverished communities that were left with diminished facilities and services:

> Charters are only for the students who are admitted to the system – an educational Green Zone. The rest of New Orleans's public-school students-many of them with special emotional and physical needs, almost all of them African American – are dumped into the pre-Katrina system: no extra money, overcrowded classrooms, more guards than teachers. An educational Red Zone.

> (Klein, 2007b: 49)

Again, what comes through strongly in her analysis is the uneven and unequal impacts of environmental harms and the significance of power and power relations in governing responses to risk incidents. Those deprived of the resources necessary for positive action to counter the storm risk where basically left in the city crossing fingers and holding tight. As we shall see, Hurricane Katrina serves of a salutary lesson of the failures of risk management and the perils of poor risk communication.

Casing risk: Hurricane Katrina through the anthropological looking glass

In the last case study section, I will be putting our outstanding theoretical perspective to work. Mobilizing the anthropological perspective, we will be examining the problems generated by the category five hurricane which hit the city of New Orleans in 2005. I will demonstrate how aspects of Douglas's perspective can be utilized to interpret the decisions, processes and practices that emerged before, during and after the disaster. As the grid/group framework (Douglas and Wildawsky, 1982) has been readily applied in risk research (see Dake, 1991; Marris et al., 1998), I would like instead to develop the underlying concepts of blame and taboo and to show how these are connected to popular notions of risk. Although the institutional failures that exacerbated the disaster have been widely covered in the media and in the academic literature, these procedural shortcomings can be better understood if we take account of underlying culturally embedded assumptions about fear and blame. Before we draw on Douglas and begin our theoretical application, it is first necessary to get a sense of the nature and the scale of the crisis.

The full course of Hurricane Katrina unravelled over a period of seven days, from the 23rd to the 30th of August 2005. What began as a low pressure system developed into a tropical storm which turned into a category four hurricane which peaked in a 12 hour period in which it hit the city of New Orleans. Several sections of the levee system protecting New Orleans from Lake Ponchartrain and the Mississippi River collapsed in the storm and the resultant water surge caused extensive damage and loss of life. Around 80 per cent of the city was flooded, 1,800 people perished, over 150,000 were evacuated and many thousands rendered homeless (see Davidson, 2006; MacAskill, 2007). Conservative estimates suggest that Hurricane Katrina damaged around 90,000 square miles of housing in total throughout Southern Louisiana, Mississippi and Alabama. Topographic factors were important in accounting for the destruction caused by the hurricane in New Orleans, in particular. The City is built on a flood plain and surrounded by water. It also resides in a natural basin seven feet below sea level on clay soils which have been sinking for many years. Given these conditions, the prospect of the city suffering serious damage in the event of a hurricane was well known. Indeed, within local folklore the arrival of the 'Big One' was a familiar topic of discussion among residents (see Kates et al., 2006). As we shall see, the full impacts of Katrina were not determined by the power of the storm itself, nor the relief of the city, but also by flimsy risk management policies and poor critical incident planning (see Hewitt, 2006; MacAskill, 2007). The lead agency involved in emergency management was the Federal Emergency Management Agency (FEMA) which was working under the direction of the National

Department of Homelands Security. As the crisis evolved, FEMA was criticized for its sluggish response to flooding, for neglecting those evacuated from the city and sizeably underestimating the amount of relief required. Images of distressed people stranded on rooftops awaiting rescue – without food, water or shelter – continued to appear in the international media days into the crisis, with many people who had survived the initial hurricane subsequently dying of heat exhaustion and dehydration. The city's major Ray Nagin was also criticized for delaying the mandatory evacuation of New Orleans and for the lack of access to food and medical provision at major evacuation sites. As Bauman (2006: 75) notes, the evacuation plans for the city were poorly thought through and privileged those with private transport: 'it was a simpler task for affluent families to evacuate their homes as they had places to go to, cars to get them there, enough money to afford motels and flight tickets. The poor of New Orleans did not'. Around 20,000 citizens without access to cars – the vast majority of whom were Black Americans – were directed to the Louisiana Superdome (Comfort, 2006: 501). Those that arrived found a site without structured medical provision and food and water supplies locked in cages. In the aftermath of Katrina, issues of fragmented command structure, political bias and skewed security priorities all surfaced. FEMA was accused of being poorly organized and staffed by jobbing civil servants without relevant expertise in disaster management. Michael Brown, the FEMA director who oversaw the agencies response to Katrina, had previously been employed as an overseer of judges for the International Arabian Horse Association (see Swain, 2005: 14). While a lack of thorough preparation and a failure to implement effective emergency management procedures exacerbated the severity of the disaster, the question which may preoccupy anthropological thinkers is not so much why risk management procedures were so disjoined, but rather which preconceived values and assumptions underpinned the institutional response. Drawing on some of the cultural principles established by Douglas, I will offer a reply to this question shortly, but we should first note the uneven impact of the storm on different populations in New Orleans.

In most cases of environmental disaster, a range of antecedent factors shape both the severity of the risk and the reactions of institutions and individuals to crisis. Availability of – and access to – resources, institutional organization and preparedness all influence the impacts that disasters have on regions and populations (Elliott and Pais, 2006: 296). At the time of the hurricane, New Orleans had approximately 485,000 inhabitants, with two thirds of the city's population being Black Americans. Unsurprisingly, it was largely – but not exclusively – Black low income citizens that lived in the areas below sea level that were worst hit both during and after the storm (Kunreuther and Pauly, 2006: 113). As Colten (2002: 237) observes, housing in New Orleans was visibly segregated by race: 'with greater means and power, the White population occupied the better drained sections of New Orleans, while Blacks typically inhabited the swampy rear districts'. There were also large disparities between affluent and poor areas in terms of property insurance. Of the parishes worst affected by the disaster, in St. Bernard's, nearly 60 per cent of occupants had insurance cover, while in Tangipahoa that number was less than 10 per cent (Kunreuther and Pauly, 2006: 103). These pre-existent material conditions set the lived terrain on which the force of Hurricane Katrina was felt. As Elliott and Pais (2009: 296) note: 'communities and regions are not homogeneous, unified systems but rather mosaics of overlapping subsystems, cross-cut by social and economic inequalities'. Although Hurricane Katrina damaged the entire city of New Orleans, certain areas and certain groups were more exposed to harm than others. In the aftermath of the storm, it became clear that race and racial politics were critical in understanding the contrasting experiences of the disaster and the differential treatment of inhabitants of the city. As Reed's (2005: 31) analysis demonstrates, race was a factor which affected, among other things, capacity to survive, evacuation rates and re-housing post the storm. Evidently, racial inequalities are not annulled nor equalized in the event of environmental disasters, rather they become more pronounced. It is at this point that the anthropological perspective allows us to make a firm entry point. Given the myriad parties involved, it would be rash to suggest a causal link between preconceptions about race and institutional (in)action. Nevertheless, we can hypothesize that fears about the 'other' might well have played a part in the mismanagement of evacuees and the misguided militaristic response to the crisis. Through the anthropological lens, we can begin to dig deeper to probe the prevailing anxieties circulating about social order in the city at the time of the disaster.

In advancing a structural-functionalist approach, Douglas (1996; 1992) asserts that social cohesion relies heavily on agreed norms and patterns of culturally sanctioned behaviour. To maintain order, clear lines are drawn between practices which are deemed to be acceptable and those that are seen as objectionable. What is more, these codes of behaviour are defined in binaries: good and bad, clean and dirty, pure and polluted. In situations in which the symbolic order is breached by transgressive activities, the wrath of those who determine the classificatory system is felt by those falling outside the prescribed moral order. From an anthropological point of view, what is symbolically significant about Hurricane Katrina is the extent to which the humanitarian aspects of the disaster – in terms of the plight of those suffering – became overtaken by security concerns about public order. The fears expressed by highly ranked public officials attenuated rather than quelled public anxieties and served to corroborate a series of risk rumours. The international media took up a number of these rumours, with unsubstantiated claims being made about opportunistic child abuse, escalating levels of violence and mass looting. In Douglas's view, notions of risk and pollution are fundamental to the upkeep of social order and polluting influences or peoples are seen as threats to the status quo. Taboo breakers deemed to be 'in sin' are a threat to cultural harmony and seen as damaging to the established social fabric. For Douglas, taboos arise *post hoc* and serve as a rationalizing force for making sense of activities or incidents that puncture normality. Linking up with Katrina, the prevailing media view of New Orleans at the time was more of a city under siege than one in crisis, with frequent reports of rapists, muggers and killers running amok in the city. In Britain, the *Daily Mail* reported that 'shoot to kill orders' had been issued in New Orleans to 'stop rampant looting and arson by armed gangs' (see Reid, 2005: 1). On the one hand we can malign the media for inciting hysterical fears and ramping up a climate of fear. Yet on the other, erroneous risk communications originated very close to the site of the disaster. On the *Oprah Winfrey Show*, Eddie Compass, then the Chief of Police of New Orleans, claimed that babies were being raped by strangers, while the Mayor Ray Nagin stated that evacuees from the Superdome had been 'watching hooligans killing people, raping people' (see Carr, 2005). It later transpired that no official reports of rapes or murders were lodged by members of the public nor recorded by the police. The comments made on *CNN News* by the Governor of Louisiana at the time, Kathleen Blanco (2005) encapsulate the deep seated nature of these fears and offer a disquieting view of a humanitarian crisis that was being treated as a war zone: 'these troops are fresh back from Iraq, well trained, experienced, battle tested and under my orders to restore order in the streets ... they have M-16s and they are locked and loaded. These troops know how to shoot and kill and they are more than willing to do so if necessary'. Looking back on the disaster, given the number of displaced, traumatized and hungry people in the area the situation in the city was remarkably calm. Rather than running out of control, levels of violence and assault were actually relatively low, with the murder rate in New Orleans falling during the week of the storm (see Smith-Spark, 2006). Aside from the irresponsibility and recklessness of the comments made by public officials, the more complex question is exactly why the risk rumours were started and why they were so widely and unquestioningly accepted. Did perceived unruliness of Black people by Whites play a part? Were assumptions about race and dangerous criminal classes factors in the institutional response? Following Douglas's theory it is clear that different moral and political values – in this case founded on race and class – may influence human responses to disaster, but so too do they shape institutional responses. Arguably *a priori* fears linking race to crime played a part in the mythology of lawlessness surrounding the disaster. Reflecting on the abject conditions endured by 1,000s of Black Americans during the disaster, Molotoch (2005: 1) pointedly asks: 'would so many Whites struggling for life be ignored for so long?' As Douglas (1992: 58) reminds us, individuals both encounter and build understandings of risk with a pre-existent package of beliefs and assumptions. In the case of Katrina, both symbolic and physical boundaries between Black and White people – indexed to binary categories of safety and danger – served to steer particular understandings of the disaster and how it might be best managed. Although this takes us into the murky realm of cognitive speculation, it is arguable that deep seated fears about the criminality of Black people impacted on the way in which the crisis was managed. The malicious reports of rape, violence and child abuse acted as symbolic markers of a feral and amoral Black population. Certainly, vulnerable Black citizens of New Orleans who were desperate for food, water and medical assistance would have been somewhat surprised to see the spectacle of soldiers arriving in the city in combat fatigues carrying machine guns. Not only did the risk rumours that surfaced reproduce White fears about a disordered Black population, they served to mythically reinforce longstanding boundaries between those defined as safe and risky. As Elliott and Pais (2009: 300) argue, 'people respond to disasters not as isolated individuals but as members of overlapping forms of social affiliation, which interpret, affirm and support particular definitions and responses to the situation'. At the least, emergency management procedures were saturated by assumptions about race, with reports of preferential evacuation for White people and the establishment of police road blocks being erected to stop evacuees entering privileged areas of the city. In effect, these road blocks were designed to protect the private property of affluent citizens in high lying areas and keep out unwanted 'others'. Douglas's approach seeks to index notions of risk to those of blame and this relationship is consolidated in the Hurricane Katrina case – from the taboo sexual behaviour inscribed in mythical risk rumours, to accusations of violent criminal behaviour levelled at unruly populations. Following Douglas, those rumoured to engage in taboo activities are cast as blameworthy and invariably lie outside or on the margins of the community.

Yet to the extent that threats to established moral codes of behaviour can be defined as threatening and deviant, the castigation of sinners serves to shore up the identity and structure of dominant groups. In the anthropological perspective the consolidation of group cohesion operates through the process of labelling and punishing others. As receptacles of risk, these outlying groups perform the function of reinforcing in group identity and provide a vent for pent up anxieties. As Arnoldi (2009: 39) notes, 'risks give a community a shared problem or enemy and can therefore be used to mobilize the community'. The attribution of blame to groups associated with danger, pollution and taboo is highly apposite to the case study in hand. The anthropological perspective provides the requisite theoretical tools that enable us to understand well the ideological fashion in which culpability for Hurricane Katrina was ascribed: 'disasters that befoul the air and soil and poison the water are generally turned to political account: someone already unpopular is going to get blamed for it' (Douglas, 1992: 5).

In summary, in the case of Katrina, both race and class were important indicators of susceptibility to risk and factors which shaped institutional responses to the hurricane. The majority of no or low-income families in New Orleans lived in areas vulnerable to severe flooding, with all but two of the city's public housing projects being below sea level. Given the extent of the damage to property, many poor uninsured individuals and families who did survive the storm literally had nothing to return to. The Katrina disaster tells us much about the gearing of vulnerability and the extent to which exposure to risk is filtered through race and class. At a wider level, the incident speaks of the fractional nature of environmental justice. Low income, minority communities often live with a disproportionate amount of environmental risk and bear the brunt of disaster impacts, while more affluent indigenous families have the necessary economic and social capital to place themselves in less risky locations and/or to draw readily on resources in order to make a swift escape. What is both revealing and regrettable about the Hurricane Katrina case is that Black Americans were predominantly labelled by primary defining agencies – including the police, politicians and the media – as risk carriers rather than victims that required help. Central to this process of labelling was the transposition of an environmental problem characterized by institutional deficiencies to a problem of law and order generated by unruly classes. The adding of these extra layers of risk by public officials and the media not only unhelpfully shifted the focus of the relief effort, but also unnecessarily ramped up fears and anxieties. Following the curve of Douglas's argument, it is clear that preconceptions, misperceptions and cultural biases played a significant role in the social construction of risk in the Hurricane Katrina case. The risks which are deemed to be important to a particular culture and how these dangers are managed tells us a lot about the setting of values and priorities (see Fischhoff and Kadvany, 2011: 136).

Casting back to the broader regulation of security, there is a final issue of importance to raise around comparative methods of risk assessment and management. As noted in Chapter 5, pre-emptive forms of intervention have become relatively commonplace in the regulation of national security. Given that the Hurricane Katrina disaster happened some years after 9/11 – and allowing for the ample evidence that the city of New Orleans was susceptible to a severe hurricane – it is surprising that the countermeasures put in place were so limited. The levees in New Orleans were erected to defend against the force of a category three hurricane. Yet it was well known by experts before the disaster that that a category four storm was possible and that this would, in all probability, breach the levee system (see Comfort, 2006: 512). Given the range of existing knowledge about the possibility – if not the probability – of serious harm eventuating one has to ask why, in post 9/11 America, clear evidence of vulnerability of the city and its inhabitants was ignored. While the established trend of managing the terrorist threat at the time was solidly bound up with imagining the worst case scenario, the institutional thinking and action around environmental disaster was distinctly hands off. Arguably, the lack of investment in structural storm defence was a result of shifting priorities and budgets with counter-terrorism being prioritized in an all hazards approach under the National Response Plan developed after 9/11 (Comfort, 2006: 503). In Swain's (2005: 14) view, 'pressure to divert resources to anti-terrorism efforts in other parts of the new homelands security department accelerated the deterioration of FEMA's natural disaster capabilities'. Seeking to defend the US Government, George Bush claimed that at the time that no one had anticipated a breach of the levee system. It later emerged that FEMA had been involved in running a super computer exercise called Hurricane Pam designed to simulate hurricane conditions that had predicted levee failure and consequent serious flooding. In 2001 FEMA had rated a hurricane induced flood of New Orleans in its top three most probable catastrophic disasters.

Douglas's (1985: 52) theoretical approach shows us that distinctions between in and out groups can lead to the attribution of blame for a range of social ills. The perceived threat to social order presented by the 'other' serves as an opportunity for the channelling of anxieties and also presents an opportunity for dominant groups to reassert control. Hurricane Katrina stands as a grisly memorial which has served to signify failures in risk management, security policy and disaster planning. This case shows that vulnerability to environmental risks is shaped not only be geophysical but also by social factors (Colten, 2006). Contra the democratizing logic of risk expressed in the risk society thesis, Bauman (2006: 78) discerns a very different pattern:

> Katrina may not have been choosy, may have struck the guilty and the innocent, the rich and the poor with the same cool equanimity – and yet that admittedly natural catastrophe did not feel 'natural' in the same way to all its victims. Whereas the hurricane itself was not a human product, its consequences for humans obviously were.

As we have seen, race and class were key factors in determining who managed to flee the city, who sank beneath the waters and who was left wallowing in the aftermath of the storm. Almost a decade after the initial impact, the shockwaves of the hurricane continue to reverberate. Many families were geographically split after Katrina, with children staying with relatives and parents in other areas while parents with salvageable dwellings attempted to rebuild and repair property (see Hewitt, 2006). Un-housed displaced families living together in crowded trailers have proven to be a recipe for social corrosion with relationship break-ups, depression and suicides being appendage risks that have spun out of the disaster (see MacAskill, 2007). Disasters such as Hurricane Katrina are important sites of social learning which tell us much about not only risk management but also about the wider world. We have not had to scratch too far beneath the surface to reveal the connections between prejudice, institutional intransigence and injustice. Aside from the human trauma caused by the incident itself, the way in which Black

Americans were treated in the wake of Hurricane Katrina brought to the fore partially concealed conditions of poverty and deprivation: 'in the aftermath of the storm, the reality of the third-world conditions in which many in the world's wealthiest nation live was literally washed up for the world to see' (Younge, 2006: 25).

Challenging consumption: The greenshoots of global subpolitics?

Having elucidated the extent to which anthropogenic factors affect the damage caused by so-called 'natural disasters' such as Hurricane Katrina, I want now to examine the extent to which human actions can positively impact upon the environment and limit the process of ecological degradation. In as much as it is tempting to imagine problems of pollution, depletion of the environment and the using up of finite resources as the fault of multinational companies and an intransigent State, it is important to remember that our own personal consumption habits are causing substantial damage to the environment. As Beck (2009: 25) extols, environmental risks are ultimately 'a product of human hands and minds'. Capitalist systems are populated by people and it is people's decisions and choices that have brought about the present malaise. Although we do not elect to be born into a system that degenerates the environment and places a higher value on profit than equality, our actions and market choices are a vital cog that turns the wheels of capitalism. While consumption choices are partly governed by the resources available to us and the market options that we are presented with, our consumer habits, levels of energy usage and modes of transportation all directly affect the quality of the environment we inhabit and in which future generations will live. As the Spanish philosopher Jose Ortega y Gasset (1914: 22) observed almost a century ago: 'I am I plus my surroundings, and if I do not preserve the latter I do not preserve myself'. In the contemporary world, the disposable culture of consumption and rising rates of car and airplane use pollute the atmosphere with CO_2 and other harmful gases. In Europe, cars are responsible for around 12 per cent of total emissions of CO_2, the main greenhouse gas (European Commission, 2012). A return flight taken to a holiday destination 1500 miles away, for instance, causes the release of greenhouse gases that amount to 1.3 tonnes of CO_2 per passenger travelling (Greenpeace International, 2012: 7). Since 1990, UK electricity consumption from consumer electronics increased by 74 per cent with home computing rising by 356 per cent between 1990 and 2011. (Department of Energy and Climate Change, 2012: 4). Meanwhile, domestic usage of non renewable energy sources such as coal, oil and gas not only shortens the time span in which finite fossil fuels will be available to us, they also produce harmful emissions which compounds the greenhouse effect. The challenge to convert to renewable energy sources is a demanding one, but there are reasons for optimism. At the micro level, individual patterns of energy consumption have improved in many advanced industrialized nations since the 1990s. In addition, greater use is now being made of renewable energy sources such as solar power, water and wind and energy saving products are becoming more popular. Yet the bigger picture remains one in which vast quantities of energy are used up by businesses, industries and government (see Held et al., 2011). Far from encouraging the development and dispersal of innovative renewable energy solutions and the advancement of low carbon technologies, the State's preference for leaving the market to its own devices is retrogressive. It is thus with good reason that Urry (2011) posits that impactful environmental changes have to be determinedly advocated by an 'ensuring State' that intervenes to harness the free market and oversees environmentally effective tax systems that challenge rather than give free play to neo-liberal laissez-faire policies. In Europe between 80 and 90 per cent of greenhouse gases and acidifying gases are generated by industry (Eurostat, 2010: 18). Meanwhile, in the United Kingdom, domestic energy consumption accounts for just a quarter of total UK consumption (Department of Energy and Climate Change (2012: 1). While individual consumption and energy preferences are thus an important part of the picture, if the environment is to be restored a huge collective effort is required and the systemic production of environmental harm must be halted. In order to keep the rise in global temperature below 2 degrees Celsius, CO_2 emissions will have to be cut by 50 per cent across the piece and by up to 80 per cent in majorly industrialized countries (Greenpeace International, 2012: 3). The last statistic is sobering as it infers that a dramatic scaling down of production and major changes in energy usage. Disregarding the issue of whether such actions will be sufficient to reverse the tide of environmental despoliation, the targets agreed at Earth Summits to reduce emissions have all too frequently been lapsed on (see Weltzer, 2012). Although the Kyoto Protocol set legally binding emissions-reduction targets several countries that ratified the treaty such as Spain and Italy are way behind schedule and have not met their pledges (Harvey, 2012). Moreover, the principles agreed at global conferences and summits can become contorted by politicians post hoc to meet prevailing short-term goals. Monbiot's (2012b) observations of the two decades of linguistic reverse engineering that transpired between the 1992 and 2012 Rio Earth Summits aptly captures the process of discursive manipulation:

> In 1992, world leaders signed up to something called 'sustainability'. Few of them were clear about what it meant; I suspect that many of them had no idea. Perhaps as a result, it did not take long for this concept to mutate into something subtly different: 'sustainable development'. Then it made a short jump to another term: 'sustainable growth'. And now, in the 2012 *Rio+20* text that world leaders are about to adopt, it has subtly mutated once more: into 'sustained growth'.

In the context of capitalism, growth has historically proven to be the antithesis of sustainability, demonstrating that greenwash can be an activity engaged in by politicians as well as corporations. Nonetheless, as Monbiot's contribution illustrates, the media can serve as a moral and ethical watchdog on the environment, revealing attempts at mystification and visualizing cases of harm (Beck, 2009: 83). Clearly, the presence of environmental issues in the media has had a positive impact in terms of raising public consciousness of environmental issues over the last three decades (see Anderson, 2006; 2009). Alongside a net rise in environmental awareness in Western cultures, the nature and objects of concern have also changed. Macnaghtan (2006) posits that a gradual transformation has occurred from a focus on global nature that prevailed in the 1980s to a more individualized emphasis on how the local environment has been impacted by large-scale pollution. This transition from seeing the environment as something that exists 'out there' to seeing it as internal to us and 'in here' has ramifications for human behaviour and notions of responsibility (see also Jacobs, 1999). While the 1970s and 1980s saw NGOs battling against denials that climate change was being accelerated by human activity, this struggle for proof has given way in the new millennium to debates about the extent of anthropogenic climate change. This is what Macnaghtan (2006: 137) describes as a shift from a concern about saving the environment to a sense that it may somehow *save us* if we are able to nurture and protect it properly. As perceptions of the environment as something distant and abstract are replaced by the acknowledgement that it cannot be detached from social life, political potentialities are enhanced. Arguing in a similar groove, Beck (2009: 81) canvasses for a shift in sociological focus away from the environment as conceived as the surrounding world (*Umwelt*), towards understandings which are rooted in the inner word (*Innenwelt*). But what does the increased physical and mediated visibility of environmental risk mean for public attitudes and behaviour in the future? Again, one's response to this question will be influenced by political values and one's view of human nature. Those adopting pessimistic positions tend to see individuals as atomized, self-interested actors who will continue to make instrumental decisions. Those of a more optimistic persuasion suggest that collective public concern about environmental issues will continue to rise and greater numbers of people will actively campaign against major polluters and challenge the intransigence of political decision makers (see Beck, 2009: 94). For risk society thinkers such as Giddens (1999a; 2009) and Strydom (2002) environmental politics is a crucial site of political contestation. Despite the apparent disconnect between formal politics and everyday life indicated by record lows in votes cast at general elections, Beck himself remains sanguine about the capacity of humans to forge an environmentally sustainable system via the development of a 'new future-oriented planetary ethics of responsibility' (2009: 15). In effect, as major environmental threats become manifest, citizens become compelled to act. Beck (2009: 93) draws an important distinction between globalization from above – as epitomized by the kinds of international treaties agreed at global summits – and globalization from below, which involves transnational actors engaging with environmental issues outside of the formal parliamentary process and in opposition to party politics. In his purview, a transnational global subpolitics which takes place from the bottom up is taking shape:

> It is the reflexivity of world risk society that founds the reciprocal relation between publicity and globality. With the constructed and accepted planetary definition of threats, a joint space of responsibility and action is being created across all national boundaries and divisions, a space that potentially ... founds political action between strangers in an analogous way to national space.
>
> (Beck and Grande, 2010: 182)

Such a movement has the capacity to challenge corporate interests, institutions and agencies which generate environmental risk. Through the application of direct political pressure, members of the public have begun to transform society from the bottom-up, leading to shifts in political power away from an unresponsive formal democratic system towards active issue-based engagement. For Beck, various forms of environmental sub-politics have solidified, where citizens have used oppositional political tactics and direct protest as a means of holding polluters directly accountable for the consequences of their actions. As reflexive globalization transforms the nexus of political decision-making, local actions can produce global impacts. In the risk society, protest marching, boycotting products, picketing, petition signing and awareness raising campaigns, all serve as contemporary methods of 'direct balloting' (Beck, 1999: 42). The active lobbying of *Greenpeace* and *Friends of the Earth* has successfully kept environmental issues high on the agenda and these organizations have had notable successes in keeping polluting companies in check (see Clifford and Edwards, 2012: 23). Alongside these developments looser networked groups such as *Occupy* and *Climate Camp* have used direct actions to expose and stymie the business activities of major polluters. A number of camps for climate action have drawn attention to major carbon emitters, with campaigners descending on polluting companies to set up camps which disrupt working practices and attract media attention. In the United Kingdom, climate camps have been sited at Heathrow Airport, Drax Power Station in North London, the City financial district of London and outside the Royal Bank of Scotland Headquarters in Edinburgh. But how widespread and how well supported are environmental protests? To what extent is a green consciousness solidifying among the general public? Empirical studies do suggest a net rise in awareness of environmental risks over the last two decades (see Eurostat, 2010; Macnaghtan, 2003; ONS, 2001). Yet there is, of course, something of a lacuna between cognizance and action and awareness of environmental issues is not necessarily converted into environmentally friendly behaviour, nor indeed active political opposition. As the 'value-action gap' identified by Blake (1999) indicates, changing values do not always equate with changing practices, meaning that knowledge of environmental harm does not mechanically translate into ecologically sound behaviour. Rather, there are a range of quotidian factors which obstruct the conversion of environmental awareness into greener practices. The grass which is most difficult to see may well be that which we are standing on. To this end, a greater degree of reflexivity and a stronger commitment to change are pre-cursors to improving the quality of the environment in the short and the long term. Despite knowing about the scale of carbon emissions produced by airplane travel many of us still choose to board the flight. In some instances, this kind of behaviour may well be a reflexive process of risk trade-off. In this case the tranquillity and recuperation provided by a holiday in a remote location as against the wider damage caused to the environment. The task here is no longer to impress upon people that the environment is at risk. Rather it is to convince them that the long-term future of the planet is more important than the short-term benefits of leisure and pleasure. It must also be acknowledged that for many people – in the West and elsewhere – engaging in practices to restore the environment remains a low priority amidst the management of more prosaic and unceasing demands of working, maintaining family relations and paying off a mortgage. As Robinson and Holdsworth (2013: 65) point out: 'people living in poverty are more likely to be preoccupied with immediate concerns such as keeping their job, paying their rent, and their own and their children's safety, rather than the chance of developing an illness in 20 years time'. Acknowledging preoccupation with the realm of necessity, the 'value-action gap' and corporate inertia, Hajer (1995) suggests that alongside ethical and moral appeals, strategies of incentivization must be implemented. Adopting a more liberal position than Beck, he believes that macro regulation and anti-growth measures will simply stifle capitalism. Hajer (1995) instead suggests the introduction of a range of positive incentives designed to encourage business and industry to internalize limits and self-regulate via internal regulation.

If ecological solutions are made economically viable Hajer believes there is no reason why both companies and citizens would not engage in greener practices or embrace ecological friendly consumption choices.

Conclusion

It is important to recognise that the distribution of environmental risks remains patchy and public awareness of green issues varies considerably over time and space (see Hannigan, 2012). Although citizens in the West have become more conscious of environmental issues over the last three decades, knowledge about environmental risks is not evenly layered within countries and may be relatively sparse in regions where the simple need to survive on a day-to-day basis trumps the cultivation of environmentally friendly practices. In the West, the admixture of life-world demands presented by balancing personal relationships, family life and work reduces the time available to engage in environmental politics. Although the dystopic prospect of an imperilled planet is justified by the scientific evidence, at present and in the medium term, environmental damage will continue to affect certain areas, regions and people more than others (see Body-Gendrot, 2011; Dominelli, 2012). Disasters such as hurricanes, floods and earthquakes occur more frequently and more intensely in some regions than others and, as the Katrina disaster shows, localized exposure to harm can be variable (see Howes, 2005: 57). The effects of global warming and excessive carbon emissions are more apparent in some places than others. The quality of the air that people breathe in tastes very different in Cubatoa or Beijing, than it does in Winturthur or Richmond. Against the curve of the boomerang effect, affluent countries retain the capacity to ship their environmental toxins and waste to the shores of poorer countries. As Monbiot (2012c) observes: 'those who consume far more resources than they require destroy the life chances of those whose survival depends upon consuming more'. The task of restoring environmental balance is historically unprecedented and it requires determination to implement sweeping changes at both the macro and micro level (see Held et al., 2011). Top level institutions must undergo a reflexive process of ecological modernization that prioritizes environmental responsibility over profit. At ground level, citizens themselves will need to fundamentally alter their economic and cultural activities, from consuming for need not want, to limiting energy usage and buying green products.

As Urry (2011) urges, we must avoid presuming that the local and the global dimensions of climate change can be decoupled. Despite his optimism, Beck (2009: 92) does recognize that an 'ecological conversion' will need to materialize if global subpolitics is to produce a transition towards a more sustainable ways of living. It is hard to see how all this can come to fruition under the framework of a capitalist system given that the goals appear to be diametrically opposed: the environment over the economy, frugality over consumption, people over profit. Yet it is clear that the future of the environment rests on whether or not we can take up this challenge (see Sutton, 2007; Weltzer, 2012). It involves changing our approach to work and leisure, reducing production and consumption of goods, using renewable energy sources and modifying modes of transportation. Rather than merely accepting a scintilla of responsibility, we need instead to seriously reconfigure the way we think, act, work and play. If we fail to do this the habitat that awaits future generations looks hostile and unwelcoming (see Hannigan, 2012). As if to increase the urgency with which we confront such problems, we should perhaps remind ourselves that initial predictions regarding the rate of environmental despoliation are having to be revised and scaled up in the light of contemporary evidence of harm (see Giddens, 2009; Žižek, 2010). Casting back to the pioneering work of the environmentalist Donella Meadows, the task ahead is as simple as it is surmountable: 'we humans are smart enough to have created complex systems and amazing productivity; surely we are also smart enough to make sure that everyone shares our bounty, and surely we are smart enough to sustainably steward the natural world upon which we all depend' (Meadows, cited in Kevany, 2007: 107). It is important to stress that environmental problems are no longer a threat that is only just visible in the rear view mirror. Rather, they confront us in the here and now, meaning that complacency and delay will simply compound the problems we face. This is not the time to be rearranging the deckchairs on the Titanic. Besides endangering the planet, environmental risks raise to the surface questions of human rights and responsibilities. As Beck (2009: 95) succinctly puts it:

> Analysed in terms of social policy, therefore, the ecological crisis involves a systematic violation of basic rights, whose long-term socially destabilizing effects can scarcely be overestimated. For dangers are being produced by industry, externalized by economics, individualized by the legal system, legitimized by the natural sciences and downplayed by politics.

Given an appropriate range of information, relevant incentives and just forms of regulation there is no reason why human beings cannot modify their behaviours and place a greater value on the environment in everyday decision making. But an effective plan for economic transformation that foregrounds restoration of the environment rather than sanctions its despoliation is required (see George, 2011; Lewis, 2013). The speed with which the US Government responded to bail out ailing banks in the early stages of the 2008 financial crisis is striking when considered against their reluctance to commit to reducing pollution levels and to invest in renewable energy. On a single day the Federal Reserve made $1.2 trillion available – more than the entire world has committed to addressing climate change in 20 years (see Monbiot, 2012c). The continued privileging of markets over nature, of the interests of the affluent over the poor, impoverishes the present quality of the environment and stores up big trouble for future generations.

7 Contesting Risk

In previous chapters I have upheld the virtues of adopting an open, critical approach to risk. Assuming such an aspect involves acknowledging the undoubted impact of risk within the social sciences and wider society, while being alert to institutional misuses of risk and some of the pitfalls of using risk as an academic tool for understanding social problems. In the case study sections in particular, I have endeavoured to demonstrate that theories of risk have utility in illuminating specific incidents, actions and processes. This open aspect of approach has been developed alongside a more hawkish line of inquiry that has involved tracking the potential drawbacks of utilizing risk as a tool of analysis and regulation. In this final chapter I wish to press the critical aspects of the argument further by examining the conceptual capacity of risk to illumine macro-social processes and contemporary cultural practices in the round.

As an academic who has reproduced the grammar and syntax of risk, it is not without some navel-gazing – and a degree of unease – that I undertake the task of contesting the place of risk in the social sciences and wider society. I would, for the record, line up alongside O'Malley (2006) and concur that risk is an open-ended and plastic concept. I am thus suitably mindful of the dangers of reifying 'risk' such that it becomes a generic 'thing' that is seen to beget either negative or positive social outcomes. Risks are constructed and labile incidents, objects and processes. Yet the unified nature in which risk has sometimes been treated in sociology, social policy and criminology textbooks – typified by loose references to 'risk theory' – belies a messy history and overlooks disconnected roots. It would seem that the desire to make risk meaningful has sometimes overridden the desire to question both its conceptual content, empirical utility and theoretical potential. As I have stressed through an appreciation of competing perspectives, the congregation of risk is wide. Yet insofar as I am sensitive to the polysemic quality of risk as it manifests itself in different circumstances, the staking out of divergent positions on risk should not inhibit us from trying to critically evaluate the impact of risk in and on the social sciences more generally. Nor should it allow us to shy away from uncomfortable debates about our own roles as academics, practitioners and students. In engaging with debates about risk and using risk as an analytical frame we need to be aware that we are reproducing particular ways of looking at the world. Having discussed the uneven distribution of risks across different social spheres – and considered the implications of this for equality and social justice – I wish now to further develop the critical angles of the argument by evaluating the explanatory power of risk. Drawing attention to some of the dangers that lurk in the background when risk is prioritized as a mode of social analysis, I will maintain that while macro theories of risk may equip us with a camera to take snapshots of the world, they do not necessarily enable us to see the bigger societal picture. Bringing together the shortcomings of theoretical perspectives on risk,

I will be suggesting that the valorization of risk has created three inter-layered problems around the ways in which agency, power and experience are understood. First, I posit that social science perspectives on risk have served to construct an insufficiently differentiated notion of human agency. I will argue that the insensitivity of distinct theories of risk to issues of diversity and difference has led to the reproduction of a subject that is devoid of affect and identity; a subject who is presumed to function as a mechanical rational actor and micro-manager of risk. A lack of empirical attention to the contrasting ways in which risk is embedded in everyday life – in both positive and negative ways – masks the diversity and unevenness of lived experiences of risk. Second, I will be suggesting that theories of risk have tended to present an incomplete account of power relations that often evacuates important debates about social inequalities. Addressing this hollow, I wish to explicate the connections between risk, power and discourse and to develop questions of who speaks about risk, how and for whom? To be clear, my concern here is not simply about the conceptual limits to risk, although these are important. Rather, I am upper-mostly concerned about the way in which risk has been liberally applied in the social sciences and the extent to which this has dislodged traditional categories of analysis that remain socially significant. Third, I want to express some reservations about the extent to which risk research accurately represents the lived experiences of the majority of people living in the world today. As Gorz (2009: 69) counsels, we should avoid 'taking refuge in the realm of ideas where all things are merely incidental illustrations of a general idea'. The fashion in which we academically categorize risk can itself be interpreted as a form of power and control that brings with it the responsibility of faithfully reflecting the experiences of those that we claim to speak for.

Casting back to the early chapters of the book, one of the key problems we encounter when we talk of and about risk is the all encompassing nature of the concept. As Beck (2009: 138) notes: 'the category of risk exhibits an expansive logic. It embraces everything'. In sharp contrast to the contemporary vogue for treating risk as a broad ranging concept, for classical economists such as Frank Knight (1922), risk was reserved solely for instances in which harm can be calibrated, rather than those in which it remained indeterminate. For others, risk also envelops situations of uncertainty when the possible harms remain inestimable. On this point, it is interesting to note Beck's (2009) recent clarification of his theoretical position, in which measurable and manifest harms are dubbed 'catastrophes' and potential future dangers are classified as 'risks'. As well as an indicator of possible material harm, risk is, in many senses, a technology for planning and limiting upcoming adversities. In principle, once institutions distinguish risks forming on the horizon they are able to set about organizing policies and technologies to manage such dangers. As both Beck (1995) and Foucault (1991b) note – albeit pursuing different paths of inquiry – the development and advance of the capitalist neo-liberal State has produced a barrage of institutional processes and practices designed to reduce danger and to encourage individualized risk management strategies. Of course, risk – as both a macro form of structural regulation and a micro form of self-management – has a long tradition of featuring in social categorization and ordering, for instance, in areas around immigration, asylum, policing, detention, sentencing, probation and human rights (see Bosworth and Guild, 2008; Kemshall, 2003; McGhee, 2008; O'Malley, 2008). While the debate about risk that we are engaged in may be distinctly theoretical, it is evident that risk is hugely important in informing and shaping public policy and these debates themselves raise broader questions about the nature and reach of social science perspectives that take risk as their analytical entry point.

Theoretical blind spots: Factoring in agency

Over the course of the last decade it has been common for social scientists to advocate and apply various risk theories to shed light on social occurrences. As noted in Chapter 1, risk traverses a range of subject areas and has served as a something of an academic commons on which academics have been able to engage in cross-disciplinary debate. Broadly speaking, the consolidation of risk as a leitmotif in the social sciences has occurred through the furtherance of the two branches identified earlier: one which has advanced largely empirical forms of risk analysis and another which has favoured theoretical approaches. Researchers involved in risk analysis have sought to understand public perceptions and human decision making around the communication and management of risk. Meanwhile, the more narrative-based branch of risk theory has involved working up perspectives that seek to account for the relationship between structural shifts, social processes and human behaviour. Along the axis of risk analysis, risk is something that can be explicitly identified and managed and the effects of policies to combat risk can be measured and evaluated. For those developing the theoretical axis, risk is foremostly approached in relation to its connection to underlying social processes and cultural phenomena. Despite the combined range of this work – and travelling from one axis to the other – studies which adequately synthesize social structure and individual agency have been rare. While risk analysis has fixed too tightly on individual processes of cognition, the major theory-builders have tended to either skirt around empirical evidence or to draw on a smattering of secondary data. As Leiss (2000: 7) reasons, 'fragments from the empirical world intrude only as illustration or example'. Perhaps the time consuming and laborious nature of large-scale empirical research – plus the difficulties of acquiring sufficient funding for major projects – has led to a paucity of work documenting the ways in which problems of risk feature in the everyday experience of individuals. In as much as conceptual debates about risk undoubtedly have their place, the meta-theoretical bent of the grand theories of risk leaves them somewhat detached from the humdrum nature of existence and the experiences of those motivated primarily by the need to grub out a living. On this point, Dave Haslam's (2000: 29) account of the mundane realities of life for many working class people living in inner city Manchester is instructive:

> Life is a wait. For a job, or a better job. For a change in the weather, for a sugar daddy, or a National Lottery win. Time flies when you're having fun, but when you're not, then it drags. You skin up, shut up, lie down, can't be bothered; feel alienated, poverty-stricken, sad. Maybe you have the luck and the wherewithal to shape your own destiny, with a job you love and enough money to please yourself. But most likely, you don't. More likely you're trapped in a job you don't much like and which pays a wage you can't live off; insurance, telesales, shelf-stacker.

For our purposes, the chord that Haslam's observations strike relates to the relative salience of global risks for the individual amidst more mundane aspirations and fears.

In as much as the spectre of the global bads of the risk society – such as environmental disaster or a serious terrorist attack – may occasionally flitter across consciousness, many people are bound up with managing more humdrum risks: finding and keeping a job, paying the rent, having enough money to feed and clothe the kids. Without doubt, the importance – or otherwise – of large-scale risks within the wider construction of personal biographies remains underexplored (see Parkhill et al., 2011: 325). This is a black box which social scientists would do well to prize open. When theories of risk gain currency the suppositions they make about human behaviour can become taken for granted social facts which are all too often assimilated rather than empirically validated. Broadening this point of critique out, what is common to competing strands of risk theory is a lack of attention to the *differentiated* nature of populations and the importance of social stratification in shaping vulnerability to and experience of risk (see Mythen, 2005b; Vandecasteele, 2010). If we take the financial crisis as an example, within Europe there are large gulfs between people's levels of exposure to harm. Austerity measures have been severe and intense in some places, with economic policies designed to reduce debt having devastating effects on welfare health-care provision. In Greece a 200 per cent increase in HIV cases has been reported since 2008, while in the United States more than five million people have lost access to health care (see Henley, 2013). Meantime, in Britain an estimated 10,000 families have been rendered homelessness as a result of housing benefit cuts (Stuckler and Basu, 2013). In other countries with considerable financial reserves, such as Switzerland and Norway, the structural damage and the private pain has been much more limited.

As with all theories, those that are oriented towards risk imagine a particular kind of social context and a particular kind of individual. Indubitably, the types of citizens conceived in specific theories of risk tell us something about their historical moment of origin and the proclivities of their progenitors. The perspectives on risk we have discussed do capture something of the epoch in relation to trends in political ideology, modes of governance, national security management, environmental regulation and crime science. However, in each perspective – risk society, governmentality, anthropological and culture of fear – the human and experiential dimensions of risk remain under-analysed. In short, the question of how risk is understood, lived and *felt* is talked around, not about. Borrowing C. Wright-Mills's (1959) sociological phraseology, the 'public issues' within which risk surfaces – such as crime, unemployment and domestic violence – are well recognized, but the 'private troubles' that underlie and shape them are yet to be properly excavated. In my view, foundational theories of risk – and the sub-theories which they have informed – do not properly address the symbiotic relationship risk and the self. This is a point to which I will return, but for now I wish to distinguish between the different types of individual imagined in competing risk perspectives.

The major perspectives on risk offer quite different interpretations of risk as a concept, from the risk society emphasis on tangible manufactured harms to the anthropological view of risk as a device for establishing (dis)order and the governmentality position in which risk is constructed through discourse. What these perspectives share in common is the view that pre-occupations with risk go hand in hand with the process of modernization and the elevation of expert systems. As Lupton (2006: 13) observes, 'expert knowledges are central to neo-liberal government, providing the guidelines whereby citizens are assessed, compared against norms and rendered productive'.

Although macro theoretical perspectives tend to perceive agency as a static universal – in the sense that little differentiation is made between the behaviour of social actors across time and space – the type of human being they imagine differs markedly. As I have argued in my work with Sandra Walklate (Walklate and Mythen, 2010), the theoretical perspectives on risk propose an ideal type of social actor with variegated preoccupations and proclivities. The risk society thesis assumes a politically activated citizen, the culture of fear a neurotic citizen and the governmentality thesis a prudential citizen. These contrasting types of citizen represent the competing views of their advocates about the capacity of human beings to express agency and autonomy in the modern world. The disciplined prudential citizen hailed by Foucauldians is one who dutifully takes on the assorted tasks of self-management demanded by the structures of the Western capitalist system. Such a citizen is able to assume responsibility for their health, educational trajectory, career and finances. Such micro activity is actively encouraged by the State as it reduces both the span of direct governance and the financial costs of managing populations. As Cruikshank (1993: 327) reasons, the prudential citizen is rendered governable by 'quietly placing themselves in the hands of society and by mobilizing themselves in society's interest'. This type of citizen is the thoughtful and careful citizen who assesses hazards and subjects their life to the strictures of cost/benefit analysis. As Kemshall (2006: 65) puts it: 'prudentialism requires the citizen to adopt a calculating attitude towards most if not all of his/her decisions, whether these be decisions over healthy eating options or the installation of burglar alarms.'

In the fluctuating context of modernity, making disciplined decisions in all facets of live becomes a systemic requirement for the upwardly mobile. Although the prudential citizen possesses agency in terms of life choices, the parameters of these decisions are set by disciplinary discourses and the regulatory practices of State and market.

In contrast to the rational and calculating approach of the prudential citizen envisaged by followers of Foucault, the culture of fear approach recounts a more troubled subject who is less the active risk-manager and more an anxious receptacle of risk. It is a decidedly neurotic citizen plagued by worry that inhabits Furedi's culture of fear. This is the citizen who is overwhelmed by the relentlessness bombardment of information, images and warnings about the dangerous aspects of modern existence. The neurotic citizen cannot escape the decisions that the prudential citizen is asked to make, but does so with trepidation. As Isin (2004: 223) describes it, the neurotic citizen, 'is incited to make social and cultural investments to eliminate various dangers by calibrating its conduct on the basis of its anxieties and insecurities rather than rationalities'. Thus, as Isin suggests, the neurotic citizen can effectively be seen as a malfunctioning prudential citizen, defined as irrational and unable to manage the trials and tribulations of everyday life. Overwhelmed by the pressures and tensions exacted on the individual, the neurotic citizen is left in a constant state of apprehension, fretful about her or his health, safety and security. The neurotic self imagined in the work of Furedi and Isin is effectively wrapped up in the fruitless search for biographical solutions to systemic problems. Rather than perceiving personal troubles as the result of structural deficiencies, the individual instead turns inward. This neurotic citizen stands in sharp contrast to the politically charged individual imagined in the risk society thesis. Far from being pulverized by risk, Beck's preferred citizen is one who is catalysed by global problems and looks outwards to challenge the system and resolve structural problems. As the continual 'social explosion' of risks in the mass media raises public awareness, the man-ufactured 'bads' of the risk society act as a trigger for political action. Beck is convinced that a global public sphere populated by citizens with a cosmopolitan outlook is possi-ble. The 'cosmopolitan moment' (Beck, 2009: 97) brought about by an environmental crisis that transcends nation state policies and discourses can serve to activate agency and re-energize individuals long disenchanted by party politics. Of course, what is over-played here is the capacity of individuals to politically mobilize and what is understated is our tendency to close down anxieties that we feel may be beyond our ambit of control or simply too 'big' to contemplate. Insofar as the preoccupations of the risk society loom large for Beck, in the ebb and flow of life people become adept at emotionally 'bracketing off' risks which they would rather not think about (Parkhill et al., 2012).

Each of the ideal types of citizen captured in competing perspectives on risk captures something of some people some of the time. Yet the rigidity with which citizens are imagined in each of these perspectives raises to the fore the issue of representation. The hailing of the *l'homme moyen* by the pioneering Belgian statistician Adolphe Quételet (1835) is instructive in this regard. In grappling with the idea of the average man – under-stood as possessing mean values of measured variables – Quételet realized that human beings were far more complex than statistical formula would allow. His acknowledge-ment that that *l'homme moyen* in one culture and location would be quite different from that in another picks out a thorn that sticks deep in the side of macro theories of risk. As ideal type constructs, the neurotic, prudential and active citizen do not exist in the real world where mutability, inconsistency and capriciousness mark attitudes, values and behaviours towards risk. Returning to the empirical holes alluded to earlier, the outstanding task is to interrogate and flesh out these constructs in order to develop a more nuanced understanding of how different people approach and understand differ-ent risks at different times, under different conditions. The mapping of such risk-scapes is undoubtedly a colossal task, but it may well be one which is worth pursuing in the long run.

Who speaks about risk? Danger, power and geopolitics

Having cogitated on the agential gaps that exist in theoretical accounts of risk, I now wish to flag up a second shortcoming around the role of power and power relations in shaping communication about risks, patterns of risk distribution and modes of risk governance. Through the course of the book I have sought to stress that – despite bold claims made within the natural sciences regarding objective 'scientific' assessment processes – risks are often difficult to quantify. Techniques of data analysis and risk assessment are themselves partial and constructed rather than neutral and objective. The analogy used by the first Director of the United States Environmental Protection Agency William Ruckelshaus (1984: 157) is enlightening in this regard: 'we should remember that risk assessment data can be likened to the captured spy: If you torture it long enough, it will tell you anything you want to know'. As Ruckelshaus indicates, where risk anal-ysis is concerned, neutrality is impossible to achieve and political, moral and cultural values inevitably influence evaluative frameworks. As we saw in Chapter 6, discourses of risk – and the methods of calibration they yield – are saturated with power and engender particular ways of seeing humans, objects and the wider environment. As Heyman and Henriksen (1998) astutely observe, risk is not so much a tangible property of the real world as a 'simplifying heuristic'. Such reflections notwithstanding, important debates have been opened up by scholars that have used risk as an anchor, specifically those around environmental despoliation (Strydom, 2002), shifting modes of social control (Garland, 2001), new methods of surveillance and intelligence gathering (Amoore, 2011; McCulloch and Pickering, 2009) and the changing nature of security (Bajc and de Lint, 2011; Zedner, 2009). Yet there is a curious reluctance among risk scholars to engage with – less still interrupt – a range of harmful activities and processes. Indeed, in typically reflexive mode, Beck (2009: 50) himself confronts the issue of relative risk:

> Wouldn't an external observer of European societies be forced to conclude that the risks we are getting worked up about are exclusively luxury risks? After all, our part of the world seems a lot safer than the war-torn regions of Africa and the Middle East, for example, or Afghanistan and Iraq.

Perhaps the time has come then for scholars to exhibit bravery in their thinking and to break free from the somewhat worn patterns of thinking that have become consolidated in the two branches of risk research. Opening up to new conceptual approaches and fresh currents may light some new pathways down which to travel. Speaking about England, Dorling (2006: 28) argues that a research agenda concerned with social harm, rather than crime or risk might lead to a much needed reorientation of priorities in academia: 'in the past 75 years, millions of short lives were begun and ended in this country. Almost none of these deaths were the result of a crime as conventionally understood, but many if not most were preventable and were largely the product of social harm'. Arguing for a shift in focus away from risk and towards harm, Dorling proposes a renewed focus on major social problems such as mass unemployment, intergenerational poverty and drug and alcohol abuse. Branching out from the national to the global, the environmental crimes of multinational corporations, the land-grab taking place in parts of Africa, genocide, fratricide, dire problems of poverty and famine exacerbated by corrupt regimes, major human rights abuses and various forms of unjust and illegal detention are obvious areas where the seriousness of the social crisis is not matched by comprehensive programmes of research nor academic attention. These palpably pressing problems appear as elephants in the room that must surely be seen, but are considered too unwieldy or too difficult to broach within established disciplinary boundaries. When using risk as a tool of analysis or a form of classification, there is a need to appreciate that we are making a selective choice about our trope that has consequences which extend beyond the priorities and conventions of the academy. I am reminded here of the American Cartoonist Jules Feiffer's remarks regarding the impacts of labelling on the social conditions of those who are economically excluded from society:

> I used to think I was poor. Then they told me I wasn't poor, I was needy. Then they told me it was self-defeating to think of myself as needy, I was deprived. Then they told me deprived was a bad image, I was underprivileged. Then they told me

> underprivileged was overused, I was disadvantaged. I still don't have a dime. But I sure have a great vocabulary.
>
> (Feiffer, 1929, cited in Andrews, 1987: 205)

Feiffer's ironic musings bring to the surface a very serious point about the relationship between language, categorization and inequality. The application of risk as a social label to define groups and to describe cultural experiences necessarily generates a play of power. Scholars, researchers, tutors and students are not outside of – but are active parties in – the production of knowledge. With this in mind, it is no coincidence that the discourse of risk has been popularized in Western universities and colleges across the United Kingdom, in Germany, America, Australia and Canada. Such a turn to risk has produced a somewhat tendentious and decidedly Westocentric focus. This rather begs the question of how different the social sciences might look and feel if writers and researchers in Africa, Asia and South America were afforded an equal platform to speak about world affairs in Anglophone books, websites and journals (see Body-Gendrot, 2011). Doubtless, the field of risk research would require some fairly serious structural revision and dire global problems such as starvation, malnutrition and disease may appear somewhat higher up the agenda. Although the unexpected spectacle of 9/11 produced seismic geopolitical reverberations, such events are, to borrow from Taleb (2007), Black Swans. The happenings of 9/11 were difficult to predict, exceptional in nature and have had major impacts on public attitudes, State policy and security practices. Yet the ways in which the State chooses to regulate in the aftermath of Black Swan events such as 9/11 is connected to culture, history, power and geopolitical priorities. As Wilkinson (2009: 96) notes, the fact that more people die every day from diarrhoea than were killed in 9/11 serves as 'a graphic and worthwhile reminder that the scale of discussions about many Western "catastrophes" still pale in comparison with daily conditions in less economically developed parts of the world'.

While the subject of risk has acted as a constructive intersection point which has encouraged dialogue between academics working in different disciplines, the turn to risk is a movement that should be scrutinized rather than passively accepted (see Mythen, 2008). It is no coincidence that an enhanced emphasis on risk within the social sciences has occurred at the same time as issues of poverty, class, ethnicity and gender appear to have dropped down the pecking order. This is troubling, given that – even in the arguably misnamed 'advanced democracies' – vast inequalities endure (see Wilkinson and Pickett, 2009). The fallout from the global financial crisis – in large part generated by the avarice of individuals in the West – has caused food costs to spiral and plunged millions of people into hunger. While dominant political discourses surrounding the 'global' financial crisis have couched the problem as general and collective – witness the British Conservative Party's mantra: 'we are all in this together' – as we have seen, the effects of the economic downturn are scattered and partial. While political elites demand to be heard, but refuse to listen, the famished have no voice. As Robert Zoellick the former president of the World Bank observes: 'the credit crunch has created a human crisis in many of the poorest countries. The number of malnourished people is expected to rise by 44 million to 967 million as a result of high food prices' (cited in Stewart and Elliott, 2008). Grumbling over supper about the price of tinned tomatoes these days is a world away from the dire food shortages affecting countries such as Zimbabwe where people are reduced to scrabbling for edible roots in the ground in order to stay alive. The Governments of affluent nations have been decidedly slow to broach the problem in the developing world and the aid that has been provided has barely scratched the surface of the problem. Clearly the trickle-down model of capitalism whereby the wealth at the top percolates down to those at the bottom is nothing but a myth (see Bauman, 2013). The price of staple foods such as corn meal, sugar and rice has continued to rise and widespread public protests – dubbed by the media as 'food riots' – have occurred in many countries, including Haiti, Cameroon, Somalia, Bangladesh, Mozambique, Kenya and India. If we take a detailed look at issues such as the global financial crisis in the round – factoring in the experience of the majority – we may well end up posing a very different set of questions about risk, security and welfare. As Boaventura de Sousa Santos (2007) observes, 'hegemonic epistemologies' in the social sciences act to define and determine what counts as valid knowledge. The sets of knowledge that academics produce do not reside in a vacuum and produce not only dialogue but also reconfigured activities and practices in the public realm (see Cohen, 2010). The Austrian social theorist Alfred Schütz (1962) argues that items only become facts through the selective choices of human actors. Clearly, academics have both a vested interest and have a weighty responsibility in the process of knowledge production. The ideas we (re)produce are, in Schutz's (1962: 2) terms, 'world-making'. We do not have to stretch this point too far to see that risk has become a taken for granted way of seeing the world, generating bodies of knowledge that categorize and shape not just threatening incidents and responses to them but also a spectrum of social experiences. It is with some vindication that Bourdieu and Wacquant (1992: 228) warn of the dangers of fetishizing concepts: 'of theory born of the propensity to study theoretical instruments . . . in themselves and for themselves, rather than to put them in motion and make them *work*'. With this caveat in mind, opening our ears to a plurivocal range of discourses drawn from a wider global geographic would seem to be a simple but meaningful step forward for risk research. In terms of debates in the Anglophone countries, as the turn to risk has gained momentum, traditional modes of analysis such as class, power and gender have regrettably receded.

Despite the apparent eagerness with which academics have embraced risk, questions remain about the analytical reach of risk and its exploratory power. What is concerning is that the rapid ascent of risk has been accompanied by a relative decline in the use of less fashionable analytical concepts. Further, Tombs and Whyte (2006) note that the drift towards risk has segued with the prevailing neo-liberal political agenda which conceals forms of exploitation and glosses over fundamental inequalities. Sharing such sentiments, I would agree that greater attention needs to be directed to issues that are obscured or displaced when we use the language of risk. While the most ardent riskophiles have merrily considered there paean to be a panacea, the desire to utilize and apply risk as a catch-all concept has led to vital societal issues – about which theories of risk may ultimately have relatively little to say – being marginalized. Thus, the current vogue for risk in the social sciences has arguably nudged out valuable modes of analysis that seek to reveal the operation of power relations, the securing of social reproduction and the consistent generation of forms of stratification and inequality. As Coleman and McCahill (2011: 181) point out, in the context of surveillance and crime control, 'powerful groups, and their proximity to taken-for-granted assumptions concerning the priorities relating to political and economic interests and their greater command of resources and information, have greater affective power over the meaning and deployment of terms like public safety and risk'. At a time of austerity when the State is seeking to drastically reduce expenditure on social welfare, the criminalization of the poor becomes more pronounced and risk attribution is operationalized with renewed vigour (see Wacquant, 2009).

(Mis)applying risk: Avoiding catachresis

Theoretical advances in the field of risk research have undoubtedly produced some note-worthy insights and generated important debates about human security and the nature of social change. However, as I have argued above there are reasons to be cautious when deploying risk as a unit of analysis. In my view, the overuse of risk as an analytical device has, in some quarters resulted in a process of *catachresis* (see Campbell, 2011). In addition to individualizing risk and sequestrating it from context, the turn to risk has been marked by cases of misuse in both academic and policy-making arenas. In some cases the concept of risk has been applied in and to situations where it is not germane or useful. Taking this issue up O'Malley (2006: 49) observes that 'crime prevention has succeeded in marrying risk with a more traditional social and behavioural form of criminology by translating the old causes of crime into risk factors'. In this way a multitude of activities – such as alcohol and substance abuse, parental violence and gang involvement – all become redefined as free-floating risks which are disconnected from context or structure. Focussing on the gendered nature of risk-based policies, Hannah-Moffatt (2005; 2006) points to the way in which the underlying assumptions implicit in risk assessments have been transformed into similarly unacknowledged 'needs assessments' for females 'at risk' of offending. Davidson and Chesney-Lind (2009) add that such transformations may unwittingly result in a simultaneous over-classification and under-classification of women at risk. In both examples, risk has replaced cause and/or need and this may serve to shroud social experience. Thus, the danger with over-applying risk is that what may be only one part of picture is presented as the whole. Further, at a time in which there is great pressure on academics to 'capture' research funding, the perils of dancing to a risk agenda defined by the State, private funders and security industries is palpable. In an age of austerity, independent and critical social science needs to be promoted if we are not to fall into the trap of performing perfunctory paid social research and perpetuating a risk industry that sometimes appears curiously disconnected from the travails of people in the real world. The warning bell sounded by Wright-Mills (1959: 180) over half a century ago remains just as resonant today:

> The individual social scientist tends to become involved in those many trends of modern society that make the individual a part of a functionally rational bureaucracy, and to sink into his [*sic*] specialized slot in such a way as not to be explicitly concerned with the structure of post-modern society . . . the role of

reason in human affairs tends to become merely a refinement of techniques for administrative and manipulative uses.

With Wright-Mills's admonition still reverberating, it is important to be chary of the ways in which risk can be politically harnessed as a tool for governance. As Wilkinson asserts (2009: 92), the identification and labelling of risks by social institutions is an ideological exercise that invariably brings with it attempts to shape opinions and behaviour.

Conclusion

In this chapter I have taken the liberty of assuming a panoramic view in order to express some reservations about the advance of risk in academic and policy arenas. Our discussion has been oriented to three major problems that need to be considered when the currency of risk is prioritized. First, I have pointed to the partial view of human agency reproduced in theoretical accounts of risk. Second, I have voiced concerns about the limited visibility of power in accounts of social relations and processes which are primarily defined in terms of risk. To this end, I have suggested that the lionization of risk may have the effect of reducing the use of socially relevant analytical prisms such as class, power and violence. Third, I have discussed the problem of catachresis through which risk has been overstretched and in some cases misapplied. Taken as an ensemble, these shortcomings amount to more than the sum of their parts and churn up uncomfortable questions about how we as social scientists represent the world and the lived experience of others.

To return to a theoretical plain, in many respects the extant perspectives we have considered here may well possess descriptive power in accounting for the production of risk in contemporary society, but have weaker purchase in answering the underlying questions of whether, when, how and why regulation of risk occurs. Travelling against the turn to risk, a case can be made for a renewed focus on classical concepts and a return to more traditional modes of analysis within the social sciences. The link between poverty, social deprivation and crime is well established, yet we live in a world in which huge inequalities remain. In the formally 'affluent, advanced' United Kingdom, national surveys reveal not so much gaping divides in wealth and income between the *nonpareil* and *les autres* but veritable canyons (see Daffin, 2009). There is a clear link between health risks generated by lifestyles and social class, with people in the most economically affluent groups in the United Kingdom living on average seven years longer than those in lower income categories (see Buck and Frosini, 2013). As Mike Davis (1990) observed in his study of Los Angeles, people are reclining on the beaches while others are left to beg in the streets. In conditions in which luxury and poverty exist cheek by jowl, it is not difficult to see why those at the bottom of the economic pile may be attracted to committing crime, whether for financial gain, status uplift or simply to release some of the frustrations generated by an otherwise monotonous existence. As they have historically been utilized, institutional technologies of risk – policies, programmes, legislation, surveillance – have been directed as much *at* as *for* marginalized groups. In the context of crime control risk governance functions more as a device to label and police classes determined as dangerous than a tool for tackling the conditions of poverty in which criminality flourishes. As critical criminologists have argued, such labelling not only attaches negative stereotypes, it simultaneously renders certain crimes associated with the middle and upper classes more actionable and permissible, less heavily policed and less likely to attract punitive sentencing (see Coleman and McCahill, 2011; Hillyard, 2009; Tombs and Whyte, 2007).

Conclusion

The time has come to reflect on the paths that have been trodden, the cul-de-sacs ventured into and the emergent horizons that are yet to be explored. In drawing the book – but certainly not the argument – to a close, I want to offer some final reflections on the place of risk in the social sciences and to suggest some potentially rich seams of future inquiry. It has been my primary intention to provide a critical account of the emergence and consolidation of 'risk' in the modern world. This account has sought to engage with contemporary processes and trends and to examine the extent to which perspectives on risk provide constructive tools for scrutinizing society. I hope firstly to have erected some signposts to allow smoother navigation through the maze of approaches on risk in the social sciences. Second, it has been my intention to encourage further reflection on the difficulties and dilemmas that arise when human experiences and social processes are viewed through the lens of risk. I have argued that the reification of risk has created a range of problems, including a lack of empirical engagement with the human experience of 'risk', a tendency to use the concept too liberally and in areas in which it is not apposite, the underplaying of the positive dimensions of risk-taking and a tendency to overlook the limits to risk as both a unit idea and a policy tool. Nevertheless, in line with the open critical approach I have championed, rather than calling for the banishment of risk in the social sciences, I would instead advocate greater understanding of its operation in pre-charged power bound spaces. Without diminishing the possibility of human agency, the situations and contexts in which risks emerge are dynamic but exist a priori. As such, in encountering – and, indeed, contesting risk – we are situated in what Althusser (1970) fittingly described as the 'always-already': a realm in which established ideologies and hegemonic discourses are rooted. Moving from a largely theoretical plain to matters of public policy and intervention, I have posited that – partly as a product of the uncritical reproduction of 'risk' as a political discourse – a disquieting institutional preference for pre-emptive intervention has taken hold in certain areas of crime, welfare and security management. It is only by laying bare cases of manipulation that we can identify misuses of risk and consider the traps that are set when risk takes centre stage in academic, media and political discourse. This is in no way to assume the position of Jeremiah, proclaiming with a glum full stop that risk functions as ideological screen that conceals relations of domination and subordination. Sometimes it does. Sometimes it doesn't. Hence there is a need to be receptive to what O'Malley (2008) has called the 'uncertain promise' of risk. We must remember that there have been notable interventions and deployments with risk that have produced positive social outcomes. Few would argue that interventions such as cervical cancer screening, client-centric drug rehabilitation or sex education programmes to prevent the spread of HIV have been socially damaging. It is necessary then to maintain distance from a reductive position that seeks to dismiss the apparatus of risk – both theoretical and operational – and to appreciate some of the potentialities of risk. As I hope to have elucidated, an open critical approach permits the identification of progressive risk-based interventions but also enables critique of more dubious deployments of risk. To demonstrate the possibilities of such an approach, let us revisit the theoretical perspectives on risk with which we began.

Theoretical perspectives: Promises fulfilled or risky seductions?

The allure of risk theory in the social sciences can be explained in many ways, some of which are material and context specific, and others which are ideational. Following on from searching questions being asked in the late 1980s about whether Marxist theories of class were able to grapple with the changing nature and structure of contemporary society, the concept of risk appeared relatively attuned to the dynamics of the globalizing world and its attendant uncertainties and oscillations. As the subjects to which it has been applied in this book attest, risk has an inherent malleability, and it also taps into the prevailing anxieties of a harm-averse society. The attraction of totalizing theories of risk is that they both provide an all-embracing narrative of the present while promising a glimpse into the future that is not yet upon us. The worldview minted by Beck for instance both describes the contemporary impacts of environmental risks and acts as a catch-cry for upcoming dangers. In his words: 'the dynamics of risk society are beyond status and class because global threats ultimately affect everybody, even those responsible for them' (Beck, 2009: 22). The idea that trans-boundary risks equalize harm and democratize vulnerability has appealed to diverse audiences, from far left academics to right inclined neo-liberal governments. At a surface level, there are good grounds to endorse the idea that we inhabit a 'risk society'. In modern life, the trapdoors of risk do seem to be permanently underfoot. The range of humanly generated hazards that exist in the contemporary world, coupled to our cultural and psychological preoccupation with future threats, seems to indicate that risk is a strong emblem of the epoch. Yet if we go beyond the 'risk society' as a moniker and relate it to the specific tenets of the risk society perspective – for instance, those regarding the 'global' and 'democratic' nature of threats – some unconcealable blemishes appear. Although we are all endangered and all at threat in the event of the 'worst imaginable accidents' that haunt the keepers of the Doomsday Clock, the weight of social research indicates that layering of risk in the present is uneven and unequal. Problems arise when, instead of engaging in the process of empirical investigation across the piece, a stock set of 'icons of destruction' are taken as indicative of the risk-producing tendencies of contemporary Western cultures (Mythen, 2004: 181). Yet constructing a general argument about the trajectory of society on the basis of exceptional examples is a questionable strategy. Sociological research has shown that in many areas of life, from health and housing to employment and education, exposure to risk is structured and patterned rather than individualized and random.

Similarly, criminological research indicates that propensity to commit crime, probability of being a victim and punishment and sentencing tariffs are all influenced by underlying socio-economic factors. Thus, risk is far from a democratic leveller in either causation or effect. Traditional determinants of goods stratification – of class, gender, ethnicity, age and geography – remain primary indicators of life chances and relative propensity to be a perpetrator and/or victim of crime. While we are all theoretically equal in the event of a worst imaginable accident, in the realm of criminal victimization – as in wider society – some remain more equal than others (see Moss, 2011). We can also question whether Beck's cosmopolitan optimism about the transformative capacity of risk is well founded. Rather than being an aide of the powerful, as both Foucault and Furedi intimate, Beck conceives risk as 'an unreliable ally or even a potential antagonist, as a hostile force confronting the power both of the nation-state and of global capital' (Beck, 2009: 79). There is no doubt that risk conflicts can and do de-stabilize power interests, yet the extent to which risks can be harnessed via (sub)political activity to transformative ends remains a moot point.

Sharing some of the concerns of the risk society thesis, the culture of fear perspective is also pitched at a somewhat general level and is rather short on empirical grist. Although Furedi's description of a cementation of a generalized culture of fear is example rich, more detailed, comparative empirical evidence is required to determine the extent and the effects of fear and anxiety across populations and regions. As Douglas's grid-group model proposes, different personalities and worldviews will lead to the production of heterogeneous perceptions of risk. While Douglas's emphasis on culture and meaning making adds depth and geographical diversity to our understanding of how risks are interpreted and what their function is for different groups and peoples, her typology of cultural types is very broad. Typologies can give us a rudimentary view of social matters, but they are ill equipped to grasp the nuances of individual behaviour. Human dynamics and the minutiae of social action also evades the governmentality thesis. Indeed, one of the most common criticisms levelled at Foucault's micro-physical work is that it misses the sentient, reflective actions of human actors and treats individuals as tabula rasa, passively inscribed by disciplinary discourses. The capacity to resist discourses and to dispute dominant ideologies of risk is under emphasized in work that has followed the Foucauldian tradition. This tendency to gloss over human feelings and actions is not only common to foundational theories of risk, it has also emerged in later conceptual incarnations of risk inspired by Beck and Foucault. For example, Feeley and Simon's 'new penology' – which draws on elements of both risk society and governmentality perspectives – charts a managerial process through which risk becomes central in the identification and monitoring of specific social groups. In the vision of proponents of the new penology, risk is one aspect of a broader sweep away from rehabilitation and transformation of the offender towards containment. Thus, although the 'new penology' has implications for the individual – from the professional pressures of risk assessment for criminal justice practitioners to the uneasy experience of being monitored for suspect populations – for Feeley and Simon (1992), these factors are an outcome of the process rather than a key focus. Aside from whether a 'new penology' has gained a foothold, it is the ways in which this changes the everyday life experiences of victims, offenders and criminal justice professionals that remain unexcavated. Along with Feeley and Simon (1992), Garland's culture of control is similarly attuned to the structural transformations characteristic of the risk society and the way in which changing social conditions engender a 'process of adaption' (Garland, 2001: 7). Despite being cognizant of its limits, Garland's theory is more consentient with the governmentality tradition in its emphasis on the quest for control through a mix of punitive sanctions, incitement and responsibilization. For Garland, the implications of the proliferating culture of control for the individual are manifold, ranging from populist responses to criminality and a renewed emphasis on the victim to the self-management of crime risks. Yet along with Feeley and Simon, Garland is concerned chiefly with conditions rather than subjects. Concrete evidence of the impacts of the burgeoning 'crime complex' on individuals and discrete groups remains very much on the margins rather than at the core, leaving the argument rather depopulated. Despite these lacuna, followers of Foucault are certainly correct in flagging the ascent of risk governance and the shifting locus of responsibility for risk management from the State to citizens. One can see the Foucauldian penumbra of responsibilization in the policy trend of 'nudging', whereby citizens are encouraged towards 'better choices' about health, finance and welfare (see Thaler and Sunstein, 2008). Under Tony Blair health promotion campaigns in Britain to limit risky behaviour such as smoking, alcohol consumption and drug taking appear to have impacted on the more affluent whose net addictions may have been tempered, but not the poor (see Buck and Frosini, 2013). Comprehending the stresses and strains of the immediate life-world for people living on low incomes reveals often entirely understandable 'risk-taking' in relation to particular lifestyle choices. As a respondent in Robinson and Holdsworth's (2013: 47) study of attitudes towards smoking responded when asked about her feelings about anti-smoking campaigns: 'they don't live in my house every day'.

In the United Kingdom the Behavioural Insights Team (BIT) set up by the current Prime Minister, David Cameron, is very much the fulcrum of policies designed to encourage people towards certain choices by compliance rather than direct coercion. Commonly referred to as the 'nudge unit', the BIT has produced a string of policies designed to 'incentivize' individuals in disparate areas including diet, tax returns, energy efficiency and consumer debt. If effective the economic benefits of 'nudging' for the State are considerable. On inception those invited as part of the BIT were tasked with achieving a tenfold return on the costs of their salaries. Up to press this return has been achieved and the present interventions made by the BIT are expected to save the Government £300 million over the next five years (see Chater, 2013: 38). For modern governmentality thinkers, risk assessment and risk management are part and parcel of a broadening of systems of classification and control that seek to bolster neo-liberal governance and promote the expansion of market capitalism. Certainly risk governance is one form of activity that has been rolled out in response to the legitimacy crisis that has settled deep in Western nation states in a period of prolonged economic crisis. Yet we should be aware that the turn to risk in policy making and regulation is cross-culturally variable (see Rothstein, 2003; Rothstein et al., 2006). In as much as the British Government has advanced risk governance as an explicit strategy for managing the health and security of the population, social policy in countries with more corporatist traditions such as Holland and France has been less pronounced. Establishing regulatory limits and agreeing standards on risk are exercises which look different across space and place and are linked to moral, political and religious views. Returning to the key theoretical frames, each offers us a way into understanding risk, but we should be mindful that the direction of travel is quite distinct.

I have argued here that the plasticity of risk as a concept may be a strength, but it is simultaneously a weakness. In a world in which risk potentially explains everything then somehow it also explains nothing. Thus, it is sensible to keep a handle on some of the limits to risk theory. While the field of research has become somewhat tribal with thinkers keen to nail their flags to particular masts, given the problems that bedevil theories of risk it is perhaps sagacious to remain agnostic. No single theory of risk is capable of providing a flawless entrée into the social and cultural world. As such, the perspectives on risk we have unpacked do not provide a panoramic vista, but they do offer us portals through which we can peek in on the social world. The risk society thesis has both political prescience and environmental clout, yet the historical narrative is too neat and universalizing. Further, Beck's view of the threats which are the most important to resolve to prevent societal meltdown are not absolute. Rather than environmental, nuclear and terrorist threats, one could make an equally compelling case that the most pressing issues facing us today are global poverty, warfare and human rights abuses (see Grayling, 2007: 65). In light of the advancement of grand theories of risk, the issue of how they actually reflect and/or (dis)articulate with the experiences, needs and outlooks of people can become oblique. As suggested in Chapter 7, one of the generic shortcomings of theories of risk has been their tendency to treat specific features of Western modernity as globally apparent. Spectacular one-off risk incidents – such as the terrorist attacks in New York, Madrid and London – are eminently more reportable than ongoing global problems of grinding poverty and inequality (Anderson, 2006; Boyne, 2003: 33). Indeed, it is quite possible that imbalanced media coverage has in part contributed towards the skewing of public concerns, with extensive reporting of new terrorism, MRSA and Avian Flu catapulting risk forward as a politically hot issue (see Furedi, 2002; Ungar, 2001). The tendency in the academic literature to focus on singular risk incidents rather than pernicious creeping processes that cause fatal harm is a hindrance. As Rose (2000: 65) argues, it is likely that an unstinting focus on one-off risk incidents has served to cloud the importance and persistence of endemic and systemic inequalities. For the poor in continents such as Africa, Asia and South America, prioritizing the political management of technological risks may smack of decadence. Beyond the West, dangers to public health are both more rudimentary and more pressing than those illuminated in the risk society thesis. In this sense, foundational theories of risk devote insufficient attention to the cultural geography of risk. There is perhaps something perverse about the post-scarcity politics of risk when positioned against the backdrop of persistent and marked global inequalities. In many regions, the disenfranchised have little option but to continue to exhaust natural resources and literally swallow the environmental consequences. The global political failure to meet fundamental human needs serves as a sharp reminder to those absorbed with the possibilities of a high-tech risky future. Recent statistics generated by the United Nations (2012) in a detailed report on hunger security are alarming. A staggering 870 million people in the world presently suffer from chronic hunger and malnutrition, the vast majority of this number – some 852 million – living in developing countries. Translated across the world's population this figure means that more than one person in eight is unable to consume enough food each day to be sufficiently nourished to ward off ill-health. Childhood malnutrition remains a cause of death for more than 2.5 million children every year. It is a consideration of the global context in the round that perhaps leads Bauman (2012: 27) to warn of the perils of becoming oblivious to major problems in the social world. In all of this we need to contest the present primacy of narrowly defined crime and security concerns, when considered against the struggle to survive. Within the social sciences more broadly, the rise of risk has come at a time of relative hush about issues of poverty, pain and suffering. What is missing, it seems, is a human frame to understand and evaluate the consequences of risk. The concept of risk may be useful as is an abstract technology of description, but it fails to properly attend to the consequences of suffering – what we might call the lived experience of harm (see Cohen, 2001).

While I have expressed my reservations about the unfettered application of risk, the baby must not be thrown out with the bath water. Using the concept of risk and its analytical tools sensibly, sensitively and, crucially, in situations in which it is socially relevant can further our understanding of human behaviour, the environment we live in and our rotating social worlds. Giddens's (1984) 'double hermeneutic' serves as a useful compass here. As social actors make sense of their own actions and life-worlds, social scientists must interpret people's interpretations of their own circumstances. This is a complex task and we must be steered by the sense-making of actors, rather than the lure of parading with the academic fashionistas. The time has come then to take some meaningful strides towards exploring alternate or hybridous interpretive frameworks that are capable of grasping prescient social problems and issues. It may well be that these frameworks develop in a synergistic manner and explore the combined operations of, say, class, risk and power or gender, risk and suffering. Taking a view across a landscape that is truly global, we can see that the world remains blighted by vast inequalities, pain, disease and human rights abuses. It is the task of critical social scientists to try to lay bare the nature and the causes of these different forms of human harm and to propose possible solutions that can contribute to a more just and equal society. While some may find this a reductionist blueprint for scholarly activity, prevalent trends within the academy may not fully articulate with either the need to connect with social problems in a tangible way or the attention to detail involved in providing a dependable account of the lives of others. The grand theories that we create and labour to establish should – if they are to speak about and for society – resemble what life is like for most of the people, most of the time. Amidst an instrumental academic agenda driven by research assessment exercises, grant capture, demonstrating impact and student satisfaction surveys, there is an acute danger that we lose sight of the broader social responsibility we have. Kelly and Burrows (2012) refer to the pervasive audit culture which has seeped into the academy and, in particular, the process of 'performative metricization', as exemplified by journal raking systems, starred output systems and the publication of league tables. Without doubt, some career driven academics are acutely mindful that their findings do not, as Ericson (1996: 19) puts it: 'antagonise potential institutional audiences and sponsors'. At a time when major conflicts and crises bespeckle the globe, the social sciences are perhaps at something of a crossroads moment when important decisions have to be made individually and collectively about what it is that we do, and, moreover, what it is that we ought to be doing. As debates regarding the future of 'pubic sociology' provoked by Burawoy (2005) endures – followed up latterly in the context of Criminology by

Loader and Sparks (2010) – the time has arrived for some honest reflection and recognition of omissions and lapses. Yet it is also a time to discuss re-organized priorities and to recast understandings of the social. In 2007 the panel assembled to oversee the establishment of standards in teaching and learning in Criminology warned of the need to 'guard against attempts to foreclose ... dialogue with the premature creation of theoretical or methodological protocols favouring particular sub-discipline fields, whether endorsed by State officials, by the mass media or by fashions of academic thought' (QAA, 2007). Echoing these sentiments, it is critical that social science disciplines value and defend academic freedom. The task is to retain social relevance, but also to be bold enough to be reflexive, self-critical and to resist dominant political agendas. With the demand from Government that academics demonstrate real world 'impact', there is a need to avoid the temptation of responding to a preset research agenda and reducing complex and contested phenomena into simple digestible missives designed to 'inform' policy. To this end, Foucault's endeavour to make windows where there were once walls would seem to sum up well both the intellectual and the material challenge for social science academics.

In the course of the book I have asked what the turn to risk in the social sciences embraces and what it may exclude. I have identified some of the problems that emerge out of the popularization of risk and raised uncomfortable questions about the capacity of risk to adequately reflect and/or explain contemporary social problems. In adopting an open critical position regarding the value of risk, I would want to acknowledge that the mapping out of grand narratives – and their adjustment to capture specific processes or moments – has historically been a productive means of opening up fresh ways of thinking about the world. The offering up of risk perspectives by key thinkers has generated a dialogic space for discussion about how we perceive and characterize the world that we live in. While these discussions trundle on, my concern is that rather than treating theories of risk as imperfect but potentially useful discussion tools, there has been a perceptible degree of conflation between the ideational and the experiential, that is between risk as a narrative and risk as it is beds into and filters through lived social practices. In short, there has been a presumption in weaker narrative versions that risk theory *reflects* reality, and in stronger versions that it actually *is* reality. Work in the latter category ignores the dilemma at the nub of Giddens's double hermeneutic and brings to mind the apocryphal tale of the two Ming dynasty philosopher's conversing while staring into a pond in the Summer palace in Beijing. The first cheerfully declares that the fish looked happy, to which the second responds: 'How could you know? You're not a fish.' Whereupon the first replies, 'And you are not me, so how do you know I don't know?' (Lewis, 2008: 107). In speaking for others, it is vital that social theories do not simply assume perception, reflection or behaviour and that knowledge voids are admitted rather than papered over. Macro perspectives are always wont to trace the shape of society in a loose style and with broad brushstrokes. Nevertheless, to ensure that such theories have relevance in the real world, there is a need to measure up the bigger pictures theory produces with the smaller, fine-grain pictures of the individual that empirical inquiries allow. In putting one next to the other, we can sincerely advance theory for its ability to capture the diversity of human experience rather than because it is considered *de rigueur* to do so. In the field of risk theory, the reification of the subject matter and the tendency towards catachresis has detracted from the task of situating human experience within the appropriate economic, cultural and political context. Theoretically and empirically social sciences disciplines are equipped with the methodological techniques and the capability to rigorously scrutinize the uses and the abuses of risk. Yet many working in Sociology and Criminology have been somewhat parochial and selective in their grasp and utilization of risk. If we were to ask a cross-section of people to make a list of the most pressing risks in society – defined as those that potentially lead to death, serious injury and/or psychological trauma – my suspicion is that the list may not correlate very well with the somewhat narrow focus of risk research in general and risk analysis in particular. In many senses, the problem then is not about what risk captures, but more about what it obscures.

As Cluey (2012: 205) points out, we need to keep a trained eye on not only the subjects, concepts and objects that readily present themselves for social scientists to study, but also those remain concealed or untapped. The example given by the late Howard Becker was the tendency to study criminality by researching convicted felons rather than those that manage – for various reasons – to evade imprisonment. As far as 'risk' is concerned, it is likely that its ubiquity and applicability at least partly explains its popularity, rather than any inherent rise in the day-to-day dangerousness of everyday life. Thus, the place at which we situate our 'observation post' in Becker's terms (1986: 143) will not only shape our view but also inform the aspect from which we present our findings. The labelling of social issues as problems of 'risk' is thus not a neutral process. What risk means, who it gets attached to and who is able to slope-shoulder responsibility for it are all important issues that are worthy of greater focus. In this regard, the consequences of large-scale financial corruption, the harms produced by policies that put economic over human interests and crimes of the State all appear to be fertile areas for further research. No matter which avenues of inquiry are pursued, contesting risk is likely to be an ongoing endeavour in the social sciences in coming years.

Bibliography

9/11 Commission Report (2004) Washington DC: Department of Homelands Security.

Abbas, T. (2011) *Islamic Radicalism and Multicultural Politics*. London: Routledge.

Abbinnett, R. (2000) 'Science, Technology and Modernity: Beck and Derrida on the Politics of Risk', *Cultural Values*, 4(1): 101–26.

Adam, B., Beck, U. and van Loon, J. eds. (2000) *The Risk Society and Beyond*. London: Sage.

Adams, J. (1995) *Risk*. London: UCL Press.

Agamben, G. (2005) *State of Exception*. Chicago: University of Chicago Press.

Allan, S., Adam, B. and Carter, C., eds. (2000) *Environmental Risks and the Media*. London: Routledge.

Allen, J. (2004) 'Power in its Institutional Guises', in G. Hughes and R. Fergusson, eds. *Ordering Lives: Family, Work and Welfare*. London: Routledge.

Almond, P. (2013) *Corporate Manslaughter and Regulatory Reform*. Basingstoke: Palgrave Macmillan.

Altheide, D. (2002) *Creating Fear: News and the Construction of a Crisis*. New York: Aldine.

Althusser, L. (1970) *Lenin and Philosophy and Other Essays*. New York: Monthly Review Press.

Amis, M. (2008) *The Second Plane: September 11, Terror and Boredom*. London: Vintage.

Amoore, L. (2011) 'Data Derivatives: On the Emergence of a Security Risk Calculus for our Times', *Theory, Culture and Society*, 28: 24–43.

Amoore, L. (2007) 'Vigilant Visualities: The Watchful Politics of the War on Terror', *Security Dialogue*, 38: 215–32.

Amoore, L. and de Goede, M. eds. (2008) *Risk and the War on Terror*, London: Routledge.

Anderson, A. (2009) 'Media Politics and Climate Change: Towards a New Research Agenda', *Sociology Compass*, 3/2: 166–82.

Anderson, A. (2006) 'The Media and Risk', in G. Mythen and S. Walklate, eds. *Beyond the Risk Society*. Berkshire: OUP.

Andrews, R. (1987) *Routledge Dictionary of Quotations*. London: Routledge.

Aradau, C. and Van Munster, R. (2008) 'Governing Terrorism Through Risk: Taking Precautions, (un)Knowing the Future', *European Journal of International Relations*, 13(1): 89–115.

Arnoldi, J. (2009) *Risk*. Cambridge: Polity Press.

Atkinson, W. (2007) 'Beck, Individualization and the Death of Class: A Critique', *British Journal of Sociology*, 58(1): 349–66.

Atman, C.J., Bostrom, A., Fischhoff, B. and Morgan, M.G. (1994) 'Designing Risk Communications: Completing and Correcting Mental Models: Part I', *Risk Analysis*, 14 (1): 779–88.

Ayto, J. (1990) *Dictionary of Word Origins*. London: Bloomsbury.

Bajc, V. and de Lint, W. (2011) *Security and Everyday Life*. London: Routledge.

Banks, M. (2005) 'Spaces of (in)Security: Media and Fear of Crime in a Local Context', *Crime, Media, Culture*, 1(2): 169–87.

Barnaby, F. (2002) *How to Build a Nuclear Bomb and Other Weapons of Mass Destruction*. London: Granta.

Baudrillard, J. (2003) *The Spirit of Terrorism*. London: Verso.

Baudrillard, J. (1995) *The Gulf War Did Not Take Place*. Indiana: Indiana University Press.

Bauman, Z. (2013) *Does the Richness of the Few Benefit Us All?* Cambridge: Polity.

Bauman, Z. (2012) 'The Only Permanence in Society is Change', *Network*, no. 111. London: BSA: 26–27.

Bauman, Z. (2011) 'Privacy, Secrecy, Intimacy, Human Bonds – and Other Collateral Casualties of Liquid Modernity', *Hedgehog Review*, 13(1): Spring Edition.

Bauman, Z. (2007) *Consuming Life*. Cambridge: Polity Press.

Bauman, Z. (2006) *Liquid Fear*. Cambridge: Polity Press.

Bauman, Z. (2005) *Liquid Life*. Cambridge: Polity Press.

Bauman, Z. (2002) *Society Under Siege*. Cambridge: Polity Press.

Bauman, Z. (2000) *Liquid Modernity*. Cambridge: Polity Press.

Bauman, Z. and Lyon, D. (2013) *Liquid Surveillance: A Conversation*. London: Polity.

BBC News Online (2010) 'The Perfect Storm', viewable at http://news.bbc.co.uk/1/hi/8213884.stm. Accessed 14 February 2011.

BBC News Online (2004) 'Blair Urges New Era in Crime Fight', viewable at http://news.bbc.co.uk/1/hi/uk/3905547.stm. Accessed 25 August 2012.

Beck, U. (2009) *World at Risk*. Cambridge: Polity Press.

Beck, U. (2007) 'Beyond Class and Nation: Reframing Social Inequalities in a Globalizing World', *British Journal of Sociology*, 58(4): 679–705.

Beck, U. (2006) *Cosmopolitan Vision*. Cambridge: Polity Press.

Beck, U. (2005) *Power in the Global Age*. Cambridge: Polity Press.

Beck, U. (2002) 'On World Risk Society', *Logos*, 1(4): 1–18.

Beck, U. (2000) 'Risk Society Revisited: Theory, Politics and Research Programmes', in B. Adam, U. Beck and J. van Loon, eds. *The Risk Society and Beyond: Critical Issues for Social Theory*. London: Sage.

Beck, U. (1999) *World Risk Society*. Cambridge: Polity Press.

Beck, U. (1997) *The Reinvention of Politics: Rethinking Modernity in the Global Social Order*. Cambridge: Polity.

Beck, U. (1996) 'Risk Society and the Provident State', in B. Szerszinski, S. Lash and B. Wynne, eds. *Risk, Environment and Modernity: Towards a New Ecology*. London: Sage.

Beck, U. (1995) *Ecological Politics in an Age of Risk*. Cambridge: Polity Press.

Beck, U. (1992) *Risk Society: Towards a New Modernity*. London: Sage.

Beck, U., Giddens, A. and Lash, S. eds. (1994) *Reflexive Modernization: Politics, Tradition and Aesthetics in the Modern Social Order*. London: Sage.

Beck, U. and Grande, E. (2010) 'Varieties of Second Modernity: Extra-European and European Experiences and Perspectives', *British Journal of Sociology*, 61(3): 409–43.

Beck, U. and Sznaider, N. (2006) 'Unpacking Cosmopolitanism for the Social Sciences: a Research Agenda', *The British Journal of Sociology*, 57(1): 1–23.

Beck, U. and Willms, J. (2004) *Conversations with Ulrich Beck*. Cambridge: Polity Press.

Becker, G. (1976) *The Economic Approach to Human Behavior*. Chicago: University of Chicago Press.

Becker, H. (1986) *Doing Things Together: Selected Papers*. Illinois: Northwestern University Press.

Begley, S. (2004) 'Afraid to Fly After 9/11, Some Took a Bigger Risk – In Cars', *Wall Street Journal*, 23 March: 4.

Behringher, W. (2013) *A Cultural History of Climate Change*. Oxford: Polity.

Belasco, A. (2009) *The Cost of Iraq, Afghanistan and Other Global War on Terror Operations Since 9/11*. Washington: Congressional Research Service.

Benjamin, W. (1974) *Gesammelten Schriften I:2*. Suhrkamp Verlag: Frankfurt am Main.

Bennett, J. (2010) *Vibrant Matter: A Political Ecology of Things*. North Carolina: Duke University Press.

Bennett, S. (2012) *Innovative Thinking in Risk, Crisis and Disaster Management*. Aldershot: Ashgate.

Benson, M. and Simpson, S. (2009) *White Collar Crime*. London: Routledge.

Bernstein, P. (1998) *Against the Gods: The Remarkable Story of Risk*. London: Wiley.

Biello, D. (2011) 'Human Population Reaches 7 Billion', *Scientific American*, 27 October.

Biglino, I. (2002). *Anti-Terrorism Legislation in Britain*. London: Liberty.

Bigo, D. (2002) 'Security and Immigration: Towards a Critique of the Governmentality of Unease', *Alternatives: Global, Local, Political*, 27(1): 63–92.

Blackwood, L., Hopkins, N. and Reicher, S. (2012) 'I Know Who I am, But Who do They Think I am? Muslim Perspectives on Encounters with Airport Authorities', *Ethnic and Racial Studies*, DOI:10.1080/01419870.2011.645845: 1–19.

Blair, T. (2005) *Common Sense Culture, Not a Compensation Culture*, speech to University College London, 26 May.

Blake, J. (1999) 'Overcoming the Value-Action Gap in Environmental Policy: Tensions Between National Policy and Local Experience', *Local Environment*, 4(3): 257–78.

Blanco, K. (2005) *CNN News*, 2 September, viewable at http://edition.cnn.com/2005/WEATHER/09/02/katrina.impact. Accessed 13 July 2012.

Boden, D. (2000) 'Worlds in Action: Information, Instantaneity and Global Futures Trading', in B. Adam, U. Beck and J. van Loon, eds. *The Risk Society and Beyond: Critical Issues for Social Theory*. London: Sage.

Body-Gendrot, S. (2011) *Globalization, Fear and Insecurity: The Challenges for Cities North and South*. Basingstoke: Palgrave Macmillan.

Borger, J. (2006) 'Cost of Wars Soars to $440bn for US', *The Guardian*, 4 February: 3.

Bostrom, A., Fischhoff, B. and Morgan, M.G. (1992) 'Characterizing Mental Models of Hazardous Processes', *Journal of Social Issues*, 48(4): 85–100.

Bosworth, M. and Guild, M. (2008) 'Governing through Migration Control: Security and Citizenship in Britain', *British Journal of Criminology*, 48(6): 703–19.

Bottoms, A. and Brownsword, R. (1982) 'The Dangerousness Debate after the Floud Report', *British Journal of Criminology*, 22(3): 229–54.

Bourdieu, P. and Wacquant, L. (1992) *An Invitation to Reflexive Sociology*, Chicago: University of Chicago Press.

Bourke, J. (2006) *Fear: a Cultural History*. London: Virago.

Bourke, J. (2005) 'The Politics of Fear are Blinding Us to the Humanity of Others', *The Guardian*, Saturday 1 October: 12.

Bowling, B. (1998) *Violent Racism: Victimization, Policing and Social Context*. Oxford: Clarendon.

Boykoff, M. (2011) *Who Speaks for the Environment? Making Sense of Media Reporting on Climate Change*. Cambridge: Cambridge University Press.

Boykoff, M. (2007) 'From Convergence to Contention: United States Mass Media Representations of Anthropogenic Climate Change Science', *Transactions of the Institute of British Geographers*, 32(4): 477–89.

Boyne, R. (2003) *Risk*. London: Sage.

Bradshaw, M. (2013) *Global Energy Dilemmas*. Oxford: Polity.

Branigan, T. (2006) 'Britons Would Trade Civil Liberties for Security', *The Guardian*, 22 August: 3.

British Crime Survey (2011) 'The British Crime Survey', viewable at https://www.gov.uk/government/publications/crime-in-england-and-wales-2010-to-2011. Accessed 21 May 2012.

British Crime Survey (1982) London: HMSO.

British Meteorological Office (2012) 'Met Office in the Media: 14 October 2012', viewable at http://metofficenews.wordpress.com/2012/10/14/met-office-in-the-media-14-october-2012. Accessed 9 January 2013.

Bronner, S.E. (1995) 'Ecology, Politics and Risk: The Social Theory of Ulrich Beck', *Capitalism, Nature, Socialism: A Journal of Socialist Ecology*, 6(1): 67–86.

Bruckner, P. (2013) *The Fanaticism of the Apocalypse: Save the Earth, Punish Human Beings*. Oxford: Polity.

Buck, D. and Frosini, F. (2013) *Clustering of Unhealthy Behaviours Over Time*. London: Kings Fund.

Bukovansky, M., Clark, I., Eckersley, R., Reus-Smit, C. and Wheeler, N. (2012) *Special Responsibilities: Global Problems and American Power*. Cambridge: Cambridge University Press.

Bulletin of the Atomic Scientists (2012) 'Doomsday Clock Moves to Five Minutes to Midnight', viewable at http://www.thebulletin.org/content/media-center/announcements/2012/01/10/ doomsday-clock-moves-to-five-minutes-to-midnight. Accessed 10 January 2012.

Burawoy, M. (2005) 'For Public Sociology', *American Sociological Review*, 70(1):1–28.

Burgess, A. (2008) 'Risk, Precaution and the Media', in R. Mueller, ed. *Risk Society and the Culture of Precaution*. London: Routledge.

Burgess, A. (2005) 'Mobiles and Health: What are We Scared Of?' *Spiked Online*, viewable at http://www.spiked-online.com/articles/0000000CADC3.htm. Accessed 15 November 2009.

Burgess, E. (1936) 'Protecting the Public by Parole and Parole Prediction', *Journal of Criminal Law and Criminology*, 27: 491–502.

Burgess, E. (1928) 'Factors Making for Success of Failure on Parole', *Journal of Criminal Law and Criminology*, 19: 239–306.

Burgess, E. and Park, R. (1921) *Introduction to the Science of Sociology*, University of Chicago Press: Chicago.

Burgess, A., Donovan, A. and Moore, S. (2009) 'Embodying Uncertainty? Understanding Heightened Risk Perception of Drink Spiking', *British Journal of Criminology*, 49(6): 848–62.

Burke, J. (2005) *Al-Qaeda: The True Story of Radical Islam*. London: IB Taurus.

Burkitt, I. (2005) 'Powerful Emotions: Power, Government and Opposition in the War on Terror', *Sociology*, 39(4): 679–95.

Burn-Murdoch, J. (2013) 'UK was World's Most Phished Country in 2012', *The Guardian*, 7 February: 11.

Burnett, J. and Whyte, D. (2005) 'Embedded Expertise and The New Terrorism', *Journal for Crime, Conflict and the Media*, 1(4): 1–18.

Bush, G. (2005) *State of the Union Address*. Washington DC, 2 February.

Cameron, D. (2011) Speech Delivered at Whitney, 15 August, *New Statesman*, viewable at http://www.newstatesman.com/politics/2011/08/society-fight-work-rights. Accessed 7 November 2012.

Campbell, P. (2011) *A Catachresis of Creativity? Liverpool 2008, Culture-Led Regeneration and the Creative Industries*. PhD Thesis, University of Liverpool.

Caplan, P. ed. (2000) *Risk Revisited*. London: Pluto.

Carr, D. (2005) 'More Horrible than Truth', *New York Times*, 19 September, viewable at http://www.nytimes.com/2005/09/19/business/media/19carr.html?pagewanted=all&_r=0. Accessed 4 November 2010.

Carrabine, E., Iganski, P., Lee, M., Plummer, K. and South, N. (2004) *Criminology: A Sociological Introduction*. London: Routledge.

Castel, R. (1991) 'From Dangerousness to Risk', in G. Burchell, C. Gordon and P. Miller, eds. *The Foucault Effect: Studies in Governmentality*. London: Harvester Wheatsheaf.

Chadee, D., Austen, L. and Ditton, J. (2007) 'The Relationship Between Likelihood and Fear of Criminal Victimization: Evaluating Risk Sensitivity as a Mediating Concept', *British Journal of Criminology*, 47: 133–53.

Chadee, D. and Ditton, J. (2005) 'Fear of Crime and the Media: Assessing the Lack of Relationship', *Crime, Media, Culture*, 1(3): 322–32.

Chater, N. (2013) 'Big Problems, Small Solutions', *Core*, 1: 37–38.

Christie, N. (2004) *A Suitable Amount of Crime*. Routledge, London.

Clark, D. (2012) 'Has the Kyoto Protocol made Any Difference to Carbon Emissions?', *The Guardian*, 26 November, viewable at http://www.theguardian.com/environment/blog/2012/nov/26/kyoto-protocol-carbon-emissions. Accessed 15 July 2013.

Clifford, M. and Edwards, T. (2012) *Environmental Crime*. Basingstoke: Jones and Bartlett.

Cluey, R. (2012) 'Art Words and Art Worlds: The Methodological Importance of Language Use in Howard S. Becker's Sociology of Art and Cultural Production', *Cultural Sociology*, 6(2): 201–16.

Cohen, A. (1955) *Delinquent Boys: The Culture of the Gang*. Glencoe: The Free Press.

Cohen, S. (2010) 'Ideology? What Ideology?' *Criminology and Criminal Justice,* 10(4): 387–93.

Cohen, S. (2001) *States of Denial: Knowing About Atrocities and Suffering.* Cambridge: Polity Press.

Cohen, S. (1979) 'The Last Seminar', *The Sociological Review,* 27(1): 5–20.

Cohen, S. (1972) *Folk Devils and Moral Panics.* London: MacGibbon and Kee.

Coleman, J.S. (1990) *Foundations of Social Theory.* Cambridge: Belknap Press.

Coleman, R. and McCahill, M. (2011) *Surveillance and Crime.* London: Sage.

Coleman, R., Sim, J., Tombs, S. and Whyte, D. eds. (2009) *State, Power, Crime.* London: Sage.

Colten, C. (2006) 'Vulnerability and Place: Flat Land and Uneven Risk in New Orleans', *American Anthropologist,* 108(4): 731–34.

Colten, C. (2002) 'Basin Street Blues: Drainage and Environmental Equity in New Orleans, 1890–1930', *Journal of Historical Geography,* 28(2): 237–57.

Comfort, L. (2006) 'Cities at Risk: Hurricane Katrina and the Drowning of New Orleans', *Urban Affairs Review,* 41: 501.

Cooper, M. (2008) *Life as Surplus: Biotechnology and Capitalism in the Neoliberal Era.* Washington: University of Washington Press.

Copeland, T. (2001) 'Is the New Terrorism Really New? An Analysis of the New Paradigm for Terrorism', *Journal of Conflict Studies,* 21(2): 91–105.

Cornish, D. and Clarke, R. (1987) 'Understanding Crime Displacement: An Application of Rational Choice Theory', *Criminology,* 25(4): 933–48.

Cottle, S. (1998) 'Ulrich Beck, Risk Society and the Media', *European Journal of Communications,* 13: 5–32.

Crime Survey of England and Wales (2012) Newport: Office for National Statistics.

Criminal Injuries Compensation Authority (2010) *Annual Report 2008–2009,* viewable at http://www.cica.gov.uk/Documents/publications/Reports/Annual%20report%20 and%20accounts%2008-09.pdf. Accessed 13 February 2010.

Cruikshank, B. (1993) 'Revolutions within: Self-government and Self-esteem', *Economy and Society,* 22(3): 327–44.

Culpitt, I. (1999) *Social Policy and Risk.* London: Sage.

Curtis, A. (2004) 'Fear Gives Politicians a Reason to be', *The Guardian,* 24 September: 9.

Daffin, C. (2009) *Wealth in Great Britain 2006–2008.* London: ONS.

Dake, K. (1991) 'Orienting Dispositions in the Perception of Risk: An Analysis of Contemporary Worldviews and Cultural Biases', *Journal of Cross-Cultural Psychology,* 22: 61–82.

Davidson, C. (2006) Insurance Firms Weather the Storm, *BBC News,* viewable at http://news.bbc.co.uk/1/hi/business/5273974.stm. Accessed 7 April 2012.

Davidson, D. (2012) 'Analysing Responses to Climate Change Through the Lens of Reflexivity', *The British Journal of Sociology,* 63(4): 616–38.

Davidson, J. and Chesney-Lind, M. (2009) 'Discounting Women: Context Matters in Risk and Need Assessment', *Critical Criminology,* 17: 221–45.

Davies, G.H. (2010) *The Financial Crisis: Who is to Blame?* Basingstoke: Palgrave Macmillan.

Davis, M. (1990) *City of Quartz: Excavating the Future in Los Angeles.* London: Vintage.

Davis, P., Francis, P. and Greer, P. (2007) *Victims, Crime and Society.* London: Sage.

Davis, R., Lurigo, A. and Herman, S. (2013) *Victims of Crime*. London: Sage.

Dawdy, S. (2010) 'Clockpunk Anthropology and the Ruins of Modernity', *Current Anthropology*, 51(6): 761–93.

Dean, M. (1999a) 'Risk, Calculable and Incalculable', in D. Lupton, ed. *Risk and Socio-cultural Theory: New Directions and Perspectives*, Cambridge: Cambridge University Press.

Dean, M. (1999b) *Governmentality: Power and Rule in Modern Society*. London: Sage.

de Dijn, H. (2004) 'The Terrorist Threat: A Postmodern Kind of Threat', *Ethical Perspectives*, 11(2): 122–29.

de Lint, W. and Virta, S. (2004) 'Security and Ambiguity: Towards a Radical Security Politics', *Theoretical Criminology*, 8(4): 465–89.

Denney, D. (2005) *Risk and Society*. London: Sage.

Department of Energy and Climate Change (2012) *Energy Consumption in the United Kingdom*. London: HMSO.

de Sousa-Santos, B. (2007) *Another Knowledge Is Possible: Beyond Northern Epistemologies*. London: Verso.

Dick, P.K. (1956) *The Minority Report*. New York: Victor Gollancz.

Dodd, V. (2006) 'Police May Let Muslims see Terrorism Intelligence', *The Guardian*, 17 June: 9.

Dodd, V. (2005) 'Asian Men Targeted in Stop and Search', *The Guardian*, 17 August: 1.

Doig, A. (2010) *State Crime*. London: Routledge.

Dolan, P. and Peasgood, T. (2007) 'Estimating the Economic and Social Costs of the Fear of Crime', *British Journal of Criminology*, 47(1): 121–32.

Dominelli, L. (2012) *Green Social Work: From Environmental Crises to Environmental Justice*. London: Polity.

Dorling, D. (2006) 'Policing the Borders of Crime: Who Decides Research', *Criminal Justice Matters*, 62: 28–29.

Douglas, M. (1996) *Purity and Danger: An Analysis of Concepts of Pollution and Taboo*. London: Routledge.

Douglas, M. (1992) *Risk and Blame: Essays in Cultural Theory*. London: Routledge.

Douglas, M. (1985) *Risk Acceptability According to the Social Sciences*. New York: Russell Sage.

Douglas, M. and Wildavsky, A. (1982) *Risk and Culture: An Essay on the Selection of Technical and Environmental Dangers*. Berkeley: University of California Press.

Dupont, D. and Pearce, F. (2001) 'Foucault Contra Foucault: Rereading the Governmentality Papers', *Theoretical Criminology*, 5: 123–58.

Durkheim, E. (1984) *The Division of Labor in Society*. Basingstoke: Macmillan.

Durodie, B. (2006) 'Tempted by Terror', *Spiked Online*, 14 November.

Durodie, B. (2004) 'The Limitations of Risk Management: Dealing With Disasters and Building Social Resilience', *Argang*, 8(1): 14–21.

Edmunds, J. (2011) 'The New Barbarians: Governmentality, Securitization and Islam in Western Europe', *Contemporary Islam*, 6: 67–84.

Ekberg, M. (2007) 'The Parameters of the Risk Society: A Review and Exploration', *Current Sociology*, 55: 342–66.

Elliott, A. (2009) 'Series Editors Foreword', in I. Wilkinson, ed. *Risk, Vulnerability and Everyday Life*. London: Routledge.

Elliott, A. (2002) 'Beck's Sociology of Risk: A Critical. Assessment', *Sociology*, 36(2): 293–315.

Elliott, J.R. and Pais, J. (2006) 'Race, Class and Hurricane Katrina: Social Differences in Human Responses to Disaster', *Political Journal of Social Science Research*, 35: 295–21.

Ericson, R. (1996) 'Making Criminology', *Current Issues in Criminal Justice*, 15: 14–25.

Ericson, R.V. (2007) *Crime in an Insecure World*. Cambridge: Polity Press.

Ericson, R.V. (2006) 'Ten Uncertainties of Risk-Management Approaches to Security', *Canadian Journal of Criminology and Criminal Justice*, 48(3): 345–57.

Ericson, R. and Haggerty, K. (1997) *Policing the Risk Society*. Oxford: Clarendon.

European Commission (2012) *Climate Action*. Brussels: European Commission.

Eurostat (2010) *Environmental Statistics and Accounts in Europe*. Brussels: European Commission.

Ewald, F. (2002) 'The Return of Descartes's Malicious Demon: An Outline of a Philosophy of Precaution', in T. Baker and J. Simon, eds. *Embracing Risk: The Changing Culture of Insurance and Responsibility*. Chicago: University of Chicago Press.

Ewald, F. (1991) 'Insurance and Risk', in G. Burchell, C. Gordon and P. Miller, eds. *The Foucault Effect: Studies in Governmentality*. London: Harvester.

Fardon, R. (2007) 'Obituary: Dame Mary Douglas', *The Guardian*, May 18: 12.

Farrall, S., Bannister, J., Ditton, J. and Gilchrist, A. (2000), 'Social Psychology and the Fear of Crime; Re-examining a Speculative Model', *British Journal of Criminology*, 40(3): 414–36.

Farrall, S. and Gadd, D. (2004) 'Research Note: The Frequency of the Fear of Crime', *British Journal of Criminology*, 44: 127–32.

Fattah, E. (1991) *Understanding Criminal Victimization*. Ontario: Prentice-Hall: Canada.

Feeley, M. and Simon, J. (1995) 'True Crime: The New Penology and Public Discourse on Crime', in T.G. Blomberg and S. Cohen, eds. *Punishment and Social Control: Essays in Honor of Sheldon L. Messenger*. New York: Aldine De Gruyter.

Feeley, M. and Simon, J. (1994) 'Actuarial Justice: The Emerging New Criminal Law', in D. Nelken, ed. *The Futures of Criminology*. New York: Sage.

Feeley, M. and Simon, J. (1992) 'The New Penology: Notes on the Emerging Strategy of Corrections and its Implications', *Criminology*, 30(4): 449–74.

Ferrell, J. (2006) *Empire of Scrounge: Inside the Urban Underground of Dumpster Diving, Trash Picking and Street Scavenging*. New York: New York University Press.

Ferret, J. and Spenlehauer, V. (2009) 'Does Policing the Risk Society Hold the Road Risk?' *British Journal of Criminology*, 49(2): 150–64.

Field, A. (2009) 'The New Terrorism: Revolution or Evolution?' *Political Studies Review*, 7: 195–207.

Fischhoff, B. and Kadvany, J. (2011) *Risk: A Very Short Introduction*. Oxford: Oxford University Press.

Flood, C., Hutchings, S., Miazhevich, G. and Nickels, H. (2012) *Islam, Security and Television News*. Basingstoke: Palgrave Macmillan.

Floud, J. (1982) 'Dangerousness and Criminal Justice,' *British Journal of Criminology* 22(1): 213–28.

Floud, J. and Young, W. (1981) *Dangerousness and Criminal Justice*. London: Heinemann.

Flusty, S. (2000) 'Thrashing Downtown: Play as Resistance to the Spatial and Representational Regulation of Los Angeles', *Cities*, 17(2): 49–58.

Flynn, J.H., Slovic, P. and Mertz, C.K. (1993) 'Decidedly Different: Expert and Public Views of a Radioactive Waste Repository', *Risk Analysis*, 13(1): 643–48.

Ford, R. (2009) 'Blacks Bear Brunt of Rise in Stop and Search', *The Times*, 1 May: 3.

Ford, J., Burrows, R. and Nettleton, S. (2001) *Home Ownership in a Risk Society: A Social Analysis of Mortgage Arrears and Possessions*. Policy Press: London.

Fothergill, A., Maestas, E. and Darlington, J. (1999) 'Race, Ethnicity and Disasters in the United States: A Review of the Literature', *Disasters*, 23(2): 156–73.

Foucault, M. (1993). 'About the Beginnings of the Hermenuetics of the Self: Two Lectures at Dartmouth', *Political Theory*, 21(1): 198–227.

Foucault, M. (1991a) 'Questions of Method', in G. Burchell, C. Gordon and P. Miller, eds. *The Foucault Effect: Studies in Governmentality*, London: Harvester Wheatsheaf.

Foucault, M. (1991b) 'Governmentality', in G. Burchell, C. Gordon and P. Miller, eds. *The Foucault Effect: Studies in Governmentality*, London: Harvester Wheatsheaf.

Foucault, M. (1984) 'What is Enlightenment?', in P. Rabinow, ed. *The Foucault Reader*, New York: Pantheon.

Foucault, M. (1982) 'The Subject and Power', in H. Dreyfus and P. Rabinow, eds. *Michel Foucault: Beyond Structuralism and Hermeneutics*. Chicago: University of Chicago Press.

Foucault, M. (1980) *Power/Knowledge*. Brighton: Harvester.

Foucault, M. (1979) *Discipline and Punish: The Birth of the Prison*. London: Penguin.

Foucault, M. (1978) *The History of Sexuality*. Harmondsworth: Penguin.

Fox, C. and Albertson, K. (2011) 'Payment by Results and Social Impact Bonds in the Criminal Justice Sector: New Challenges for the Concept of Evidence-based Policy?' *Criminology and Criminal Justice*, 11(5): 395–413.

Fox News (2007) 'Cops: Superdome Violence Reports Exaggerated', viewable at http://www.foxnews.com/story/0,2933,170569,00.html. Accessed 6 May 2012.

Furedi, F. (2009) 'Be Afraid . . .', *Sunday Herald*, 3 May 2009, viewable at http://www.frankfuredi.com/index.php/site/article/304/ Accessed 15 November 2010.

Furedi, F. (2007a) *Invitation to Terror: The Expanding Empire of the Unknown*. London: Continuum.

Furedi, F. (2007b) 'The Only Thing We Have to Fear is the Culture of Fear Itself', viewable at http://www.spiked-online.com/index.php?/site/article/3053. Accessed 1 October 2010.

Furedi, F. (2005a) 'Terrorism and the Politics of Fear', in C. Hale, K. Hayward, A. Wahidin and E. Wincup, eds. *Criminology*. Oxford: Oxford University Press.

Furedi, F. (2005b) 'Bird Flu Prophets of Doom Spread Nothing but Needless Alarm', *Daily Express*, 18 October: 9.

Furedi, F. (2002) *Culture of Fear: Risk Taking and the Morality of Low Expectation*. London: Continuum.

Gaba, J. (1999) 'Environmental Ethics and Our Moral Relationship to Future Generations: Future Rights and Present Virtue', *Columbia Journal of Environmental Law*, 249: 285–86.

Gabriel, U. and Greve, W. (2003) 'The Psychology of Fear of Crime: Conceptual and Methodological Perspectives', *British Journal of Criminology*, 43(1): 600–14.

Gadd, D. and Jefferson, T. (2007) *Psychosocial Criminology*. London: Sage.

Gallup (2005) *What Frightens America's Youth?* Viewable at http://www.gallup.com/poll/15439/What-Frightens-Americas-Youth.aspx. Accessed 14 February 2011.

Gardner, D. (2009) *Risk: The Science and Politics of Fear.* London: Virgin.

Garland, D. (2001) *The Culture of Control: Crime and Social Order in Contemporary Society*. Oxford: Oxford University Press.

Garland, D. (1997) 'Governmentality and the Problem of Crime', *Theoretical Criminology*, 1(2): 173–214.

Garland, D. (1990) *Punishment and Modern Society*. Oxford: Oxford University Press.

Garside, R. (2013) *UK Justice Policy Review*. London: Centre For Crime and Justice Studies.

Garside, R. (2008) 'Knife Crime: Perception v Reality', *The Guardian*, 18 July, viewable at http://www.theguardian.com/commentisfree/2008/jul/18/knifecrime1. Accessed 20 July 2011.

George, S. (2011) *Whose Crisis? Whose Future?* Cambridge: Polity.

Giddens, A. (2009) *The Politics of Climate Change: National Responses to the Challenge of Global Warming*. London: Policy Network.

Giddens, A. (1999a) 'Risk and Responsibility', *The Modern Law Review*, 62(1): 1–10.

Giddens, A. (1999b) *Risk*. Hong Kong: BBC Reith Lecture.

Giddens, A. (1998) 'Risk Society: The Context of British Politics', in J. Franklin, ed. *The Politics of Risk Society*. Cambridge: Polity Press.

Giddens, A. (1984) *The Constitution of Society: Outline of the Theory of Structuration*. Cambridge: Polity Press.

Gigerenzer, G. (2002) *Reckoning With Risk: Learning to Live With Uncertainty*. London: Penguin.

Gilbert, P. (2003) *New Terror, New Wars*. Edinburgh: Edinburgh University Press.

Gill, P. (2009) 'Intelligence, Terrorism and the State', in R. Coleman, J. Sim., S. Tombs and D. Whyte, eds. *State, Power, Crime*. London: Sage.

Gill, P. (2006) 'Not Just Joining the Dots But Crossing the Borders and Bridging the Voids: Constructing Security Networks After 11 September 2001', *Policing and Society*, 16(1): 27–49.

Gilmore, J. (2010) 'Policing Protest: An Authoritarian Consensus', *Criminal Justice Matters*, 82(1): 21–23.

Glassner, B. (1999) *The Culture of Fear: Why Americans Are Afraid of the Wrong Things*. New York: Basic Books.

Goode, E. and Ben-Yehuda, N. (1994) *Moral Panics: The Social Construction of Deviance*. Oxford: Blackwell.

Goodey, J. (2005) *Victims and Victimology: Research, Policy and Practice*. Harrow, England: Pearson Longman.

Goodin, R. (2006) *What's Wrong With Terrorism?* Oxford: Polity Press.

Gorz, A. (2009) *Letter to D: A Love Story*. Cambridge: Polity Press.

Gorz, A. (1994) *Capitalism, Socialism, Ecology*. London: Verso.

Gorz, A. (1982) *Ecology as Politics*. London: Pluto Press.

Gottfredson, M. (1984) *Risk of Victimisation: Findings from the 1982 British Crime Survey*. London HMSO.

Gray, J. (2003) *Al Qaeda and What it Means to be Modern*. London: Faber and Faber.

Gray, L. (2012) 'Doha: Latest Figures Show Global CO_2 Emissions are Rising', *The Daily Telegraph*. 2 December: 11.

Grayling, A.C. (2007) *The Choice of Hercules: Pleasure, Duty and Moral Culture*. London: Weidenfeld and Nicolson.

Green, D. (2006) *We're (Nearly) All Victims Now*. London: Civitas.

Green, P. and Ward, T. (2009) 'Violence and the State', in R. Coleman, J., Sim, S., Tombs and D. Whyte, eds. *State, Power, Crime*. London: Sage.

Green, P. and Ward, T. (2004) *State Crime: Governments, Violence and Corruption*. London: Pluto Press.

Green, T. (2003) 'The Shock of the True', *Independent Magazine*, 14 June: 8.

Greenpeace International (2012) *How to Save The Climate*. Greenpeace: Amsterdam.

Greenwood, P. and Abrahamse, A. (1982) *Selective Incapacitation*. Santa Monica: RAND Corporation.

Greer, C. ed. (2009) *Crime and Media: A Reader*. London: Routledge.

Greer, C. (2007) 'News Media, Victims and Crime', in P. Davies, P. Francis and C. Greer, eds. (1997) *Victims, Crime and Society*. London: Sage.

Gregory, F. and Wilkinson, P. (2005) 'Riding Pillion for Tackling Terrorism is a High-risk Policy', *Security, Terrorism and the UK*. London: ISP/NSC.

Grusin, R. (2004) 'Premediation', *Criticism*, 46: 17–39.

Hacking, I. (1990) *The Taming of Chance*. Cambridge: Cambridge University Press.

Hajer, M. (1995) *The Politics of Environmental Discourse: Ecological Modernization and the Policy Process*. Oxford: Oxford University Press.

Hale, C. (1996) 'Fear of Crime: A Review of the Literature', *International Review of Victimology*, 3: 195–210.

Hall, M. (2009) *Policy and Practice in Criminal Justice*. Devon: Willan.

Hall, S. (1980) 'Cultural Studies: Two Paradigms', *Media, Culture and Society*, 2: 57–72.

Hall, S., Crichter, C., Jefferson, T. and Roberts, B. (1978) *Policing the Crisis*. London: Macmillan.

Hammond, P. (2004) 'Postmodernity Goes to War', viewable at http://www.spiked-online.com/Articles/0000000CA554.htm. Accessed 20 July 2012.

Hannah-Moffatt, K. (2006) 'Pandora's Box: Risk/Need and Gender Responsive Corrections', *Criminology and Public Policy*, 5(1): 183–91.

Hannah-Moffatt, K. (2005) 'Criminogenic Needs and the Transformative Risk Subject', *Punishment and Society*, 7: 29–51.

Hanman, N. (2009) 'Explainer: Terrorism Legislation', *The Guardian*, 22 January: 4.

Hannigan, J. (2012) *Disasters Without Borders*. London: Polity.

Harvey, F. (2012) 'UK Makes Biggest Emissions Cuts in Europe', *The Guardian*, 24 October: 4.

Haslam, D. (2000) *Manchester, England: The Story of the Pop Cult City*. London: Fourth Estate.

Hebenton, B. and Thomas, T. (1996) 'Sexual Offenders in the Community: Reflections of Problems of Law, Community and Risk Management in the USA, England and Wales', *International Journal of the Sociology of Law*, 24: 427–43.

Heckenburg, D. (2009) 'Studying Environmental Crime: Key Words, Acronyms and Sources of Information', in R. White, ed. *Environmental Crime: A Reader*. Cullompton: Willan.

Hegerl, G., Zwiers, F., Braconnot, P., Gillett, N., Luo, Y., Marengo Orsini, J., Nicholls, N., Penner, J. and Stott, P. (2007) 'Understanding and Attributing Climate Change', in K.B. Averyt, M. Tignor and H.L. Miller, eds. *Climate Change 2007: The Physical Science Basis. Contribution of Working Group I to the Fourth Assessment Report of the Intergovernmental Panel on Climate Change.* Cambridge: Cambridge University Press.

Held, D., Theros, M. and Fane-Hervey, A. (2011) *The Governance of Climate Change.* London: Polity.

Henley, J. (2013) 'Recessions can Hurt, but Austerity Kills', *The Guardian*, viewable at http://www.guardian.co.uk/society/2013/may/15/recessions-hurt-but-austerity-kills. Accessed 15 May.

Hesse, B., Rai, D., Bennett, C. and McGilchrist, P. (1992) *Beneath the Surface: Racial Harassment.* Aldershot: Avebury.

Hewitt, G. (2006) 'Deep Frustration in New Orleans', *BBC News*, 30 August.

Heyman, B. and Henrikson, M. (1998) 'Probability and Health Risks', in B. Heyman, ed. *Risk, Health and Health Care: A Quantitative Approach.* London: Arnold.

Hillyard, P. (2009) 'The Exceptional State', in R. Coleman, J. Sim, S. Tombs and D. Whyte, eds. *State, Power, Crime.* London: Sage.

Hillyard, P. (2005) 'The War on Terror: Lessons from Ireland', *European Civil Liberties Network*, 1: 1–4.

Hillyard, P. and Percy-Smith, C. (1988) *The Coercive State.* London: Macmillan.

Himmelweit, S. and Simonetti, R. (2004) 'Nature for Sale', in S. Hinchliffe and K. Woodward, eds. *The Natural and the Social: Uncertainty, Risk, Change.* London: Routledge.

Hinchliffe, S. (2004). 'Living with Risk', in S. Hinchliffe and K. Woodward, eds. *The Natural and the Social: Uncertainty, Risk, Change.* London: Routledge.

Hinchliffe, S. and Woodward, K. eds. (2004) *The Natural and the Social: Uncertainty, Risk, Change.* London: Routledge.

Hoeksema, T. and ter Laak, J. eds. (2003) *Human Rights and Terrorism.* Holland: NHC/OSCE.

Hoffmann, B. (2006) *Inside Terrorism.* New York: University of Columbia Press.

Hollway, W. and Jefferson, T. (1997) 'The Risk Society in an Age of Anxiety: Situating Fear of Crime', *British Journal of Sociology*, 48(2): 255–66.

Holton, R. (2011) *Globalization and the Nation State.* Basingstoke: Palgrave Macmillan.

Hope, T. and Sparks, R. eds. (2000) *Crime, Risk and Insecurity.* London: Routledge.

Hough, M. and Mayhew, P. (1983) *The British Crime Survey.* London: HMSO.

Howes, M. (2005) *Politics and the Environment.* London: Earthscan.

Hudson, B. (2006) 'Beyond White Man's Justice: Race, Gender and Justice in Late Modernity', *Theoretical Criminology*, 10(1): 1362–4806.

Hudson, B. (2003) *Justice in a Risk Society.* London: Sage.

Hudson, B. (2000) 'Punishment, Rights and Difference', in K. Stenson and R. Sullivan, eds. *Crime, Risk and Justice: The Politics of Crime Control in Liberal Democracies.* Cullompton: Willan.

Hughes, G. (2007) *The Politics of Crime and Community.* Basingstoke: Palgrave Macmillan.

Hughes, G. (1998) *Understanding Crime Prevention: Social Control, Risk and Late Modernity*. Buckingham: Open University Press.

Hughes, G., McLaughlin, E. and Muncie, J. (2002) *Crime Prevention and Community Safety: New Directions*. London: Sage.

Hulme, M. (2009) *Why We Disagree About Climate Change: Understanding Controversy, Inaction and Opportunity*. Cambridge: Cambridge University Press.

Hutter, B. (2005) 'The Attractions of Risk-based Regulation: Accounting For the Emergence of Risk Ideas in Regulation', CARR Discussion Paper No. 33. London: LSE.

Hutton, F. (2006) *Risky Pleasures: Club Cultures and Feminine Identities*. Aldershot: Ashgate.

Institute for Economics and Peace (2013) *UK Peace Index*. Sydney: IEP.

International Energy Agency (2012) *World Energy Outlook*. Paris: OECD/IEA.

International Panel on Climate Change (2012) *Managing the Risks of Extreme Events and Disasters to Advance Climate Change Adaptation*. Geneva: IPCC.

Isin, E. (2004) 'The Neurotic Citizen', *Citizenship Studies*, 8(3): 217–35.

Jacobs, M. (1999) *Environmental Modernisation: The New Labour Agenda*. London: Fabian Society.

Jacobs, M. (1991) *The Green Economy*. London: Pluto Press.

Jackson, J. (2004) 'Experience and Expression: Social and Cultural Significance in the Fear of Crime', *British Journal of Criminology*, 44: 946–966.

Jackson, R. (2005) *Writing the War on Terrorism: Language, Politics and Counterterrorism*. Manchester: Manchester University Press.

Jackson, R., Murphy, E. and Poynting, S. (2009) *Contemporary State Terrorism: Theory and Practice*. London: Routledge.

Jackson, S. and Rees, A. (2007) 'The Appalling Appeal of Nature: The Popular Influence of Evolutionary Psychology as a Problem for Sociology', *Sociology*, 41: 917–30.

Jeffrey, S. (2005) 'The Rules of the Game are Changing', *The Guardian*, 5 August, viewable at http://www.guardian.co.uk/uk/2005/aug/05/july7.uksecurity5. Accessed 4 August 2011.

Jessop, B. (2004) 'Critical Semiotic Analysis and Cultural Political Economy', *Critical Discourse Studies*, 1: 159–74.

Joffe, H. (1999) *Risk and the Other*. Cambridge: Cambridge University Press.

Kahneman, D., Slovic, P. and Tversky, A. (1982) *Judgment Under Uncertainty: Heuristics and Biases*. Cambridge: Cambridge University Press.

Kamppinen, M. and Wilenius, M. (2001) 'Risk Landscapes in the Era of Social Transition', *Futures*, 33: 307–17.

Karmen, A. (2009) *Crime Victims: An Introduction to Victimology*. California: Cengage Learning.

Kasperson, J. and Kasperson, R. (2001) *Global Environmental Risk*. London: Earthscan.

Kates, R. W., Colten, C., Laska, S. and Leatherman, S.P. (2006) 'Reconstruction of New Orleans after Hurricane Katrina: A Research Perspective', *Proceedings of the National Academy of Sciences*, 103(40): 14653–60.

Katz, J. (1998) *The Seductions of Crime: Moral and Sensual Attractions in Doing Evil*. New York: Basic Books.

Katz, J. (1988) *Seductions of Crime: Moral and Sensual Attractions in Doing Evil*. New York: Basic Books.

Kearon, T. and Leach, R. (2000) 'Invasion of the Body Snatchers: Burglary Reconsidered', *Theoretical Criminology*, 4: 451–73.

Kellner, D. (2002) 'September 11 and Terror War: The Bush Legacy and the Risks of Unilateralism', *Logos*, 1(4): 19–41.

Kelly, A. and Burrows, R. (2012) 'Measuring the Value of Sociology? Some Notes on Performative Metricization in the Contemporary Academy', *The Sociological Review*, 60(2): 130–50.

Kemshall, H. (2006) 'Social Policy and Risk', in G. Mythen and S. Walklate, eds. *Beyond the Risk Society*. Maidenhead: Open University Press.

Kemshall, H. (2003) *Understanding Risk in Criminal Justice*. Buckingham: Open University Press.

Kemshall, H. (2002) *Risk, Social Policy and Welfare*. Buckingham: Open University Press.

Kevany, K.D. (2007) 'Building the Requisite Capacity for Stewardship and Sustainable Development', *International Journal of Sustainability in Higher Education*, 8(2): 107–22.

Kibbe, J. (2012) 'Conducting Shadow Wars', *Journal of National Security Law and Policy*, 5: 373–92.

Klein, N. (2007a) *The Shock Doctrine*. New York: Allen Lane.

Klein, N. (2007b) 'Disaster Capitalism: The New Economy of Catastrophe', *Harpers*, October Edition: 49–58.

Knight, F. (1922) *Risk, Uncertainty and Profit*. Boston: Houghton Mifflin.

Krieger, K. (2012) 'The Limits and Variety of Risk-based Governance: The Case of Flood Management in Germany and England', *Regulation and Governance*. Advance Access Archive. doi:10.1111/rego.12009.

Kunreuther, H. and Pauly, M. (2006) 'Rules Rather than Discretion: Lessons from Hurricane Katrina', *Journal of Risk and Uncertainty*, 33: 101–16.

Lambert, R. and Spalek, B. (2008) 'Muslim Communities, Counter-terrorism and Counter-radicalisation: A Critically Reflective Approach to Engagement', *International Journal of Law, Crime and Justice Studies*, 36(4): 257–70.

Lanchester, J. (2010) *Whoops! Why Everyone Owes Everyone and No One Can Pay*. London: Penguin.

Laqueur, W. (2003) *No End to War: Terrorism in the 21st Century*. New York: Continuum.

Laqueur, W. (1997) 'Postmodern Terrorism', *Global Issues: An Electronic Journal of the US Information Agency*, 2(1): 1–8.

Laqueur, W. (1996) 'Postmodern Terrorism: New Rules For An Old Game', *Foreign Affairs*, September Edition, 1–12.

Lash, S. and Wynne, B. (1992) 'Introduction', in U. Beck, ed. *Risk Society: Towards a New Modernity*. London: Sage.

Law, R. (2009) *Terrorism: A History*. London: Polity.

Lea, J. and Young, J. (1984) *What is to be Done About Law and Order: Crisis in the Eighties*. London: Penguin.

Leach, B. (2008) 'Knife Crime Worst Than Thought, Figures Show', *Daily Telegraph*, 20 September: 1.

Le Coze, J.C. (2005) 'Are Organisations too Complex to be Integrated in Technical Risk Assessment and Current Safety Auditing?' *Safety Science*, 43(8): 613–38.

Lee, M. (2007) *Inventing Fear of Crime: Criminology and the Politics of Anxiety*. Cullompton: Willan.

Lee, M. (2001) 'The Genesis of Fear of Crime', *Theoretical Criminology*, 5(4): 467–86.

Lee, M. and Farrall, S. eds. (2009) *Fear of Crime: Critical Voices in an Age of Anxiety*. London: Routledge.

Leiss, W. (2000) 'Book Review: Risk Society', *Canadian Journal of Sociology Online*, 25(3), viewable at www.ualberta.ca/cjscopy/articles/leiss.html. Accessed 8 November 2013.

Leitzinger, A. (2004) 'Postmodern Terrorism?', *The Eurasian Politician*, January Edition: 1–3.

Lesser, I., Hoffman, B., Ronfeldt, D., Zanini, M. and Jenkins, B. (1999) *Countering the New Terrorism*. California: RAND.

Lester, L. (2010) *Media and Environment*. London: Polity.

Levenson, J. and Cotter, P. (2005) 'The Effect of Megan's Law on Sex Offender Reintegration', *Journal of Contemporary Criminal Justice*, 21(1): 49–66.

Levi, M. (2010) 'Proceeds of Crime: Fighting the Financing of Terrorism', *Criminal Justice Matters*, 81: 38–39.

Lewis, J. (2013) *Beyond Consumer Capitalism*. London: Polity.

Lewis, S. (2008) *The Rough Guide to Beijing*. London: Penguin.

Liberty (2011) *Liberty's Submission to the Joint Committee on Human Rights on the Replacement Power to Stop and Search without Reasonable Suspicion*. London: Liberty.

Lievrouw, L. (2012) *Alternative and Activist Media*. London: Polity.

Lindquist, J. and Duke, J. (1982) 'The Elderly Victim at Risk: Explaining the Fear-Victimisation Paradox', *Criminology*, 20(1): 115–26.

Loader, I. and Sparks, R. (2010) *Public Criminology?* London: Routledge.

Loader, I. and Sparks, R. (2002) 'Contemporary Landscapes of Crime, Order and Control: Governance, Risk and Globalization', in M. Maguire, R. Morgan and R. Reiner, eds. *The Oxford Handbook of Criminology*. Oxford: Oxford University Press.

Loader, I. and Walker, N. (2007) *Civilizing Security*. Cambridge: CUP.

Lodziak, C. (1995) *Manipulating Needs: Capitalism and Culture*. London: Pluto Press.

Lombardi, M. (2004) 'Are We Getting it Right?' *Social Science Information Sur Les Sciences Sociales*, 43(3) 361–70.

Lupton, D. (2006) 'Sociology and Risk', in G. Mythen and S. Walklate, eds. *Beyond the Risk Society*. Maidenhead: Open University Press.

Lupton, D. (1999a) *Risk*. London: Routledge.

Lupton, D. (1999b) *Risk and Sociocultural Theory: New Directions and Perspectives*. Cambridge: Cambridge University Press.

Lutz, B. and Lutz, J. (2007) 'Terrorism' in A. Collins, ed. *Contemporary Security Studies*. Oxford: Oxford University Press.

Lynch, M., Burns, R. and Stretesky, P. (2008) *Environmental Crime, Law and Justice: An Introduction*. New York: LFB Scholarly.

Lyon, D. (2013) *The Culture of Surveillance*. London: Polity.

Lyng, S. (2005) *Edgework: The Sociology of Risk Taking*. New York: Routledge.

Lyng, S. (1990) 'Edgework: A Social Psychological Analysis of Voluntary Risk Taking', *American Journal of Sociology*, 95(4): 851–56.

MacAskill, E. (2007) 'Summertime – and after Katrina, Life Still ain't Easy', *The Guardian*, 7 29 August, p.7.

Macionis, J. and Plummer, K. (1998) *Sociology: A Global Introduction.* New Jersey: Prentice Hall.

Mackey, E. (1999) 'Constructing an Endangered Nation: Risk, Race and Rationality in Australia's Native Title Debate', in D. Lupton, ed. *Risk and Sociocultural Theory: New Directions and Perspectives.* Cambridge: Cambridge University Press.

Macnaghtan, P. (2006) 'The Environment and Risk', in G. Mythen and S. Walklate, eds. *Beyond the Risk Society.* Berkshire: OUP.

Macnaghtan, P. (2003) 'Embodying the Environment in Everyday Life Practices', *Sociological Review,* 51(1): 63–84.

Manzi, T. and Jacobs, K. (2008) 'Understanding Institutions, Actors and Networks: Advancing Constructionist Methods in Urban Policy Research', *Studies in Qualitative Methodology,* 9: 22–50.

Maplecroft (2009) *Energy Index CO2 Emissions from Land Use Change Index.* Maplecroft: Bath.

Maras, H. (2013) *Counterterrorism.* New York: Jones and Burlington.

Marris, C., Langford, I. and O'Riordan, T. (1998) 'A Quantitative Test of the Cultural Theory of Risk Perceptions: Comparison with the Psychometric Paradigm', *Risk Analysis,* 18(5): 635–47.

Martin, G. (2012) *Essentials of Terrorism: Concepts and Controversies.* London: Sage.

Martin, G. (2006) *Understanding Terrorism.* London: Sage.

Matthiessen, P. (1999) 'Get Down to Earth', *The Guardian,* 30 October: 6.

Mays, J. B. (1958) *Growing up in the City.* Liverpool: Liverpool University Press.

May, T. and Powell, J. (2007) 'Foucault: Interpretive Analytics and the Constitution of the Social', in T. Edwards, ed. *Cultural Theory: Classical and Contemporary Positions.* London: Sage.

McCulloch, J. and Pickering, S. (2010) 'Future Threat: Pre-crime, State terror and dystopia in the 21st Century', *Criminal Justice Matters,* 81: 32–33.

McCulloch, S. and Pickering, J. (2009) Pre-Crime and Counter-Terrorism', *British Journal of Criminology,* 49(5): 628–45.

McGhee, D. (2010) *Security, Citizenship and Human Rights.* Basingstoke: Palgrave Macmillan.

McGhee, D. (2008) *The End of Multiculturalism? Terrorism, Integration and Human Rights.* Buckingham: Open University Press.

McGovern (2010) *Countering Terror or Counter-Productive?* Liverpool: Edge Hill.

McMillan, N. (2004) 'Beyond Representation: Cultural Understandings of the September 11 Attacks', *Australia and New Zealand Journal of Criminology,* 37(3): 380–400.

McMylor, P. (2006) 'Economics and Risk', in G. Mythen and S. Walklate, eds. *Beyond the Risk Society.* Maidenhead: Open University Press.

Meadows, D., Meadows, D. and Randers, J. (1972) *Limits to Growth.* New York: Universe.

Measham, F. and Moore, K. (2008) 'The Criminalisation of Intoxication', in P. Squires, ed. *ASBO Nation: The Criminalisation of Nuisance.* Cambridge: Policy Press.

Meer, N., Dwyer, C. and Modood, T. (2010) 'Embodying Nationhood? Conceptions of British National Identity, Citizenship and Gender in the Veil Affair', *Sociological Review,* 58(1): 84–111.

Meikle, J. (2011) 'Cyber-attacks on UK at Disturbing Levels, Warns GCHQ Chief', *The Guardian*, 31 October, viewable at http://www.guardian.co.uk/technology/2011/oct/31/cyber-attacks-uk-disturbing-gchq. Accessed 10 March 2013.

Miller, D. (2012) *Consumption and its Consequences*. Basingstoke: Palgrave Macmillan.

Miller, J. (1993) *The Passion of Michel Foucault*. Harvard: Harvard University Press.

Miller, W. (1958) 'Lower Class Culture as a Generating Milieu of Gang Delinquency', *Journal of Social Issues*, 14: 5–19.

Mindfull (2013) *Recommendations for a New Approach to Young People's Mental Health Support*. London: HMSO.

Mlodinow, L. (2009) *The Drunkard's Walk: How Randomness Rules Our Lives*. London: Penguin.

Molotoch, H. (2005) *Death on the Roof: Race and Bureaucratic Failure*. Social Research Council: New York.

Monahan, T. ed. (2006) *Surveillance and Security: Technological Politics and Power in Everyday Life*. New York: Routledge.

Monbiot, G. (2012a) 'The Day the World Went Mad', *The Guardian*, 28 August: 7.

Monbiot, G. (2012b) 'Rio+20 Draft Text is 283 Paragraphs of Fluff', *The Guardian*, 22 June: 9.

Monbiot, G. (2012c) 'Is Protecting the Environment Incompatible with Social Justice?' 13 February: 6.

Mooney, G., Kelly, B., Goldblatt, D. and Hughes, G. (2004) *Tales of Fear and Fascination: The Crime Problem in the Contemporary UK*. Buckingham: Open University Press.

Morgan, G. and Poynting, S. (2012) *Global Islamophobia: Muslims and Moral Panic*. London: Ashgate.

Morgan, M. (2004) 'The Origins of New Terrorism', *Parameters,* Spring Edition.

Morgan, M.G., Fischhoff, B., Bostrom, A., Lave, L. and Atman, C. (1992) 'Communicating Risk to the Public', *Environmental Science and Technology*, 26(11): 2048–56.

Morton, T. (2012) *The Ecological Thought*. Harvard: Harvard University Press.

Moss, K. (2011) *Balancing Liberty and Security: Human Rights, Human Wrongs*. Basingstoke: Palgrave Macmillan.

Muncie, J. (2003) 'Youth, Risk and Victimization', in P. Davies, P. Francis and V. Jupp, eds. *Victimisations Theory, Research and Policy*. Basingstoke: Palgrave Macmillan.

Mythen, G. (2012a) 'Contesting the Third Space? Identity and Resistance Amongst Young British Pakistanis', *British Journal of Sociology*, 63(3): 393–411.

Mythen, G. (2012b) 'Who Speaks for Us?' Counter-terrorism, Collective Attribution and the Problem of Voice', *Critical Studies on Terrorism*, Special Edition on Counter-radicalization Policies in North-Western Europe, 5(3): 1–16.

Mythen, G. (2010) 'Reframing Risk? Citizen Journalism and the Transformation of News', *Journal of Risk Research*, Special Edition on 'New Media and Risk', 13(1): 45–58.

Mythen, G. (2009) 'A Conceptual Exploration of Risk: Crime, Security and Social Welfare', in J. Powell and A. Wahidin, eds. *Risk and Social Welfare*. Beijing: Casa Verde Publishers.

Mythen, G. (2008) 'Sociology and the Art of Risk', *Sociology Compass*, 2(1): 299–316.

Mythen, G. (2007a) 'Reappraising the Risk Society Thesis: Telescopic Sight or Myopic Vision?' *Current Sociology*, 55(6): 793–813.

Mythen, G. (2007b) 'Cultural Victimology: Are We All Victims Now?' in S. Walklate, ed. *Handbook on Victims and Victimology*. Devon: Willan.

Mythen, G. (2005a) 'From Goods to Bads? Revisiting the Political Economy of Risk', *Sociological Research Online*, 10(3), viewable at http://www.socresonline.org.uk/10/3/mythen.html. Accessed 18 February 2013.

Mythen, G. (2005b) 'Employment, Individualisation and Insecurity: Rethinking the Risk Society Perspective', *Sociological Review*, 53(1): 129–49.

Mythen, G. (2004) *Ulrich Beck: A Critical Introduction to the Risk Society*. London: Pluto Press.

Mythen, G. and Kamruzzaman, P. (2011) 'Counter-Terrorism and Community Relations: Anticipatory Risk, Regulation and Justice', in G. Smith, H. Quirk and T. Seddon, eds. *Regulation and Criminal Justice: Developing a New Framework for Research and Policy Development*. Cambridge: Cambridge University Press.

Mythen, G., Kemshall, H. and Walklate, S. (2012) 'Decentralizing Risk: The Role of the Voluntary and Community Sector in the Risk Management of Offenders', *Criminology and Criminal Justice,* doi: 10.1177/1748895812458295.

Mythen, G. and Walklate, S. (2010) 'Pre-crime, Regulation, and Counter-terrorism: Interrogating Anticipatory Risk', *Criminal Justice Matters*, 81(1): 34–36.

Mythen, G. and Walklate, S. (2008) 'Terrorism, Risk and International Security: The Perils of Asking What if?', *Security Dialogue*, Special Edition on 'Risk, Security and Technologies of the Political', 39(2/3): 221–42.

Mythen, G. and Walklate, S. (2006a) 'Criminology and Terrorism: Which Thesis? Risk Society or Governmentality?' *The British Journal of Criminology*, 46(3): 379–98.

Mythen, G. and Walklate, S. (2006b) 'Communicating the Terrorist Risk: Harnessing a Culture of Fear?' *Crime, Media, Culture: An International Journal*, 2(2): 123–42.

Mythen, G., Walklate, S. and Khan, F. (2013) 'Why Should We Have to Prove We're Alright?' Counter-Terrorism, Risk and Partial Securities', *Sociology*, 47(2): 382–97.

Mythen, G., Walklate, S. and Khan, F. (2009) 'I'm a Muslim, but I'm not a Terrorist': Risk, Victimization and the Negotiation of Risky Identities', *British Journal of Criminology*, 49(6): 736–54.

National Security Strategy Report (2010) *A Strong Britain in an Age of Uncertainty*. London: HMSO.

Newburn, T. (2009) *Criminology*. Devon: Willan.

Newell, P. (2012) *Globalization and the Environment*. London: Polity.

Nickels, H.C., Thomas, L., Hickman, M.J. and Silvestri, S. (2012) 'Constructing Suspect Communities and Britishness: Mapping British Press Coverage of Irish and Muslim Communities 1974–2007', *European Journal of Communication*, 27(2): 135–51.

Oborne, P. (2006) *The Use and Abuse of Terror: The Construction of a False Narrative of the Domestic Terror Threat*. London: Centre for Policy Studies.

O'Brien, T. (2012) 'Environmental Protest in New Zealand (1997–2010)', *The British Journal of Sociology*, 63(4): 641–61.

O'Malley, P. (2010) *Crime and Risk*. London: Sage.

O'Malley, P. (2008) 'Experiments in Risk and Criminal Justice', *Theoretical Criminology*, 12(4): 451–71.

O'Malley, P. (2006) 'Criminology and Risk', in G. Mythen and S. Walklate, eds. *Beyond the Risk Society*. London: McGraw-Hill.

O'Malley, P. (1999) 'Consuming Risks. Harm Minimisation and the Government of Drug Users', in R. Smandych, ed. *Governable Places: Readings on Governmentality and Crime Control*. Aldershot: Dartmouth.

O'Malley, P. ed. (1998) *Crime and the Risk Society*. Aldershot: Ashgate.

O'Malley, P. (1992) 'Risk, Power and Crime Prevention', *Economy and Society*, 21: 252–75.

ONS (2001) *Social Trends, 31*. London: The Stationary Office.

Oreskes, N. (2004) 'The Scientific Consensus on Climate Change', *Science*, 306(5702): 1686.

Ortega y Gasset, J. (1914) *Meditaciones del Quijote*. Madrid: Residencia de Estudiantes Language.

Ould Mohamedou, M.M. (2007) *Understanding Al Qaeda: The Transformation of War*. London: Pluto Press.

Owen, D. (1995) 'Genealogy as Exemplary Critique: Reflections on Foucault and the Imagination of the Political', *Economy and Society*, 24(4): 489–506.

Oxfam (2011) *Growing a Better Future: Food Justice in a Resource Constrained World*. London: Oxfam.

Oxford English Dictionary (2011) Oxford: Oxford University Press.

Pantazis, C. (2000) 'Fear of Crime, Vulnerability and Poverty: Evidence from the British Crime Survey', *British Journal of Criminology*, 40(3): 414–36.

Parkhill, K., Henwood, K., Pidgeon, N. and Simmons, P. (2011) 'Laughing it Off? Humour, Affect and Emotion Work in Communities Living With Nuclear Risk', *British Journal of Sociology*, 62(2): 324–46.

Park, R. (1952) *Human Communities: The City and Human Ecology*. Glencoe: Free Press.

Park, R. and Burgess, E. (1921) *Introduction to the Science of Sociology*. Chicago: University of Chicago Press.

Pauwels, L. and Svensson, R. (2011) 'Exploring the Relationship between Offending and Victimization: What is the Role of Risky Lifestyles and Low Self-control? A Test in Two Urban Samples', *European Journal on Criminal Policy and Research*, 17(3): 163–77.

Pearson, G. (1983) *Hooligan: A History of Respectable Fears*. London: Palgrave Macmillan.

Peelo, M. and Soothill, K. (2000) 'The Place of Public Narratives in Reproducing Social Order', *Theoretical Criminology*, 4(2): 131–48.

Peters, M. (2004) *Postmodern Terror in a Globalized World*. Glasgow: University of Glasgow.

Polanyi, K. (1944) *The Great Transformation*. Boston: Beacon Press.

Poynting, S. and Whyte, D. eds. (2012) *Counter-Terrorism and State Violence*. London: Routledge.

Presdee, M. (2000) *Cultural Criminology and the Carnival of Crime*. London: Routledge.

Prince, R. (2010) 'How Tony Blair's 12 Point Anti-terror Plan after 7/7 Came to Little', *Daily Telegraph*, 1 January: 8.

Punch, M. (2007) *Zero Tolerance Policing*. Bristol: Policy Press.

QAA Report (2007) Gloucester: Quality Assurance Agency for Higher Education.

Quételet, A. (1835) *Sur l'homme et le développement de ses facultés, ou Essai de physique sociale*. Paris: Bachelier.

Rawls, J.A. (1999) *A Theory of Justice*. Oxford: Oxford University Press.

Rebonato, R. (2007) *Plight of the Fortune Tellers: Why We Need to Manage Financial Risk Differently*. New Jersey: Princeton University Press.

Reed, A. (2005) 'The Real Divide', *The Progressive*, 69(11): 31.

Rehn, E. (2003) 'Excessive Reliance on the Use of Force Does Not Stop Terrorism', in T. Hoeksema. and J. ter Laak, eds. *Human Rights and Terrorism*. Holland: NHC/OSCE.

Reid, T. (2005) 'Battle for Survival', *The Daily Mail*, 3 September: 1.

Reith, G. (2005) 'On the Edge: Drugs and the Consumption of Risk in Late Modernity', in S. Lyng, ed. *Edgework: The Sociology of Risk Taking* New York: Routledge.

Rio Declaration (1992) *Report of the United Nations Conference on Environment and Development*. United Nations: Rio.

Roberts, B. (2008) 'Minister Warns of Peril as he Pushes for 42 day lock-up', *Daily Mirror*, 23 January, viewable at http://www.mirror.co.uk/news/top-stories/2008/01/23/minister-warns-of-peril-as-he-pushes-for-42-day-lock-up-89520-20294998. Accessed 30 May 2012.

Robinson, J. and Holdsworth, C. (2013) 'They don't Live in my House Every Day: How Understanding Lives Can Aid Understandings of Smoking', *Contemporary Drug Problems*, 40(1): 47–69.

Rock, P. (2002) 'On Becoming a Victim', in C. Hoyle and R. Wilson, eds. *New Visions of Crime Victims*. Oxford: Hart Publishing.

Rose, N. (2000) 'Government and Control', *British Journal of Criminology*, 40: 321–39.

Rose, N. (1996) 'The Death of the Social? Refiguring the Territory of Government', *Economy and Society*, 25(3): 327–64.

Rose, N. (1984) *The Psychological Complex*. London: Routledge.

Ross, J. (2000) *Varieties of State Crime and its Control*. New York: Criminal Justice Press.

Rothstein, H. (2003) 'Neglected Risk Regulation: The Institutional Attenuation Phenomenon', *Health, Risk and Society*, 5(1): 85–103.

Rothstein, H., Huber, M. and Gaskell, G. (2006) 'A Theory of Risk Colonisation: The Spiralling Regulatory Logics of Societal and Institutional Risk', *Economy and Society*, 35(1): 91–112.

Ruckelshaus, W. (1984) 'Risk in a Free Society', *Risk Analysis*, 4: 157–58.

Saeed, A. (2007) 'Media, Racism and Islamophobia: The Representation of Islam and Muslims in the Media', *Sociology Compass*, 1.

Salter, M. (2008) 'Conclusion: Risk and Imagination in the War on Terror', in L. Amoore and M. de Goede, eds. *Risk and the War on Terror*, London: Routledge.

Saner, E. (2009) 'A Day in the Life of a Terror Suspect', *The Guardian*, 13 June: 3.

Saul, B. (2006) *Defining Terror in International Law*. Oxford: OUP.

Saville, S. (2008) 'Playing with Fear: Parkour and the Mobility of Emotion', *Social and Cultural Geography*, 9(8): 891–914.

Sawer, J. (2010) Public Speech, Thursday 28 October. Reproduced in *The Guardian*, viewable at http://www.theguardian.com/uk/2010/oct/28/sir-john-sawers-speech-full-text. Accessed 7 February 2012.

Schmid, A. (2011) *The Routledge Handbook of Terrorism Research*. London: Routledge.

Schütz, A. (1962) *Collected Papers I: The Problem of Social Reality*. The Hague: Nijhoff.

Sciullo, N. (2012) 'On the Language of Counter Terrorism and the Legal Geography of Terror', *Willamette Law Review*, 48: 317–41.

Shapiro, J. (2012) *China's Environmental Challenges*. Oxford: Polity.

Shaw, C.R. and McKay, H.D. (1942) *Juvenile Delinquency in Urban Areas*. Chicago: University of Chicago Press.

Shaw, M. and Pease, K. (2000) *Research on Repeat Victimisation in Scotland*. Edinburgh: Scottish Executive.

Shearing, C. and Wood, J. (2007) *Imagining Security*. Cullompton: Willan Publishing.

Siddique, H. and Godfrey, H. (2011) 'Norway Attacks Rolling Coverage', *The Guardian*, Friday 22 July, viewable at http://www.guardian.co.uk/world/blog/2011/jul/22/oslo-explosion-live-coverage. Accessed April 2013.

Simon, J. (2000) 'Megan's Law: Crime and Democracy in Late Modern America', *Law and Social Inquiry*, 25(4): 1111–50.

Simon, J. (1998) 'Managing the Monstrous. Sex Offenders and the New Penology', *Psychology, Public Policy and Law*, 4: 452–67.

Simon, J. (1997) 'Governing Through Crime', in L. Friedman and G. Fisher, eds. *The Crime Conundrum: Issues in Criminal Justice*. Boulder: Westview Press.

Singleton, N., Bumpstead, R., O'Brien, M., Lee A. and Meltzer H. (2001) *Psychiatric Morbidity among Adults Living in Private Households 2000*. London: TSO.

Sjoberg, L. (1998) 'Worry and Risk Perception', *Risk Analysis*, 18(1): 85–93.

Sjoberg, L. (1997) 'Explaining Risk Perception: An Empirical Evaluation of Cultural Theory', *Risk, Decision and Policy*, 2(2): 113–30.

Slovic, P. (2000) *Perception of Risk*. London: Earthscan.

Slovic, P. (1987) 'Perception of Risk', *Science*, 236: 280–85.

Smith, A. (1776) *An Inquiry into the Nature and Causes of the Wealth of Nations*. London: Strahan and Cadell.

Smith, D. (2006) 'The Crisis of Management: Managing Ahead of the Curve', in D. Smith and D. Elliott, eds. *Key Readings in Crisis Management*. London: Routledge.

Smith-Spark, L. (2006) 'New Orleans Violence Overstated', *BBC News*, viewable at http://news.bbc.co.uk/1/hi/world/americas/4292114.stm. Accessed 30 August 2012.

Sparks, R. (2001) 'Degrees of Estrangement: The Cultural Theory of Risk and Comparative Penology', *Theoretical Criminology*, 5(2): 159–76.

Sparks, R., Parks, R., Genn, H. and Dodd, D. (1977) *Surveying Victims*. London: Heinemann.

Sprinzak, E. (2006) 'The Great Superterrorism Scare', viewable at www.radiobergen.org/terrorism/super-2.html. Accessed 7 June 2012.

Squires, P. and Stephen, D. (2012) 'Pre-crime and Precautionary Criminalisation', *Criminal Justice Matters*, 81: 28–30.

Stanford International Human Rights and Conflict Resolution Clinic/Global Justice Clinic (2012) *Living Under Drones: Death, Injury and Trauma to Civilians From US Drone Practices*. New York University/Stanford University.

Stanko, E. (1997) 'Safety Talk: Conceptualising Women's Risk Assessment as a Technology of the Soul', *Theoretical Criminology*, 4(1): 479–99.

Stanko, E. (1990) *Everyday Violence*. London: Virago.

Steinert, H. (2003) 'The Indispensable Metaphor of War: On Populist Politics and the Contradictions of the State's Monopoly of Force', *Theoretical Criminology* 7(3): 265–91.

Stenson, K. (2000) 'The New Politics of Crime Control' in K. Stenson and R. Sullivan, eds. *Crime, Risk and Justice: The Politics of Crime Control in Liberal Democracies*. Cullompton: Willan.

Stenson, K. and Sullivan, R. eds. (2000) *Crime, Risk and Justice: The Politics of Crime Control in Liberal Democracies*. Cullompton: Willan.

Stern, N. (2006) *Stern Review on The Economics of Climate Change: An Executive Summary*. London: HM Treasury, viewable at http://www.webcitation.org/5nCeyEYJr. Accessed 31 January 2010.

Stewart, E. (2008) 'Knife Crime not Increasing', *The Guardian*, 13 May, viewable at http://www.theguardian.com/uk/2008/may/13/ukcrime.boris. Accessed 4 January 2012.

Stewart, H. and Elliott, L. (2008) 'Tough, but no Depression', *The Guardian*, 9 October, viewable at http://www.theguardian.com/business/2008/oct/09/imf.globalrecession. Accessed 10 July 2013.

Storr, W. (2013) 'Welcome to Mousetrap City', *Esquire*, May Edition: 18.

Strydom, P. (2002) *Risk, Environment and Modernity*. Buckingham: Open University Press.

Stuckler, D. and Basu, S. (2013) *The Body Economic: Why Austerity Kills*. New York: Harper Collins.

Sunstein, C.R. (2005) *Laws of Fear: Beyond the Precautionary Principle*. Cambridge: Cambridge University Press.

Sutton, P. (2007) *The Environment: An Introduction*. London: Polity.

Swain, C. (2005) 'After Katrina: Stormy Waters', *Prospect*, October Edition: 12–15.

Szmukler, G. (2003) 'Risk Assessment: Numbers and Values', *Psychiatric Bulletin*, 27: 205–07.

Taibbi, M. (2013) 'Everything Is Rigged: The Biggest Price-Fixing Scandal Ever', *Rolling Stone*, 25 April: 2.

Taleb, N. (2007) *The Black Swan: The Impact of the Highly Improbable*. London: Penguin.

Taylor, I. (1999) *Crime in Context: A Critical Criminology of Market Societies*. Cambridge: Polity.

Taylor, I. (1996) 'Fear of Crime, Urban Fortunes and Suburban Social Movements: Some Reflections From Manchester', *Sociology*, 30(2): 317–37.

Taylor-Gooby, P. and Zinn, J. O. (2006) *Risk in Social Science*. Oxford: Oxford University Press.

Taylor, S.E. and Gollwitzer, P.M. (1995) 'Effects of Mindset on Positive Illusions', *Journal of Personality and Social Psychology*, 69: 213–26.

Thaler, R. and Sunstein, C. (2008) *Nudge: Improving Decisions About Health, Welfare and Happiness*. Yale: Yale University Press.

Thiel, D. (2009) *Policing Terrorism: A Review of the Evidence*. London: The Police Foundation.

Thomas, L. (2007) 'The Sobering Subject of Consent', *Daily Telegraph*, 28 March: 9.

Thompkins, T. (2000) 'School Violence: Gangs and a Culture of Fear', *The Annals of the American Academy of Political and Social Science*, 567(1): 54–71.

Thompson, H. (1972) *Fear and Loathing in Las Vegas*. New York: Summit Books.

Tietze, T. (2012) 'Justice Has Been Done', *The Guardian*, 25 August: 41.

Tietze, T., Rundle, G. and Humphreys, E. eds. (2012) *On Utoya: Anders Breivik, Right Terror, Racism and Europe*. London: Elguta Press.

Tillich, P. (1952) *The Courage to Be*. Glasgow: Collins.

Tombs, S. (2011), 'Which Public? Whose Criminology?', *British Journal of Criminology*, 51: 727–30.

Tombs, S. and Whyte, D. (2008) *A Crisis of Enforcement: The Decriminalisation of Death and Injury at Work*. Centre for Crime and Justice Studies, Briefing Paper 6.

Tombs, S. and Whyte, D. (2007) *Safety Crimes*. Cullompton: Willan.

Tombs, S. and Whyte, D. (2006) 'Work and Risk' in G. Mythen and S. Walklate, eds. *Beyond the Risk Society*. Berkshire: OUP.

Tomlinson, J. (2007) *The Culture of Speed*. London: Sage.

Toner, B. (2006) 'What We've Learned', *The Guardian*, 28 January: 14.

Travis, A. (2013) 'Fall in UK Crime Rate Baffles Experts', *The Guardian*, viewable at http://www.theguardian.com/uk/2013/jan/24/fall-uk-crime-rate-baffles-experts. Accessed 3 February 2013.

Travis, A. (2010a) 'Sarah's Law Pilot Scheme Prompts Revenge Fears', *The Guardian*, 3 March: 4.

Travis, A. (2010b) 'Stop and Search Powers Illegal, European Court Rules', *The Guardian*, 12 January: 1.

Tudor, A. (2003) 'A (macro) Sociology of Fear?' *Sociological Review*, 51(2): 238–56.

Tulloch, J. (2006) *One Day in July: Experiencing 7/7*. London: Little Brown.

Tulloch, J. and Lupton, D. (2003) *Risk and Everyday Life*. London: Sage.

Turner, B. (2010) 'Enclosures, Enclaves, and Entrapment', *Sociological Inquiry*, 80(2): 241–60.

Turner, E. (2013) 'Beyond Facts and Values: Rethinking Some Recent Debates about the Public Role of Criminology', *British Journal of Criminology*, 53(1): 49–66.

Tversky, A. and Kahneman, D. (1974) 'Judgements Under Uncertainty: Heuristics and Biases', *Science*, 185: 1124–31.

UN Conference on the Human Environment (1972), viewable at http://www.unep.org/Documents.Multilingual/Default.asp?documentid=97&articleid=1503. Accessed 4 January 2013.

Ungar, S. (2001) 'Moral Panic Versus the Risk Society: The Implications of the Changing Sites of Social Anxiety', *British Journal of Sociology*, 52(2): 271–91.

United Nations (2012) *The State of Food Security in the World*. Rome: Food and Agriculture Organization of the United Nations.

United Nations (2003) 'Report of the Policy Working Group on the United Nations and Terrorism', viewable at http://www.satp.org/satporgtp/southasia/documents/papers/WC_terrorism.htm. Accessed 4 December 2012.

Urry, J. (2011) *Climate Change and Society*. Cambridge, UK: Polity.

van Brunschot, E. and Kennedy, L. (2008) *Risk, Balance and Security*. London: Sage.

Vandecasteele, L. (2010) 'Life Course Risks or Cumulative Disadvantage? The Structuring Effect of Social Stratification Determinants and Life Course Events on Poverty Transitions in Europe', *European Sociological Review*, online archive, doi: 10.1093/esr/jcq005.

Vertigans, S. (2011) *The Sociology of Terrorism*. London: Routledge.

Vertigans, S. (2010) 'British Muslims and the UK Government's 'war on terror' Within: Evidence of a Clash of Civilizations or Emergent De-civilizing processes?', *British Journal of Sociology*, 61(1): 26–44.

Victor, D. (2011) *Global Warming Gridlock*. London: Routledge.

Vedby-Rasmussen, M. (2004) 'It Sounds Like a Riddle: Security Studies, the War on Terror and Risk', *Millennium: Journal of International Studies*, 30(2): 381–95.

Wacquant, L. (2009) *Punishing the Poor*. London: Duke University Press.

Wales, C. and Mythen, G. (2002) 'Risky Discourses: The Politics of GM Foods', *Environmental Politics*, 11(2): 121–44.

Walker, C. (2008) 'Know Thine Enemy as Thyself: Discerning Friend from Foe Under the Anti-terrorism Laws', *Melbourne University Law Review*, 32(1): 275–301.

Walker, L. (2010) *Recapping on BP's Long History of Greenwashing*, London: Greenpeace, viewable at http://www.greenpeace.org/usa/en/news-and-blogs/campaign-blog/recapping-on-bps-long-history-of-greenwashing/blog/26025/ Accessed 15 January 2013.

Walker, R. and Bulent, G. (2003) *11 September: War, Terror and Judgement*. London: Portland.

Walklate, S. (2007a) *Imagining the Victim of Crime*. Maidenhead: McGraw-Hill/Open University Press.

Walklate S. ed. (2007b) *The Handbook of Victims and Victimology*. Cullompton: Willan.

Walklate, S. (2002) 'Gendering Crime Prevention: Exploring the Tensions between Policy and Process', in G. Hughes, E. McLaughlin and J. Muncie, eds. *Crime Prevention and Community Safety: New Directions*. London: Sage.

Walklate, S. (1997) 'Risk and Criminal Victimization: A Modernist Dilemma?', *British Journal of Criminology*, 37(1): 35–45.

Walklate, S. and Mythen, G. (2010) 'Agency, Reflexivity and Risk: Which Citizen?', *British Journal of Sociology*, 61: 47–65.

Walklate, S. and Mythen, G. (2008) 'How Scared Are We?', *British Journal of Criminology*, 48(2): 209–25.

Wall, D. (2010) 'From Post-crime to Pre-crime', *Criminal Justice Matters*, 81: 22–23.

Weinstein, N.D. (1980) 'Unrealistic Optimism about Future Life Events', *Journal of Personality and Social Psychology*, 39(1): 806–20.

Weinstein, N.D. and Klein, W.M. (1996) 'Unrealistic Optimism: Present and Future', *Journal of Social and Clinical Psychology*, 15: 1–8.

Welsh, B. and Farrington, D. (1999) 'Value for Money? A Review of the Costs and Benefits of Situational Crime Prevention', *British Journal of Criminology*, 39(3): 345–68.

Weltzer, H. (2012) *Climate Wars: What People Will be Killed for in the 21st Century*. London: Polity.

White, R. (2009) *Environmental Crime: A Reader*. Cullompton: Willan.

Wilkinson, G. and Pickett, K. (2009) *The Spirit Level: Why More Equal Societies Almost Always do Better*. London: Allen Lane.

Wilkinson, I. (2011) 'Ulrich Beck', in G. Ritzer and J. Stepnisky, eds. *The Wiley-Blackwell Blackwell Companion to Major Social Theorists*. Oxford: Wiley-Blackwell.

Wilkinson, I. (2009) *Risk, Vulnerability and Everyday Life*. London: Routledge.

Wilkinson, I. (2001) *Anxiety in a Risk Society.* London: Routledge.

Williams, B. (2005) *Victims of Crime and Community Justice.* London: Jessica Kingsley.

Williams, K. (2004) *Textbook on Criminology.* Oxford: Oxford University Press.

Willmott, P. (1966) *Adolescent Boys of East London.* London: Routledge and Kegan.

Wilson, K. (2000) 'Communicating Climate Change through the Media: Predictions, Politics and Perceptions of Risk', in S. Allan, B. Adam and C. Carter, eds. *Environmental Risks and the Media.* London: Routledge.

Winchester, S. (2003) *Krakatoa: The Day the World Exploded.* London: Viking.

Wolf, J. and Moser, S. (2011) 'Individual Understandings, Perceptions and Engagement with Climate Change', *Wiley Interdisciplinary Reviews: Climate Change,* 2(4): 547–69.

Worcester, R. (2001) 'The World Will Never be the Same: British Hopes and Fears After September 11th 2001', *International Journal of Public Opinion Research,* viewable at www.mori.com. Accessed 6 January 2012.

World Food Programme (2011) *Climate Change: Enabling People to Adapt for the Future.* Rome: Office for Climate Change and Disaster Risk Reduction.

Wright Mills, C. (1959) *The Sociological Imagination.* Oxford: Oxford University Press.

Wynne, B. (2002) 'Risk and Environment as Legitimatory Discourses of Technology: Reflexivity Inside Out', *Current Sociology,* 50(3): 459–77.

Wynne, B. (1992) 'Misunderstood Misunderstanding: Social Identities and Public Uptake of Science', *Public Understandings of Science,* 1(3): 281–304.

Young, J. (2007) *The Vertigo of Late Modernity.* London: Sage.

Young, J. (1999) *The Exclusive Society.* London: Sage.

Young, J. (1988) 'Risk of Crime and Fear of Crime. A Realist Critique of Survey based Assumptions', in M. Maguire and J. Ponting, eds. *Victims. A New Deal?* Milton Keynes: Open University Press.

Younge, G. (2006) 'Gone With the Wind', *The Guardian,* 29 July: 19–25.

Zedner, L. (2010) 'Pre-crime and Punishment: A Health Warning', *Criminal Justice Matters,* 81: 24–5.

Zedner, L. (2009) *Security.* London: Routledge.

Zedner, L. (2007) 'Pre-crime and Post Criminology?', *Theoretical Criminology,* 11(2): 261–81.

Zedner, L. (2002) 'Victims', in M. Maguire, R. Morgan and R. Reiner, eds. *The Oxford Handbook of Criminology.* Oxford: Oxford University Press.

Žižek, S. (2010) *Living in the End Times.* London: Verso.

Index

Note: Letter '*f*' followed by locators refer to figures.